WebGL HOTSH⊕T

Create interactive 3D content for web pages and mobile devices

Mitch Williams

BIRMINGHAM - MUMBAI

WebGL HOTSHOT

First published: May 2014

Production Reference: 1200514

Published by Packt Publishing Ltd.
Livery Place
35 Livery Street
Birmingham B3 2PB, UK.

ISBN 978-1-78328-091-9

www.packtpub.com

Cover Image by Michael Harms (kunstraum@googlemail.com)

Credits

Author
Mitch Williams

Reviewers
Andrea Barisone
Dario Calonaci
Jing Jin
Vincent Lark
Todd J. Seiler

Commissioning Editor
Joanne Fitzpatrick

Acquisition Editor
Joanne Fitzpatrick

Content Development Editor
Neeshma Ramakrishnan

Technical Editors
Shruti Rawool
Aman Preet Singh

Copy Editors
Tanvi Gaitonde
Dipti Kapadia
Aditya Nair

Project Coordinator
Wendell Palmer

Proofreaders
Simran Bhogal
Maria Gould
Paul Hindle

Indexer
Mehreen Deshmukh

Graphics
Ronak Dhruv
Valentina Dsilva
Disha Haria

Production Coordinator
Shantanu Zagade

Cover Work
Shantanu Zagade

About the Author

Mitch Williams has been involved with 3D graphics programming and Web3D development since its creation in the mid 1990s. He began his career writing software for digital imaging products before moving on as Manager of Software for Vivendi Universal Games. In the late 1990s, he started 3D-Online, his own company, where he created "Dynamic-3D", a Web3D graphics engine. He has worked on various projects ranging from interactive 3D medical procedures, online 3D training for the Department of Defense, creating one of the first 3D mobile games prior to the launch of the iPhone, and graphics card shader language programming. He has been teaching Interactive 3D Media at various universities including UC Berkeley, UC Irvine, and UCLA Extension.

Gratitude and thanks to my family, friends, dogs—past and present, artists, SIGGRAPH, wonderful students, and the great math and engineering teachers who helped me along the way.

About the Reviewers

Andrea Barisone works for a leading Italian IT company and has over 13 years of experience in Information Technology, working on corporate projects as a developer using different technologies. He also has a strong experience in ECM Systems and has several J2EE certifications. He has the ability to acquire new technologies and to exploit the knowledge acquired by working with different environments and technologies.

He was the technical reviewer for the following books:

- *Agile Web Development with Rails 4, David Heinemeier Hansson, Sam Ruby, and Dave Thomas, Pragmatic Bookshelf*
- *BPEL and Java Cookbook, Jurij Laznik, Packt Publishing*
- *Learning Three.js: The JavaScript 3D Library for WebGL, Jos Dirksen, Packt Publishing*
- *Building Applications with ExtJS, Simon Elliston Ball, Packt Publishing* (yet to be published)

I would like to thank my parents, Renzo and Maria Carla; my beloved wife, Barbara; and my two wonderful little children, Gabriele and Aurora, for making every day of my life wonderful.

Dario Calonaci is a graphic designer specializing in typography and logo design. He has worked for the United Nations conference RIO+20, and has worked with Node.js, which was selected for Obama for America. His name and work has appeared in a book presentation in the Senate's library in Rome. He has been teaching Web Design since he was 23 years old. He is a member of FacultyRow, a New York-based association, as a valuable teacher and academic figure.

He has been invited to deliver talks as well as to conduct a workshop. His works have been exposed in New York, internationally published and featured, and studied in a couple of theses.

You can learn more about him and see his works at `http://dariocalonaci.com`.

Jing Jin works at a game company as a technical artist. She loves delving into new technologies that render game graphics better and more efficiently. She's also interested in innovations that enable a variety of gaming experiences and bring novelty to traditional gaming.

Vincent Lark (`@allyouneedisgnu`) is a French developer in Luxembourg with six years of experience. He worked as a full-stack developer in some large audience companies such as EuroDNS, Jamendo, and more recently, for a local news website for cross-border workers. Interested in game development and 3D modeling since his school years, he's practicing these subjects in Global Game Jams and other hackathons with friends. An open source fanatic, he shares every prototype on his GitHub account and tries to follow state-of-the-art web development.

Todd J. Seiler works in the CAD/CAM dental industry as a graphics software engineer at E4D Technologies in Dallas, Texas. He has worked as a software development engineer in Test on Games for Windows LIVE at Microsoft, and he has also worked in the mobile game development industry. He has a B.S. degree in Computer Graphics and Interactive Media from the University of Dubuque, Dubuque, Iowa with minors in Computer Information Systems. He also has a B.S. degree in Real-time Interactive Simulations from DigiPen Institute of Technology, Redmond, Washington, with minors in mathematics and physics.

In his spare time, he plays video games, studies Catholic apologetics and theology, writes books and articles, and toys with new tech when he can. He periodically blogs about random things at `http://www.toddseiler.com`.

www.PacktPub.com

Support files, eBooks, discount offers, and more

You might want to visit www.PacktPub.com for support files and downloads related to your book.

Did you know that Packt offers eBook versions of every book published, with PDF and ePub files available? You can upgrade to the eBook version at www.PacktPub.com and as a print book customer, you are entitled to a discount on the eBook copy. Get in touch with us at service@packtpub.com for more details.

At www.PacktPub.com, you can also read a collection of free technical articles, sign up for a range of free newsletters and receive exclusive discounts and offers on Packt books and eBooks.

http://PacktLib.PacktPub.com

Do you need instant solutions to your IT questions? PacktLib is Packt's online digital book library. Here, you can access, read and search across Packt's entire library of books.

Why Subscribe?

- ▸ Fully searchable across every book published by Packt
- ▸ Copy and paste, print and bookmark content
- ▸ On demand and accessible via web browser

Free Access for Packt account holders

If you have an account with Packt at www.PacktPub.com, you can use this to access PacktLib today and view nine entirely free books. Simply use your login credentials for immediate access.

Table of Contents

Preface

Welcome to *WebGL Hotshot*. Web3D was first introduced about the same time as HTML and web browsers in the early 1990s. VRML 1.0, the Virtual Reality Modeling Language, made its L.A. debut by its co-inventors, Mark Pesce, Tony Parisi, and others, as part of the VR SIG (special interest group) organized by Dave Blackburn at Kit and Sherrie Galloway's Electronic Café (`http://www.ecafe.com/`), a part of Santa Monica's 18th Street Arts Center (`http://18thstreet.org/`). Meanwhile, 3D was an emerging entertainment medium as *Toy Story* was released in 1995 about the same time as Microsoft's DirectX 3D game interface, and a few years after *Doom* launched, one of the first 3D games. VRML 2.0 adopted the tag style, `< >`, of HTML a few years later. VRML, however, required either a plugin for your web browser, common at the time with the emergence of real audio and flash, or a pure Java implementation such as Dynamic 3D.

For much of the first decade of this century, the commercial applications of 3D graphics were seen in animated movies, special effects, and video games. Web3D had little visibility and was mostly used in research centers such as the U.S. Naval Postgraduate School in Monterey, California, USC Behavioral Technology Labs, and the Fraunhofer Institute for Computer Graphics in Europe. However, two new technologies were about to bring Web3D into the foreground. XML (eXtensible Markup Language) emerged as the file format and validation system for passing data across the Internet, and shader languages provided the ability to program the GPU (Graphics Processing Unit), which was a significant boost in the performance of 3D graphics.

Behind every technology are innovative, imaginative people. Two organizations, Khronos and the Web3D Consortium, provided the implementation of Web3D to be robust and simple for both developers and artists. Khronos (`https://www.khronos.org`) is a group of major media-centric technology companies dedicated to creating open standards in computer graphics. Khronos defined WebGL and its adoption among web browser developers to enable interactive Web3D. The Web3D Consortium (`http://www.web3d.org`) defined X3D, the VRML 2.0-based file format using XML standards.

This book will introduce the two leading technologies for interactive Web3D: X3D and WebGL. Emphasis is placed on real-world applications while intertwining technical concepts. We begin with X3D and the fundamental concepts of creating 3D scenes. If you have never built anything in 3D, you'll be amazed at how quickly you can create colorful 3D environments. Then, we transition to WebGL, writing JavaScript to parse the 3D meshes, control the interactivity, and handle the interfacing to the GPU for rendering 3D meshes with texture maps. Then, GPU shader languages are applied to create various lights, free-flowing cloth, and animated waterfalls.

More advanced techniques are then demonstrated, such as integrating WebGL with content from Facebook, the social media site, and with live stock market data to show how 3D can be a more effective means of navigation and communication. We then deploy content from other 3D applications developed by architects and engineers to bring their content to the Web and as an engaging tool for education. Finally, we look at WebGL as art applied to the design of 3D websites to engage audiences like never before.

What this book covers

Project 1, *Building Great Web3D*, introduces us to 3D graphics concepts—lights, cameras, 3D meshes, and their placement in 3D space, plus animation with X3D.

Project 2, *WebGL for E-Commerce*, describes how to build e-commerce sites in 3D using existing assets while introducing WebGL technology including shader programming inside the GPU. Then, we look at the issues and opportunities in building a WebGL 3D e-commerce site.

Project 3, *User Experience, Story, Character, Visual Design, and Interactivity*, applies shader languages to texture maps in order to create effects such as flags waving in the wind and waterfalls. Then, we will create engaging night scenes with lighting and fog when navigating 3D scenes.

Project 4, *Mobile and Web3D Gaming*, builds 2D user interfaces in a 3D environment, common in video games. We will then implement features of games such as misdirection to create challenges in games and implement gravity.

Project 5, *Social Media Meets Its Destiny*, interfaces WebGL with Facebook, the social media website, in order to build 3D interfaces to visit your Facebook friends. Also, we will learn about the Facebook programming interface to expand our applications.

Project 6, *3D Reveals More Information*, demonstrates how to display data from a real-time Internet feed such as the stock market in 3D. We then demonstrate techniques to display large amounts of data and show how to navigate into the data so that we can analyze the data for a full year down to a day for a more refined display.

Project 7, Adapting Architecture, Medical, and Mechanical Engineering to Web3D, discusses the issues and solutions to porting the work of architects and engineers to the Web, given their 3D drawings. We then add the features of 3D renderings, including reflection and refraction of light to simulate windows and transparencies, other materials such as bricks with depth, and multiple cameras in a scene.

Project 8, 3D Websites, revisits X3D to create and navigate 3D websites and create engaging scenes with lighting and normal maps so that surfaces look natural. We then add portals to transport within a 3D website for faster navigation.

Project 9, Education in the Third Dimension, demonstrates how to select a specific chemical element from the periodic chart and then select countries off a wall map, demonstrating how to pick irregular shapes. Finally, we show how 3D graphics can be an effective tool to show math algorithms.

Project 10, The New World of 3D Art, recreates the complex architecture of Chicago's Art Institute, and then invents a new interactive 3D art based on the work of the famous pop artist Roy Lichtenstein.

What you need for this book

WebGL requires a basic editor such as Notepad and a web browser, preferably Firefox as it is better suited for development and testing WebGL. To build engaging 3D scenes, you will also need an image editing software such as Photoshop, but many tools will work. Also, you will need a 3D modeling tool to create content, preferably 3D Studio Max because of its simple user interface, but Blender is available for free.

WebGL is developed with JavaScript and applies math algorithms such as matrices, distance formulae, and trigonometry. For many, this will be a refresher from high school math, with quick tutorials into the math included in the book.

Who this book is for

Web developers will be particularly interested in this next wave of content. Your JavaScript and HTML5 skills are completely transferable to Web3D. Web developers will discover that creating Web3D and 3D graphics is an excellent new skill to add to your resume.

Those looking for an introduction to 3D graphics will find this book an excellent starting point. WebGL can be built quickly using technologies and techniques common to all 3D graphics applications without the complexity, from motion pictures and video games to mobile development.

2D and 3D artists will be very happy working in Web3D. They will enjoy applying their skills in creative ways and exploring the possibilities that WebGL offers, yet with simple examples from the book.

For those who are new to programming, you will find this book to be an excellent starting point. JavaScript has many constructs that are common to all programming languages, yet it does not have the overhead and learning curve of high-level languages such as Java and C++. In addition, 3D graphics is a great way to validate whether a program works and have fun experimenting in it too.

Finally, managers in marketing and research and development and producers involved with content development will appreciate learning the possibilities of WebGL. This book will be an excellent reference and will give you insights into managing Web3D's development with just enough insights into the technology. Managers can expect to learn both fundamental concepts and the capabilities of interactive Web3D for web and mobile applications.

Conventions

A hotshot book has the following sections:

Mission briefing

This section explains what you will build, with a screenshot of the completed project.

Why is it awesome?

This section explains why the project is cool, unique, exciting, and interesting. It describes the advantages that the project will give you.

Your Hotshot objectives

This section explains the major tasks required to complete your project, which are as follows:

- ▶ Task 1
- ▶ Task 2
- ▶ Task 3
- ▶ Task 4

Mission checklist

This section mentions the prerequisites for the project (if any), such as resources or libraries that need to be downloaded.

Each **task** is explained using the following sections:

Prepare for lift off

This section explains any preliminary work that you may need to do before beginning work on the task.

Engage thrusters

This section lists the steps required in order to complete the task.

Objective complete – mini debriefing

This section explains how the steps performed in the previous section (*Engage thrusters*) allow us to complete the task.

Classified intel

This section provides extra information that is relevant to the task.

After all the tasks are completed, the following sections should appear:

Mission accomplished

This section explains the task we accomplished in the project. This is mandatory and should occur after all the tasks in the project are completed.

A Hotshot challenge / Hotshot challenges

This section explains things to be done or tasks to be performed using the concepts explained in this project.

Code words in text, database table names, folder names, filenames, file extensions, pathnames, dummy URLs, user input, and Twitter handles are shown as follows: "Saturn also has a `<Transform>` node centered around the Sun and two child `<Transform>` nodes to control Saturn's day and rings that are constructed from a flat plane and a texture map with a transparency."

A block of code is set as follows:

```
<Shape>
    <Appearance>
        <ImageTexture url="./textureMaps/bassethound.jpg"/>
    </Appearance>
    <IndexedFaceSet coordIndex="0 1 2 -1   2 3 0 -1"
            texCoordIndex="0 1 2 -1   2 3 0 -1">
        <Coordinate point="-2 2 0   -2 -2 0   2 -2 0   2 2 0"/>
        <TextureCoordinate point="0 1   0 0   1 0   1 1"/>
    </IndexedFaceSet>
</Shape>
```

New terms and **important words** are shown in bold. Words that you see on the screen, in menus or dialog boxes for example, appear in the text like this: "The neon **X Y Z** display on the left turns on in a red, green, and blue sequence, and glows onto the street with a red, green, and blue tinge using point lights."

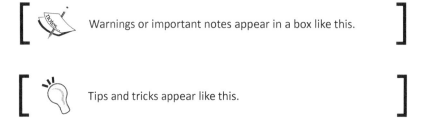

Warnings or important notes appear in a box like this.

Tips and tricks appear like this.

Reader feedback

Feedback from our readers is always welcome. Let us know what you think about this book—what you liked or may have disliked. Reader feedback is important for us to develop titles that you really get the most out of.

To send us general feedback, simply send an e-mail to feedback@packtpub.com, and mention the book title via the subject of your message.

If there is a topic that you have expertise in and you are interested in either writing or contributing to a book, see our author guide on www.packtpub.com/authors.

Customer support

Now that you are the proud owner of a Packt book, we have a number of things to help you to get the most from your purchase.

Downloading the example code

You can download the example code files for all Packt books you have purchased from your account at `http://www.packtpub.com`. If you purchased this book elsewhere, you can visit `http://www.packtpub.com/support` and register to have the files e-mailed directly to you.

Downloading the color images of this book

We also provide you a PDF file that has color images of the screenshots/diagrams used in this book. The color images will help you better understand the changes in the output. You can download this file from: `https://www.packtpub.com/sites/default/files/downloads/0919OS_ColoredImages.pdf`.

Errata

Although we have taken every care to ensure the accuracy of our content, mistakes do happen. If you find a mistake in one of our books—maybe a mistake in the text or the code—we would be grateful if you would report this to us. By doing so, you can save other readers from frustration and help us improve subsequent versions of this book. If you find any errata, please report them by visiting `http://www.packtpub.com/submit-errata`, selecting your book, clicking on the **errata submission form** link, and entering the details of your errata. Once your errata are verified, your submission will be accepted and the errata will be uploaded on our website, or added to any list of existing errata, under the Errata section of that title. Any existing errata can be viewed by selecting your title from `http://www.packtpub.com/support`.

Piracy

Piracy of copyright material on the Internet is an ongoing problem across all media. At Packt, we take the protection of our copyright and licenses very seriously. If you come across any illegal copies of our works, in any form, on the Internet, please provide us with the location address or website name immediately so that we can pursue a remedy.

Please contact us at `copyright@packtpub.com` with a link to the suspected pirated material.

We appreciate your help in protecting our authors, and our ability to bring you valuable content.

Questions

You can contact us at questions@packtpub.com if you are having a problem with any aspect of the book, and we will do our best to address it.

Project 1
Building Great Web3D

"If I have seen further it is by standing on the shoulders of giants."

– Sir Isaac Newton

Not long after the introduction of HTML, 3D for the web was launched. Web3D was a natural extension of existing technologies. Already, the first 3D games such as *Doom* were being launched and computer-generated imagery was being used for special effects in movies. Microsoft's **DirectX** game interface (originally known as Game Developers Kit) was launched and a number of 3D modeling programs such as Caligari trueSpace, 3D Studio, and Wavefront were made available to artists. In addition, programming languages such as Java and JavaScript enable web programming and Internet applications. Existing tools were also being migrated to the Web such as Macromedia's Director through the Shockwave plugin. The Web quickly went beyond just text and static images as multimedia streamed through RealAudio and RealVideo. The first modems grew from 14.4 to 28.8 and then to 56.6 kb/s. Storage increased from 1 MB floppy discs to 700 MB CD-ROMs. Memory disk prices dropped significantly, supporting the move from text to imagery. All this was driven by consumers.

A graphical revolution was taking place. The command-line operating system was finally giving way to a graphical user interface. *Toy Story*, the first animated feature film premiered, showed that 3D was a story-telling medium with engaging characters. Moreover, there was a small group of committed, talented people with visions of an interactive Web3D, combined with enthusiasm and dreams of virtual reality. So much was in place for Web3D's growth: fast technology, 3D modeling tools for creation, and talented people with vision. The first specification, **Virtual Reality Modeling Language** (**VRML**), was also born, although it served as a prototype to the soon-replaced update, **VRML 2.0**. Web3D was a small representative of the dot-com boom. A mix of startups and technology giants entered the arena with varied engineering approaches. Some opted for their own technology such as Pulse 3D and Activeworlds, which is still active as its name says. Others relied on their own VRML browsers and plugins such as Sony, Microsoft, and Silicon Graphics.

With time, however, the Web could no longer just be about fun, irrelevant stuff such as live video cameras focused on fish tanks. It had to become economically viable, and thus, the more frivolous applications gave way to search engines, online banking, and e-commerce. Among them were Yahoo!, Amazon, and America Online. The early pioneers of Web3D and VRML were ahead of their time and deserve acknowledgement for their great work. Their efforts were not futile, but Web3D's day would come another time. The public needed the familiar medium of text, photos, and streaming audio and video. Interactive 3D was finding its early adopters elsewhere—gamers—people who embraced new technology for fun.

A second coming

3D was basically an entertainment medium used in movies such as *Toy Story* and *Shrek* or in video games such as *Doom*. Game development was rather tedious. Programmers had to create software known as drivers for every model of a graphics card, similar to how peripherals today, for instance a printer and a scanner, must have their own driver device. Each video game had its own unique graphic card drivers. The industry needed a better solution to interface between video games and graphic cards. Thus, an industry standard interface was born: a set of commands that said "you game developers, build your game using these commands" and "you graphics chip makers, make sure you accept these commands". The end result was that any game could run on any graphics card.

A graphic interface can be thought of as a gas station; any car can purchase their gas from any gas station. We need not worry about our car only accepting gas from a particular vendor. The two leading graphics interfaces at the end of the millennium were **Open Graphics Library** (**OpenGL**) (1992) and **DirectX** (1995). OpenGL was from **Silicon Graphics Incorporated** (**SGI**) and was designed for computer graphics in animation or special effects, mostly in movies or commercials. Thus, OpenGL did not require interactivity from the mouse or keyboard to play video games. OpenGL also did not include sound; audio would just be combined with the computer-generated video in a film-editing process.

The other graphics interface was DirectX, originally known as Game Developers Kit from Microsoft. Launched in the early 1990s, DirectX provided additional support for programming video games such as interfaces to the mouse, keyboard, and game controllers as well as support to control audio. Game developers could use DirectX to load their 3D models; move and rotate them; specify lights and properties; and receive mouse, keyboard, and game controller commands.

OpenGL was picked up by Khronos (`www.khronos.org`), a consortium of graphics and computer companies that insured its growth. Khronos' mission is to create open standards for all computing media. It was a broad agenda that incorporated mobile graphics and the Web.

Meanwhile, file formats also needed an industry standard. It was clear that information was being shared among organizations, businesses, and over the Internet. There was a need for a worldwide standard for the World Wide Web. XML, eXtensible Markup Language, was launched in the late 1990s. It specified a format to share data and ways to validate whether the format is correct. Each industry would come up with its own standards; the most prevalent was HTML, which adopted the XML standard to become XHTML, a more rigorous standard that enabled a more consistent file format.

VRML 2.0 gained stature as a 3D mesh file-sharing format and was exported from major 3D modeling programs. Now was the time to jump on the XML bandwagon, and thus, X3D was born. It had the features of VRML but was now in a standardized XML format. VRML and X3D were under the direction of the Web3D Consortium (`http://www.web3d.org/`), a group of outstanding, intelligent, dedicated people with a vision and commitment for 3D on the Web. As an XML document, X3D could be extended for specific applications, such as medical applications, computer-aided design (CAD) for mechanical engineers, and avatars. Collada is another file format from Khronos with a broader scope for other 3D applications, but with X3D, the community is well served.

Comprehensive solutions

Khronos and the Web3D Consortium brought different companies together to produce unified standards and solutions. An issue with the standards was that companies with vested financial interests in their own technologies would have to compromise and perhaps lose a technical advantage. However, in the long run, we end up with a greater good that has standards, and some companies continue to support their own features as an extension to these standards. Often, the right path cannot be discovered until we have tried other unsuccessful paths. We learned a lot in the early days. Remarkably, the early inventors got much of it right, even for the products that had not yet been invented or conceived such as smartphones. Perhaps the only criticism seemed to be redundancy; there were multiple commands in OpenGL to accomplish the same functions. A little streamlining was in order, and thus, **OpenGL ES** (Embedded Systems, 2003) gave us a powerful 3D graphics interface for low battery power and low-level devices.

Khronos launched **WebGL** in March 2011, which was supported in Google Chrome, Safari, Firefox, and most recently, Microsoft's Internet Explorer. The ongoing evolution of HTML—the language read by web browsers to display web pages—was producing new standards for HTML5 with the goal of supporting multimedia and interactivity. 3D and, by association, WebGL were a natural fit to be embedded into HTML5. WebGL did not require a plugin to view 3D inside web pages, and by interfacing with the graphics card, WebGL could deliver high-performance graphics. Programming in **JavaScript** and **Cascading Style Sheets** (**CSS**) were languages familiar to web developers.

Technical breakthroughs are often a synergy of near-simultaneous events. The Internet had been around for nearly a quarter of a century before 1970, but was not a commercial success. A convergence of hardware and software took place. Fax modems became commonplace on most PCs. Netscape, the first web browser, was born. Consumers were introduced to the Internet via AOL (America Online), and while primitive to today's standards, the graphical user interface was ubiquitous with Windows, introduced years earlier by Macintosh (and Xerox if we wish to be precise). Web3D was undergoing its own technical breakthrough with HTML5, OpenGL ES, X3D, and one more innovation—shader languages—also known as GPU (Graphics Processing Unit) programming.

The earlier versions of OpenGL and the streamlined OpenGL ES used the *fixed-function pipeline* method. A 3D mesh, which is simply a list of vertices and how they are connected—think of a Rose Parade Float formed with chicken wire—would go through a series of steps known as the 3D graphics pipeline. The pipeline would perform the following tasks:

▶ Transform the object so that it would move (translate), rotate, and scale the 3D object

▶ Transform the object to the camera's point-of-view

▶ Convert the scene into perspective view so that it appears on the screen in the same way as we would perceive it with our eye in the real world

Traditionally, all the programming was done on the CPU, which passed the 3D meshes and object transformations to the GPU in order to draw or render the colored dots on the screen. The GPU is simply another computer chip specifically designed for this final drawing. It is programmable and its multiprocessor capability means it can operate on multiple vertices simultaneously. Innovators began programming GPUs. Eventually, a formal programming language was designed to program the GPU / shader languages.

Shader languages enabled developers to have finite control and programming over each pixel, vertex, light, and text. With the earlier fixed-function pipeline, we only controlled the final location of the vertices and let the GPU interpolate between the vertices to draw the polygons. Now, with shader languages, we can calculate lighting, shadows, rough surfaces, and blend texture maps on a pixel-by-pixel basis. A great advantage of GPU programming is that the OpenGL ES standard is shared across many products. So, the same shader language coded on an iPhone works for an Android phone. Finally, all was in place—WebGL overcame the plugin issues of the previous Web3D attempts, X3D would be the latest file format based on the XML community standard, and shader languages would give us improved performance and image quality on a pixel-by-pixel basis.

Mission briefing

We now venture into Web3D by building our first X3D objects. This will also introduce you to the 3D scene graph of how objects are specified; first, they are specified as primitives, such as boxes and spheres, and then as more complex 3D models built by artists. We will also apply textures to these 3D meshes and include cameras, lights, animation, and interactivity.

Why is it awesome?

X3D is a great language to specify a 3D scene without doing any programming. It is also a great learning tool. Best of all, it provides instant gratification. If you have never created anything in 3D, you will now be able to create something in a few minutes.

Your Hotshot objectives

- Introduction to 3D fundamentals
- Transformations – translation, rotation, and scaling
- Lights, camera, action!
- Navigating between multiple viewports
- Animation with interpolators
- Adding texture maps to 3D meshes
- Lighting a scene and shading 3D objects with normals
- Creating an animated Solar System with multiple cameras for navigation

Mission checklist

Most X3D and WebGL developments require a little more than what comes on a standard computer—be it a PC, Macintosh, or other device; I would not doubt that one can create and test Web3D on a smartphone or a tablet.

Firefox is the preferred browser for testing. Google Chrome will not allow you to read 3D objects off the hard drive due to security restrictions, which require you to upload your 3D objects, texture maps, and WebGL to your website before testing. Firefox relaxes these restrictions and will enable you to test your work on your hard drive.

As we dive deeper into Web3D creation, you may need to configure your server to enable MIME types such as `.obj` for 3D models. You may want to consult your server administrator to check this.

Some websites that are worth bookmarking are as follows:

- **The Web3D Consortium**: This website (http://www.web3d.org/) defines the X3D file format and has the latest news

- **X3Dom**: This website (http://www.x3dom.org/) has the libraries that are used for our X3D demonstrations

- **The Khronos Group**: This website (http://www.khronos.org/) is the consortium that oversees the OpenGL specification and defines WebGL

- **3D-Online**: This website (http://www.3D-Online.com) is for book demonstrations and author contact information

Introduction to 3D fundamentals

A picture is worth a thousand words, and this is, after all, a book on 3D graphics. So, let's get started with the fun stuff! Two technologies will be demonstrated: WebGL and X3D. WebGL is related to X3D, but X3D is better to demonstrate simple objects. Since we will be building the Solar System, X3D is better in order to show the three rotations of the Earth—the 24-hour day rotation, the seasonal tilts, and the 365.25 annual rotation around the Sun. The Moon is a child of the Earth. Wherever the Earth goes, the Moon follows with its own independent rotation around the Earth. To assist the parsing of these X3D files, we shall use X3DOM (X3D with the **Document Object Model** (**DOM**))—a publicly available program. WebGL, by itself, is ideal to display the 3D mesh, whereas X3D better represents the connection between objects. For example, an X3D file can show the hierarchy of an animated hand rotating at the wrist, which is connected to the lower arm that rotates at the elbow, and then the shoulder.

Programming tradition states that the first program shall be called "Hello World" and simply displays these words. 3D also has "Hello World"; however, it displays the simplest 3D object—a box.

A <Box> node is one of the several simple primitives that are included in X3D; the other shape nodes are <Cone>, <Cylinder>, and <Sphere>. While WebGL is JavaScript programming, X3D looks like HTML tags. So, angular brackets, < and >, will often be used to describe X3D.

Engage thrusters

However, we will not cover basic HTML tags, CSS, or JavaScript. There is too much to cover in 3D, and these are better addressed online. A good source for basic HTML and web programming can be found at http://www.w3schools.com/. Here is our first <Box> shape node used in the following code:

```
<!DOCTYPE html PUBLIC "-//W3C//DTD XHTML 1.0 Strict//EN" http://www.
w3.org/TR/xhtml1/DTD/xhtml1-strict.dtd">
<html xmlns="http://www.w3.org/1999/xhtml">
    <head>
<meta http-equiv="X-UA-Compatible" content="chrome=1" />
        <meta http-equiv="Content-Type"
content="text/html;charset=utf-8" />
        <title>WebGL Hotshots - chapter 01</title>
<link rel="stylesheet" type="text/css"
href="x3dom.css"/>
        <script type="text/javascript" src="x3dom.js"></script>
    </head>
    <body>
        <X3D
xmlns=http://www.web3d.org/specifications/x3d-namespace
width="400px" height="400px">
<Scene>
    <Shape>
        <Appearance>
            <Material diffuseColor='0.9 0.6 0.3'/>
        </Appearance>
         <Box/>
    </Shape>
</Scene>
</X3D>
</body>
</html>
```

Objective complete – mini debriefing

Between the `<head>` and `</head>` tags are two references that link this xhtml file to the X3DOM JavaScript code, `x3dom.js`. This code parses the X3D file and loads the data onto the graphics card using the OpenGL commands. So, it takes care of a lot of low-level coding, which we will look at later using WebGL. Also, the `x3dom.css` file sets some parameters similar to any CSS file. Thus, a basic knowledge of HTML is helpful to develop WebGL. Some of the other tags in the preceding code relate to the validation process of all XML documents such as the DOCTYPE information in the preceding code.

The heart of the matter begins with the `<X3D>` tag being embedded into a standard XHTML document. It can also include X3D version information, width and height data, and other identifications that will be used later. There are also a set of `<Scene>` and `</Scene>` tags within which all the 3D data will be contained.

The `<Shape>` tags contain a single 3D mesh and specify the geometry and appearance of the 3D mesh. Here, we have a single `<Box/>` tag and the `<Appearance>` tag, which specifies either a texture map and/or a `<Material>` tag that includes several properties, namely, the diffuse color that will be blended with the color of our scene's lights, the emissive or glow simulation color, the object's specular highlights such as a bright spot reflecting the Sun on a car's hood, and any transparency. Colors in 3D are the same as those used on the Web—red, green, and blue. Though 3D colors span between 0 and 1, the Web often uses a hexadecimal number from 0 x 00 through 0 x FF. In the preceding code, the diffuse color used is 0.9 red, 0.6 green, and 0.3 blue for a light orange color.

The box also shows some shading with its brightest sides facing us. This is because there is a default headlight in the scene, which is positioned in the direction of the camera. This scene has no camera defined; in this case, a default camera will be inserted at the position (0, 0, 10), which is 10 units towards us along the *z* axis and points towards the origin (0, 0, 0). If you run this program (which you should), you will be able to rotate the viewpoint (camera) around the origin with the default headlight attached to the viewpoint. We will address lighting later, as lighting is a very important and complex part of 3D graphics.

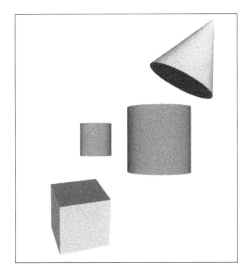

Transformations – translation, rotation, and scaling

We are off to a good start. Now, let's add two or more objects. If we don't want everything sitting in the same place, we need a way to position the objects in the vast universe of 3D space. The most common way is by using *transformation*.

Engage thrusters

We don't alter the original 3D object, but just apply some math to each point in the 3D mesh to rotate, translate (move), and/or scale the object, as follows:

```
<Scene>
    <Transform translation="-2 -3 -3"  rotation=".6 .8 0 .5">
        <Shape>
            <Appearance>
                <Material diffuseColor='0.9 0.6 0.3' />
            </Appearance>
         <Box/>
        </Shape>
    </Transform>
    <Transform translation="2 2.5 1" rotation="0 0 1 -.5">
        <Shape>
            <Appearance>
                <Material diffuseColor='0.3 0.9 0.6' />
            </Appearance>
```

```
                <Cone/>
            </Shape>
        </Transform>
        <Transform translation="-1 0 0" scale=".5 .5 .5">
            <Shape>
                <Appearance>
                    <Material diffuseColor='0.6 0.3 0.9' />
                </Appearance>
             <Cylinder/>
            </Shape>
        </Transform>
        <Transform translation="1 0 0">
            <Shape>
                <Appearance>
                    <Material diffuseColor='0.6 0.3 0.9' />
                </Appearance>
             <Cylinder/>
            </Shape>
        </Transform>
    </Scene>
```

Objective complete – mini debriefing

Each `<Shape>` tag is now embedded into a `<Transform>` tag. The first object, the box, has a translation of (-2, -3, -3), which moves it two units to the left, three units downwards, and three units backward from the origin. It also has a rotation of (0.6, 0.8, 0, 0.5), which will be discussed in more detail later, but the first three values represent the x, y, and z axes, respectively, and the fourth value is the angle of rotation in radians (*π radians = 180 degrees*). Also, note that the sum of the squares of the *x*, *y*, and *z* values equals 1: $x^2 + y^2 + z^2 = 1$.

The second object is a cone translated two units to the right, 2.5 units upwards, and one unit forward with a rotation of 0.5 radians around the *z* axis (like the hands of a clock). The third and fourth objects are both cylinders with a uniform 0.5 scale on the left cylinder, which means that it's half its default size. Note that the scale does not need to be the same value for all three axes.

Lights, camera, action!

"Lights, camera, action!" is an old Hollywood phrase to start filming, but it is just as applicable to interactive 3D graphics. So, let's add lights, cameras, and interactivity to our X3D scenes.

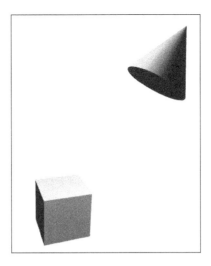

Engage thrusters

This scene retains the first two objects created previously and adds a point light that can be thought of as a light bulb—a light from a single point emanating in all directions. We turned off the headlight inside the `<NavigationInfo>` tag, and at the same time, restricted movement in the scene by setting `type` to `NONE`, simply to introduce this as part of the demo. At the same time, the `<Viewpoint>` tag or camera is introduced with its default `position` value, `orientation` (rotation) value, and `fieldOfView` value that defaults to $\pi/4$, that is, 0.785 radians. The added code is as follows:

```
<Scene>
    <NavigationInfo headlight="FALSE" type='"NONE"'/>
    <PointLight location="0 3 2"/>
    <Viewpoint position="0 0 10" orientation="0 0 1 0"
        fieldOfView=".785"/>
    <Transform …>
```

The point light is 3 units up and 2 units in front, so it clearly shines on the top of the box and to the left-hand side of the cone but not on the left-hand side of the box or the bottom of the cylinder.

Navigating between multiple viewpoints

3D space is wonderful to travel freely, but we also want specific cameras for users and ways to navigate between them. The following figure depicts the same scene from three different viewpoints with a single spotlight on the left-hand side of the image along the negative *x* axis pointing towards the origin (0, 0, 0). The image on the left shows the initial default camera, the image in the middle shows the view from the left along the *x* axis from the `<Viewpoint>` node named vp1, and the image on the right is from the `<Viewpoint>` node labeled vp2 at a 45-degree angle between the positive *x* axis and the positive *z* axis:

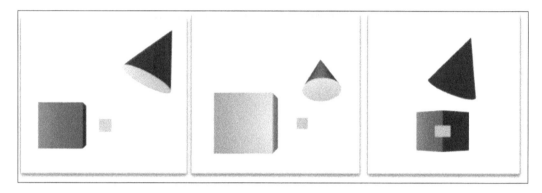

Engage thrusters

In the following code, we have three `<Viewpoint>` nodes. These cameras are in the id=origin default position, the left-hand side of the scene (id=vp1), and at a 45-degree angle on the right (id=vp2). All cameras are facing the origin. Clicking on the `<Box>` node directs us to go to the camera vp1. Clicking on the cone animates us to `<Viewpoint>` vp2, and clicking on the small blue `<Box>` sends us back to our original `<Viewpoint>`. Note that the order does matter, although the scene begins with the first `<Viewpoint>` listed:

```
<Scene>
<NavigationInfo headlight="FALSE" type='"NONE"'/>
<SpotLight location="-5 0 0" direction="0 0 0"/>
<Viewpoint id="origin" position="0 0 10"
    orientation="0 0 1 0" fieldOfView=".785"/>
<Viewpoint id="vp1" orientation="0 1 0 -1.57"
    position="-12 0 0"></Viewpoint>
<Viewpoint id="vp2" orientation="0 1 0 .785"
    position="10 0 10"></Viewpoint>
<Transform translation="-2 0 -2">
    <Shape>
```

```
        <Appearance>
            <Material diffuseColor='1 0.75 0.5'/>
        </Appearance>
        <Box onclick =
            "document.getElementById('vp1').setAttribute
            ('set_bind','true');"/>
    </Shape>
</Transform>
<Transform translation="2 2.5 1" rotation="0 0 1 -.5">
    <Shape>
        <Appearance>
            <Material diffuseColor='0.5 1 0.75'/>
        </Appearance>
     <Cone onclick =
        "document.getElementById('vp2').setAttribute
        ('set_bind','true');"/>
    </Shape>
</Transform>
<Transform scale=".25 .25 .25">
    <Shape>
        <Appearance>
          <Material diffuseColor='0 0 0'
              emissiveColor='0.75 0.5 1' />
        </Appearance>
        <Box onclick =
            "document.getElementById('origin').setAttribute
                ('set_bind','true');"/>
    </Shape>
</Transform>
</Scene>
```

Objective complete – mini debriefing

The small `<Box>` node is placed at the origin for reference. Its diffuse color is black and thus is unaffected by any lights. Instead, its emissive color is light purple, though it does not actually emit light. For this, we would need some additional lighting objects to give the impression that it glows. The `<Box>` node also has some familiar JavaScript programming, `onclick="document.getElementById('origin')`, that HTML web developers have seen while programming interactive websites. The rest of the line (`setAttribute('set_bind','true');`) is X3D's way of setting the viewpoint named `origin` to be the current or bound camera. Note that the spotlight in the image in the middle does not have a rounded edge that a flashlight typically produces. Lights without GPU or shader languages are limited to calculating the light at each vertex and interpolating the light across the polygon. By contrast, shader languages calculate these images on a pixel-by-pixel basis in the GPU's multiprocessor, so the process is quite fast. We will see more of this and shader languages' contribution to 3D graphics imagery later.

Animation with interpolators

Animation comes in the following forms:

- **Procedural**: This type of animation is controlled by a program, such as the simulation of a bouncing ball impacted by real-world physics.

- **Event-driven**: This type of animation includes motion based on events in the scene, such as a simulation of a dog that sees, smells, hears, and then reacts to it.

- **Key frame**: This type of animation is where the animated character's movement(s) and rotation(s) occur at specific times. WebGL interpolates between these key frames.

The Moon orbiting around the Earth, which in turn orbits around the Sun, has a lot of good 3D graphic concepts to review. Note that the Earth's transformation is inside the Sun's transformation, and the Moon's transform is contained inside the Earth's transform. Thus, wherever the Earth goes, rotating around the Sun, the Moon will follow. Also, not only is the Earth 10 units away from the Sun, but it's center is -10 units, which means that the center of the Earth's rotation is the Sun. Now, the Earth also rotates around its own axis for a day; we will show this later. Have a look at the following screenshot:

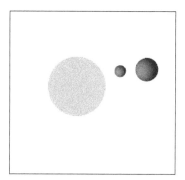

Engage thrusters

Layout the code with all the objects such as the Sun, Earth, and Moon along with all the `<Transform>` nodes, `<TimeSensor>` nodes, and interpolators before the ROUTE node. The order is important, just as we must have the `<Transform>` nodes embedded properly to represent the annual, seasonal, and daily rotations of the Earth, as shown in the following code:

```
<Scene>
<Viewpoint orientation="1 0 0 -.3" position="0 8 30"/>
    <NavigationInfo headlight="false"/>
    <PointLight/>
```

```
    <Transform DEF="Sun">
        <Shape>
            <Sphere radius="2.5"/>
            <Appearance>
                <Material diffuseColor="1 1 0"
                          emissiveColor="1 .5 0"/>
            </Appearance>
        </Shape>
    <Transform DEF="Earth" center="-10 0 0"
                           translation="10 0 0">
        <Shape>
            <Sphere radius="1.2"/>
            <Appearance>
                <Material diffuseColor=".2 .4 .8"/>
            </Appearance>
        </Shape>
    <Transform DEF="Moon" center="-3 0 0"
                          translation="3 0 0">
        <Shape>
                    <Sphere radius=".6"/>
                    <Appearance>
                        <Material diffuseColor=".4 .4 .4"/>
                    </Appearance>
        </Shape>
            </Transform>
        </Transform>
    </Transform>
    <TimeSensor DEF="yearTimer" cycleInterval="36.5" loop="true"/>
<OrientationInterpolator DEF="YRotation" key="0 .5 1"
keyValue="0 1 0 0   0 1 0 3.14   0 1 0 6.28"/>
<ROUTE fromField="fraction_changed" fromNode="yearTimer"
toField="set_fraction" toNode="YRotation"/>
<ROUTE fromField="value_changed" fromNode="YRotation"
toField="rotation" toNode="Earth"/>

<TimeSensor DEF="moonTimer" cycleInterval="2.9" loop="true"/>
<OrientationInterpolator DEF="YRotMoon" key="0 .5 1"
keyValue="0 1 0 0   0 1 0 3.14   0 1 0 6.28"/>
<ROUTE fromField="fraction_changed" fromNode="moonTimer"
toField="set_fraction" toNode="YRotMoon"/>
<ROUTE fromField="value_changed" fromNode="YRotMoon"
toField="rotation" toNode="Moon"/>
</Scene>
```

Objective complete – mini debriefing

The <TimeSensor> nodes, interpolators, and the ROUTE nodes create the key frame animation. The <TimeSensor> node specifies the duration (cycleInterval) of the animation, which is 36.5 seconds here, where each day represents one tenth of a second. Interpolators specify the key and keyValue functions such that for each key function, there must be a key value function. Since this is a rotation or change in orientation, we use <OrientationInterpolator>. Also, there are <PositionInterpolator> and <ColorInterpolator> nodes that move the 3D mesh and change its color, respectively, over time. Unlike films, where we have a fixed 30 frames per second, in real-time animations we can have more or less frames per second depending on how complex the scene is and also on the performance of our CPU.

We will break down the interpolator at the three keys when the time equals 0, 0.5, and 1, as follows:

- The <OrientationInterpolator> node says that at *time = 0*, the rotation will be (0, 1, 0, 0), meaning a rotation of 0 radians around the *y* axis.

- At *time = 0.5*, which is 18.25 seconds (half of 36.5 seconds) here, the rotation will be (0 1 0 3.14) or 3.14 radians, which is 180 degrees around the *y* axis.

- Finally, at *time = 1*, which is 36.5 seconds, the rotation will be 6.28 radians, which is a full 360-degree circle around the *y* axis.

So, why do we have to put a midpoint such as 180 degrees? The problem is that the <OrientationInterpolator> node optimizes the rotation distances to be the smallest. For example, a 120-degree rotation clockwise is the same as a 240-degree rotation counter-clockwise. However, the <OrientationInterpolator> node will take the shortest route and rotate 120 degrees clockwise. If you wanted to force a 240-degree counter-clockwise rotation, you'd need to add a midpoint.

Finally, we have to connect the timer to the interpolator with the 3D object that has to be rotated. The ROUTE node directs value(s) from a timer or sensor to another sensor or object. The first ROUTE node takes the output from yearTimer.fraction_changed to YRotation.set_fraction. Note the passing of a fraction value within the ROUTE node. The timer will count from 0 to 36.5 seconds and divide this value by 36.5 so that it is a value between 0 and 1. The orientation interpolator will receive this fraction value and interpolate between the two key values. For example, at 10 seconds, the fraction is 10/36.5 or 0.274, which is between 0 and 0.5 in the <OrientationInterpolator> node's key. This becomes a key value of (0 1 0 1.72), about 98.63 degrees (*1.72 radians * 180 degrees/π*).

The next ROUTE node sends the keyValue function from the <OrientationInterpolator> node and sets the rotation values of the <Transform> node defined as Earth, using the DEF="Earth" statement inside the <Transform> node. And with this, we nearly have our Solar System. We just have to add more planets.

Adding texture maps to 3D meshes

So far, our objects have been pretty basic shapes and in a single color. That's why they are called primitives. But of course, 3D objects are far more complex and require the talent of artists. Texture maps help us to understand how complex 3D objects are assembled based on simple ones. Have a look at the following figure:

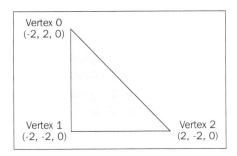

Engage thrusters

A solid colored triangle is the simplest object to draw. I often suggest drawing objects on paper and labelling the vertices depending on how they are connected because it can be very tedious to form shapes from memory:

```
<Shape>
<Appearance>
    <Material diffuseColor="1 1 0"/>
</Appearance>
    <IndexedFaceSet coordIndex="0 1 2 -1">
    <Coordinate point="-2 2 0   -2 -2 0   2 -2 0"/>
    </IndexedFaceSet>
</Shape>
```

Instead of specifying a box or sphere, the shape in the preceding code consists of `IndexedFaceSet` with three points or vertices connected in the order listed by `coordIndex = "0 1 2 -1"`. Vertex 0 is connected to vertex 1, vertex 1 is connected to vertex 2, and vertex 2 is connected back to vertex 0. The side that should face us is determined by the right-hand rule. Using your right hand, curve your fingers in the order of the vertices. The direction of your thumb is the direction that the polygon faces. So, as you curve your fingers counter-clockwise, if your thumb is pointing towards you, the polygon will be visible to you. The vertices are connected in a counter-clockwise order.

Let's add a texture map of a wonderful Basset Hound dog with a wet, pink tongue. The camera has been slightly rotated to distinguish this 3D object from a flat image. Have a look at the following screenshot:

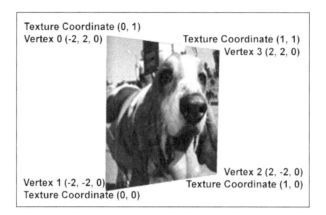

Have a look at the following code:

```
<Shape>
<Appearance>
<ImageTexture url="./textureMaps/bassethound.jpg"/>
</Appearance>
<IndexedFaceSet coordIndex="0 1 2 -1   2 3 0 -1"
    texCoordIndex="0 1 2 -1   2 3 0 -1">
    <Coordinate point="-2 2 0   -2 -2 0   2 -2 0   2 2 0"/>
    <TextureCoordinate point="0 1   0 0   1 0   1 1"/>
</IndexedFaceSet>
</Shape>
```

In the preceding code, a fourth coordinate point has been added to form two triangles. The `IndexedFaceSet  coordIndex` node now specifies two triangles. It is preferred to use triangles rather than polygons of four or more vertices for the same reason that a three-legged chair won't wobble, but a four-legged chair may wobble because one leg may be longer than the others and not sit flat on the ground. At least this is a nontechnical and noncomplex answer. Three vertex polygons will always be flat or planer and four vertex polygons can be bent. Additionally, it's often just about selecting a checkbox to export a 3D mesh using only triangles for artists.

The <Appearance> tag now has an <ImageTexture> node tag instead of a <Material> tag and specifies an image similar to how HTML would embed an image into a web page. A texture map on a 3D mesh is like hanging wallpaper on a wall. We paste the wallpaper to the corners. We need to align the corners of the walls with the correct corners of the wallpaper; otherwise, the wallpaper gets hung sideways or upside down. The <TextureCoordinate> point specifies which corner of the texture map is placed at each vertex of the 3D mesh. The lower-left corner of a texture map is (0, 0), and the upper-right corner is (1, 1). The first value is along the *x* axis, and the second value is along the *y* axis.

The <TextureCoordinate> point gets aligned to the <Coordinate> point vertices. For example, the first <Coordinate> point is (-2, 2, 0), which is the upper-left vertex, and the first <TextureCoordinate> point is (0, 1), which is the upper-left corner of the texture map.

The final texture map shows the <TextureTransform> tag, which is often used for tiling (such as repeating a brick wall pattern), but it can also be used for shifting and rotating images. For example, texture maps can also be animated to create nice water effects.

The three images in the preceding screenshot show tiling with a texture map of 3 x 2 in the upper-left 3D mesh, rotation of the texture map by 0.2 radians in the image on the right, and translation of the texture map by -0.3 units to the left and 0.6 units upwards in the image in the lower-left-hand side corner. In the following code, within the `<Scene>` tags, there are three `<Transform>` tags, one tag for each `<Shape>` node, and the `<TextureTransform>` node:

```
<Scene>
<Transform translation="-3 2 -3">
<Shape>
<Appearance>
<ImageTexture DEF="basset"
url="./textureMaps/bassethound.jpg"/>
<TextureTransform scale="3 2"/>
</Appearance>
    <IndexedFaceSet DEF="bassetIFS"
        coordIndex="0 1 2 -1   2 3 0 -1"
        texCoordIndex="0 1 2 -1   2 3 0 -1">
            <Coordinate point="-2 2 0   -2 -2 0   2 -2 0
            2 2 0"/>
                <TextureCoordinate point="0 1   0 0   1 0
                1 1"/>
    </IndexedFaceSet>
    </Shape>
        </Transform>
        <Transform  translation="2 1 -2">
    <Shape>
        <Appearance>
            <ImageTexture USE="basset"/>
            <TextureTransform rotation=".2"/>
        </Appearance>
        <IndexedFaceSet USE="bassetIFS"/>
    </Shape>
        </Transform>
        <Transform  translation="-3 -3 -4">
    <Shape>
        <Appearance>
            <ImageTexture USE="basset"/>
            <TextureTransform translation=".3 -.6"/>
        </Appearance>
        <IndexedFaceSet USE="bassetIFS"/>
        </Shape>
    </Transform>
</Scene>
```

Objective complete – mini debriefing

Since each of the 3D meshes shares the same `<ImageTexture>` and `<IndexedFaceSet>` nodes, this application is a perfect opportunity to use the `DEF` and `USE` properties. Through `<DEF>` and `<USE>`, we were able to focus on the capabilities of the `<TextureTransform>` node.

Lighting a scene and shading 3D objects with normals

One of the great effects in 3D graphics is to create surfaces such as a weathered brick wall, the bumpy skin of an orange, or ripples on the surface of water. Often, these surfaces are flat, but we can blend images together or paint the texture with these bumps. They can even be animated so that water appears to be flowing, such as in a waterfall. To create this realistic, weathered, and irregular look, we use vertex normals. A normal is simply a three-dimensional vector usually at a right angle to the polygon and often generated by 3D modeling tools.

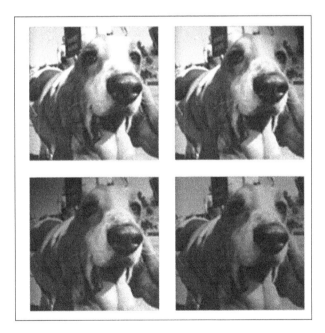

Engage thrusters

Each of the images in the preceding screenshot of the dog uses the same lighting, texture maps, and polygons. They only differ by their normals. In the upper-left image, the normals are all set to (0, 0, 1), which means that they point right back at the light and thus each corner is fully lit. However, the lower-left image has its normals randomly set and thus does not point back at the light source. The image on the upper-right-hand side has the normal in the top-right corner set 90 degrees away; therefore, this corner appears as a dark spot. Finally, the lower-right image has its normal pointing at an angle to the light and thus the entire image is dark. The following code contains four <Transform> nodes with identical shapes and texture maps, and only differs by the vector values in the <Normal> nodes (thus, much of the repeated code has been left out):

```
<Transform translation="-2.25 2.25 -2">
<Shape>
<Appearance DEF='bassetHoundImage' >
<Material diffuseColor='1 1 1' />
<ImageTexture url='textureMaps/bassethound.jpg' />
</Appearance>

<IndexedFaceSet coordIndex='0 1 2 -1   3 2 1 -1'
                normalIndex='0 1 2 -1   3 2 1 -1'
                texCoordIndex='0 1 2 -1   3 2 1 -1' >
<Coordinate DEF="coords" point='-2 -2 0, 2 -2 0,
    -2 2 0, 2 2 0'/>
            <Normal vector='0 0 1, 0 0 1, 0 0 1, 0 0 1'/>
            <TextureCoordinate DEF="textureCoord"
                point='0 0, 1 0, 0 1, 1 1' />
        </IndexedFaceSet>
</Shape>
</Transform>


<Transform translation="-2.25 -2.25 -2">
<Shape>
        <Appearance USE='bassetHoundImage' />
        <IndexedFaceSet coordIndex='0 1 2 -1   3 2 1 -1'
                    normalIndex='0 1 2 -1   3 2 1 -1'
                    texCoordIndex='0 1 2 -1   3 2 1 -1' >
            <Coordinate USE="coords" />
            <Normal vector='-.707 -.5 .5, 0 0 1,
                -.707 .707 0, 0 .8 .6'/>
            <TextureCoordinate USE="textureCoord" />
        </IndexedFaceSet>
</Shape>
</Transform>
```

```
<Transform translation="-2.25 -2.25 -2">
...
    <Normal vector='0 0 1, 0 0 1, 0 0 1, 1 0 0'/>
    ...
</Transform>

<Transform translation="2.25 -2.25 -2">
...
    <Normal vector='.63 .63 .48, .63 .63 .48,
        .63 .63 .48, .63 .63 .48'/>
</Transform>
```

Objective complete – mini debriefing

Only the X3D code for the first two images is shown. Using the DEF and USE properties allows us to share the same `<Appearance>`, `<Coordinate>`, and `<TextureCoordinate>` nodes for each shape. Only the `<Normal>` node within each `<Transform>` node for the two textured 3D meshes on the right are shown. Note that the `<Normal>` vector is a unit value, which means that it has a length of 1; its three-dimensional (x, y, z) values have the property $x^2 + y^2 + z^2 = 1$.

Normals play a major role in shader languages; they allow you to create a realistic look for complex lighting. We shall visit normals later, but let's see one small piece of math here. The amount of light on a polygon at each vertex is calculated by multiplying the (opposite direction of the) light vector and the normal vector. Both values must be unit values, which means that they should have a length of 1 unit before you multiply the two vectors. The light vector L can be multiplied with the normal vector N (known as the dot product) as $(L_x\ L_y\ L_z) * (N_x\ N_y\ N_z) = L_x * N_x + L_y * N_y + L_z * N_z$. The value will be between -1 and 1 (inclusive of both), but for any value less than zero, the light will come from behind the object, leaving the vertex in the dark. Incidentally, this amount of light at a vertex is equal to the cosine of the angle between the two vectors. For example, if the angle between the light vector and the normal vector is 30 degrees, then the dot product will equal *cosine (30) = 0.866*, or about 86.6 percent of the entire amount of light will reach this vertex.

Creating an animated Solar System with multiple cameras for navigation

We conclude this 3D graphics overview with our first application, a Solar System with several cameras and planets undergoing multiple animations. First, we will look at the organization of these objects in a condensed version of the X3D code (the `<IndexedFaceSet>` node in the Earth was removed from here since it consists of thousands of values).

Engage thrusters

Earth comprises of three <Transform> nodes for its rotation around the Sun, the seasons, and the 24-hour day. Note that in the Earth's outermost transformation, center (0, 0, 10) is at the same distance from the Sun as the Earth's translation (0, 0, -10). This is because the *center* of the Earth's yearly rotation is the Sun. The rotation for the Earth's seasons is around the *z* axis, set to 0.4 radians or 23 degrees, the actual tilt of the Earth. The final inner <Transform> node controls the Earth's daily rotation.

The Moon <Transform> is a child of the Earth's annual rotation. The Moon's rotation is centered on the Earth. Thus, the Moon's translation is 3 units (3, 0, 0) from the Earth, but its center is 3 units behind (-3, 0, 0). Of course, the Moon is unaffected by the Earth's seasonal and daily rotation, and thus the Moon's <Transform> node is a child object of the Earth's outermost year <Transform> but not a child of the Earth's seasonal or daily transformation.

```
<NavigationInfo headlight="FALSE"/>
<Viewpoint id="mainCamera" orientation="1 0 0 -.3"
position="0 8 30"/>
<Viewpoint id="aboveCamera" orientation="1 0 0 -1.57"
position="0 180 0"/>
<PointLight/>
    <Transform DEF="Sun">
        <Shape>
            <Sphere radius="6" onclick =
                "document.getElementById('aboveCamera')
                .setAttribute('set_bind','true');"/>
            <Appearance>
                <Material diffuseColor="1 1 0"
                    emissiveColor="1 .7 0"/>
            </Appearance>
        </Shape>
    </Transform>

    <Viewpoint id="EarthCamera" position=" 0 2 0"
        orientation="0 1 0 0"/>
    <Transform DEF="Earth" center="0 0 10"
translation="0 0 -10" scale="2 2 2">
        <Transform DEF="Earth-Season" rotation="0 0 1 .4">
            <Transform DEF="Earth-Day">
                <Shape>
....IndexedFaceSet and coordinates
                </Shape>
            </Transform>
        </Transform>
</Transform>
```

```
                <Transform DEF="Moon" center="-3 0 0"
    translation="3 0 0">
    <Shape>
                    <Sphere radius=".6"/>
                    <Appearance>
                <Material diffuseColor=".4 .4 .4"/>
                    </Appearance>
    </Shape>
            </Transform>
        </Transform>
```

Saturn also has a `<Transform>` node centered around the Sun and two child `<Transform>` nodes to control Saturn's day and rings that are constructed from a flat plane and a texture map with a transparency.

```
        <Viewpoint id="SaturnCamera" position=" 0 0 0"
    orientation="0 1 0 0" fieldOfView=".5"/>
        <Transform DEF="Saturn" center="0 0 20"
    translation="0 0 -20" scale="4 4 4">
            <Transform DEF="SaturnDay">
                <Shape>
                    <Appearance>
                        <Material diffuseColor='1 1 1'
                                specularColor='.1 .1 .1'
                                shininess='0.9' />
                    <ImageTexture
    url="./textureMaps/saturn.jpg"/>
                    </Appearance>
                    <IndexedFaceSet USE='Sphere_GEOMETRY' />
                </Shape>
            </Transform>
```

Saturn's rings are just a flat plane consisting of two polygons and a texture map. A `.gif` image is used to allow transparent areas in the corners and the center where Saturn sits. Saturn's rings are slightly tilted towards the Sun during the phases of its rotation around the Sun, as shown in the figure that follows this code:

```
        <Transform DEF="rings" rotation="1 0 0 .2">
            <Shape>
                <Appearance>
                    <Material diffuseColor='1 1 1'
                                specularColor='.2 .2 .2'
                                shininess='0.8'
                                emissiveColor=".1 .1 .1"/>
                    <ImageTexture
```

```
        url="./textureMaps/SaturnRings.gif"/>
                </Appearance>
                <IndexedFaceSet coordIndex="0 1 2 -1
                    2 3 0 -1    2 1 0 -1    0 3 2 -1"
    texCoordIndex="0 1 2 -1    2 3 0 -1 2 1 0 -1    0 3 2 -1">
                    <Coordinate point="-4 0 4    4 0 4
                        4 0 -4    -4 0 -4"/>
                    <TextureCoordinate point="0 0    1 0
                        1 1    0 1"/>
                </IndexedFaceSet>
            </Shape>
        </Transform>
    </Transform>
</Transform>
```

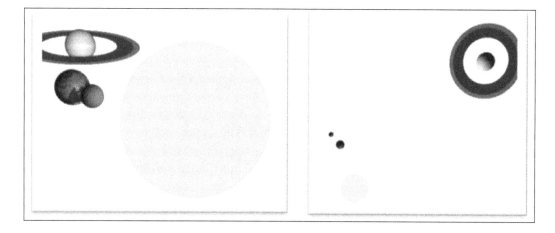

Animation is a series of `<TimeSensor>`, `<OrientationInterpolator>`, and `<ROUTE>` functions. The fraction of time is sent via the `<ROUTE>` node from `<TimeSensor>` to the interpolator, which uses another `<ROUTE>` node to update the rotation or position in the object's `<Transform>` node in order to allow rotation of the Earth around the Sun as the first four statements show in the following code. The next set of three statements control the seasonal tilt of the Earth using the same `<TimeSensor>` node with a rotation around the *z* axis of +/- *0.4* radians. The day rotation for the Earth has its own four statements to control the 24-hour day, animated as one second. The Moon has its own independent animation and finally, the camera focused on the Earth uses the same `<TimeSensor>` node as the Earth's year and seasons. However, the cameras focused on the Earth, the Earth's annual rotation, and the Earth's seasons have their own `<OrientationInterpolator>` nodes. Saturn has its own interpolators to rotate around the Sun and for its own day, but this is not shown in the following code:

```
<TimeSensor DEF="yearTimer" cycleInterval="36.5" loop="true"/>
<OrientationInterpolator DEF="yearlyRotation" key="0 .5 1"
keyValue="0 1 0 0   0 1 0 3.14   0 1 0 6.28"/>
<ROUTE fromField="fraction_changed" fromNode="yearTimer"
toField="set_fraction" toNode="yearlyRotation"/>
<ROUTE fromField="value_changed" fromNode="yearlyRotation"
toField="rotation" toNode="Earth"/>
```

Earth's seasonal rotation, which has a tilt of 0.4 radians, is demonstrated in the following code:

```
<OrientationInterpolator DEF="seasonalRotation" key="0 .5 1"
keyValue="0 0 1 .4   0 0 1 -.4   0 0 1 .4"/>
<ROUTE fromField="fraction_changed" fromNode="yearTimer"
toField="set_fraction" toNode="seasonalRotation"/>
<ROUTE fromField="value_changed" fromNode="seasonalRotation"
toField="rotation" toNode="Earth-Season"/>
```

Earth's day rotation, set to 1 second, is demonstrated in the following code:

```
<TimeSensor DEF="EarthDayTimer" cycleInterval="1" loop="true"/>
<OrientationInterpolator DEF="EarthDayRotation" key="0 .5 1"
keyValue="0 1 0 0   0 1 0 3.14   0 1 0 6.28"/>
<ROUTE fromField="fraction_changed" fromNode="EarthDayTimer"
toField="set_fraction" toNode="EarthDayRotation"/>
<ROUTE fromField="value_changed" fromNode="EarthDayRotation"
toField="rotation" toNode="Earth-Day"/>
```

The Moon's rotation around the Earth is set to 5.8 seconds and is demonstrated in the following code:

```
<TimeSensor DEF="moonTimer" cycleInterval="5.8" loop="true"/>
<OrientationInterpolator DEF="YRotMoon" key="0 .5 1"
keyValue="0 1 0 0   0 1 0 3.14   0 1 0 6.28"/>
<ROUTE fromField="fraction_changed" fromNode="moonTimer"
toField="set_fraction" toNode="YRotMoon"/>
<ROUTE fromField="value_changed" fromNode="YRotMoon"
toField="rotation" toNode="Moon"/>
```

To ensure that our camera stays focused on the Earth, the `<Viewpoint>` node is also animated using the same year timer as the Earth, as shown in the following code:

```
<OrientationInterpolator DEF="EarthCameraRotation" key="0 .5 1"
keyValue="0 1 0 0   0 1 0 3.14   0 1 0 6.28"/>
<ROUTE fromField="fraction_changed" fromNode="yearTimer"
toField="set_fraction" toNode="EarthCameraRotation"/>
<ROUTE fromField="value_changed" fromNode="EarthCameraRotation"
toField="orientation" toNode="EarthCamera"/>
```

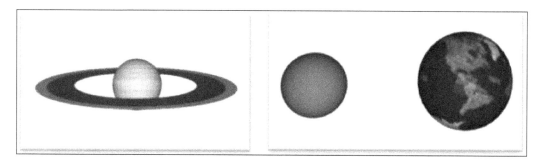

The images in the preceding figure show the views from Saturn's and Earth's cameras, two of the four cameras in the scene. To track planets, the user requires HTML buttons to navigate from one planet to the next. Clicking on the Sun or Earth will also take the user to the respective cameras. Buttons for X3D on a web page use the same buttons as any HTML page. What is unique for X3D is that element ID's such as `aboveCamera` and `mainCamera` are the ID values for the `<Viewpoint>` nodes in X3D. The `setAttribute('set_bind', 'true')` method, also a part of X3D, sets this as the new camera position, as shown in the following code:

```
<input type="button" value="Solar System View"
onclick="document.getElementById('aboveCamera').setAttribute('set_
    bind','true');" />
<input type="button" value="Sun"
onclick="document.getElementById('mainCamera').setAttribute('set_b
    ind','true');" />
<input type="button" value="Earth"
onclick="document.getElementById('EarthCamera').setAttribute('set_
    bind','true');" />
<input type="button" value="Saturn"
onclick="document.getElementById('SaturnCamera').setAttribute('set
    _bind','true');" />
```

Some of the images in the preceding figure look pixelated or tiled. This is partly due to the default shader language and will be addressed as we go further in WebGL.

Objective complete – mini debriefing

If you are new to the creation of 3D, one of the most fun aspects is the instant gratification from creating 3D scenes. In the subsequent projects, we will apply 3D graphics to familiar applications and see the places where 3D can be a more effective communication tool for users.

Mission accomplished

We covered a great deal of ground in understanding the fundamentals of 3D graphics: basic objects such as boxes and spheres, the creation of more complex objects using indexed face sets, texture maps, lights, viewpoints, animation, and interactivity. From just what was introduced here plus a little HTML and JavaScript, we can create vast worlds and applications. After all, if we can create a Solar System in an introduction, we can pretty much go anywhere.

Project 2

WebGL for E-Commerce

"I still take a lot of pride in the fact that when I went through the reviews, almost all of the reviews only mentioned in one sentence it was done on the computer, and the rest of the time, it was about the story"

— Ed Catmull, Pixar, commenting on Toy Story, from "The Story of Computer Graphics", 2000

The Web is often used as a marketing tool. However, a company website needs to pay for itself and justify its cost. It is required for virtually every commercial enterprise selling products and services to have a vibrant online business.

When deploying Web3D, it helps to ask basic questions about e-commerce first and then determine whether or not interactive 3D has a role to play. Consumers place a high value on convenience and quality. They also want to feel confident in making the right choice and have neither regrets nor buyer's remorse. Shopping can and should be a pleasurable experience. We like to spend our free time shopping, and this is highly demographic—some people prefer clothes shopping, while others like to wander the aisles of a hardware store.

The retailer wants satisfied customers. It generates avenues for repetitive business and word-of-mouth advertising, which is the best kind of advertising because it is free and reaches potential customers from trusted sources; this generates profits, fulfills entrepreneurs' dreams, and employs people. As the saying goes, we have to spend money to make money; businesses need to see a return on their investment (ROI). Thus, we cannot just deploy Web3D because it is cool and high tech, or it simply distinguishes your website from the rest. Web3D must be beneficial to the retailer and the customer. This seems fundamental, but when deploying a new technology, it never hurts to focus on the big picture.

Mission briefing

We will look at WebGL for e-commerce, but we want to be sensitive to the development costs. As a result, we begin with using existing assets before jumping into developing 3D models of the parts for sale online. Nearly all websites have existing product images. The goal here is to integrate those images in a WebGL website, while still using the features of a 3D environment to navigate the products on that website.

This project distinguishes WebGL from X3D, which was introduced in *Project 1*, *Building Great Web3D*. WebGL involves JavaScript beyond handling button clicks and shader language programming that involves coding on the graphics card. Most software programs, such as Microsoft Word and your web browser, run exclusively on the CPU. However, in the last few years, graphics applications such as video games and computer-aided design have taken advantage of the simultaneous processing capabilities of the **Graphics Processing Unit** (**GPU**).

The final demonstration will look at the opportunities in creating an actual 3D environment for an engaging shopping experience.

Why is it awesome?

E-commerce is wonderful. We can shop from home, make informed decisions, compare websites for best prices and features, and view numerous reviews of a product or service you've decided to purchase. Still, e-commerce websites are pretty utilitarian. Sometimes, this is quite nice, but few would describe their time spent on Amazon as an experience or a great story such as a video game, book, or a movie.

E-commerce is one of the few media platforms that has little emotional connection. Often, that is fine. Shopping for computer cables or headphones should be a simple act, but what if it involved an experience? After all, e-commerce websites are outlets for both advertising and order placement, and isn't advertising about creating an emotional connection with the buyer? Our buying decisions and brand loyalty are highly influenced by the portrayal of the product. Car commercials want to identify their product and the buyer as seeking freedom and luxury, successful, smart, rugged, and practical. Alcohol and soft drink commercials portray good times, friends, relaxation, refreshment, or a reward.

Web3D has the ability to make the online shopping experience fun and the user confident in their decision to buy a product. They can play with the new truck they are researching by smashing obstacles in their way or have a fun time impressing their friends in their virtual luxury car.

We understand e-commerce; it is, essentially, an electronic newspaper advertisement. The larger unchartered area of Web3D shopping is the only thing left.

Web3D as a new medium

The Internet has been revolutionary. We get our information and perform transactions remotely. We do so many things online, namely, conduct commerce, network with others, acquire education, make investments, research medical advice, and so on. However, for all these major changes, one constant has been the presentation of media using text and images, that is, never in an interactive 3D environment. In a way, the Internet is just a faster-delivery technology, but not necessarily a new medium.

Now there are interactive 3D environments. It seems intuitive; after all, we live in a 3D world. However, our screens are 2D; the mouse is a 2D device. The critical issue is that the general public has not engaged with interactive 3D environments before. It is as revolutionary as the advent of motion pictures. Of course, there are video game players engaging with 3D. Video game players may represent early adopters to Web3D, but it helps to distinguish key differences. WebGL is streamed content whereas video games reside on disk. The vast worlds within games invite you to walk around and explore; web-based 3D is downloaded in real time, so it will not have these vast worlds. The general public would not intuitively know how to use the WASD keys to navigate a scene like gamers would. So, how do we deploy Web3D to an audience who may very well be interacting with 3D for the first time? The same way audiences embraced 3D computer-generated movies—by providing great content.

Your Hotshot objectives

- ▶ Introduction to WebGL
- ▶ WebGL 3D with Perspective View
- ▶ WebGL texture mapping and animation
- ▶ Loading 3D modeled objects, the normal, and the lighting feature
- ▶ Using our mouse for interactivity
- ▶ E-commerce using existing assets
- ▶ E-commerce with 3D modeling

Mission checklist

WebGL requires very little programming to develop. Any editor, such as Textpad or Notepad, will work. Firefox is my preferred browser for development and testing. WebGL works fine on Google and Safari, but Google has security issues reading files such as 3D meshes of `.obj` or `.jpg` for texture maps off your hard drive. Once your WebGL files are uploaded to a server, Google works just fine.

We also need art tools such as Photoshop to create texture maps and resize the images so their width and height dimensions are in powers of two. Also helpful is a 3D modeling tool such as Maya; my preference is 3ds Max because I like its user interface. Blender (`http://www.blender.org/`) is a good alternative and it is free.

WebGL development requires basic knowledge of JavaScript and HTML. W3Schools (`http://www.w3schools.com/`) is a good reference (W3 is an abbreviation for World Wide Web). At the same time, WebGL may be an ideal tool to learn these languages, practice 3D modeling, and texture mapping. In many ways, WebGL is an ideal starting point to learn a number of technologies—its development is instant gratification. However, at the same time, it is useful to have a background in these related technologies.

Introduction to WebGL

In the previous project, we learned to use X3D, which declares the location of items in 3D space, including that of lights and the camera. There were additional JavaScript libraries to read (parse) X3D that links directly to WebGL. X3D is a great file format to learn 3D concepts. I regularly taught classes on X3D to students in high schools and post-graduate courses at the University of California. However, WebGL gets us closer to 3D technology and gives us more direct access to the graphics card, and offers more capabilities to control the imagery.

WebGL uses JavaScript programming in a regular HTML web page. It eventually loads the 3D models to the graphics card to draw (render) 3D scenes. Many applications can use either X3D, which is a file format, or WebGL, which involves JavaScript programming; I have had projects where I switched back and forth between the two. X3D was preferred when I had multiple transforms, such as the Earth in the Solar System demonstration in *Project 1*, *Building Great Web3D*, with animations for the year, season, and day. However, when we need absolute control over the lighting effects for individual objects, then WebGL is preferred.

Prepare for lift off

This book is involved in applications using WebGL, combining it with other media using professional tools to develop content. Along the way, we will introduce the fundamentals of WebGL. However, another good resource includes *Learning WebGL* (`http://learningwebgl.com`) originally created by Giles Thomas and now maintained by one of Web3D's legends, Tony Parisi. So, I encourage you to use the demonstrations here and keep some technical resources handy too. If 3D gets a bit confusing and too new, a good first step is to learn the HTML 2D Canvas. I often began courses introducing 2D programming as a nice lead-in to 3D programming. Thus, let us draw a 2D triangle in WebGL.

Engage thrusters

We won't cover all the code, such as basic copy-and-paste functions like `initShaders()`, which just reads a file, but let us go over the key components for drawing a basic triangle in WebGL:

We begin with the familiar `<html>`, `<head>`, and `<meta>` tags common to HTML pages:

```
<html>
<head>
<meta http-equiv="content-type" content="text/html;
charset=ISO-8859-1">
<script type="text/javascript" src="glMatrix-0.9.5.min.js"></script>
```

Now we take the first look at shader languages, which actually run inside the graphics card. A bit later, we will identify the code that sends the shader language to the graphics card and as with a high-level language such as Java, the graphics card will compile this text into zeroes and ones that computers read. The **vertex shader** with `id="shader-vs"` comes first in processing 3D graphics. Vertex shaders, as the name implies, work on the vertices of a 3D mesh. Often this moves the object into 3D space based on any transformations (placements, rotations, and scaling) in the vertices. We are not performing any transformations and instead pass the vertices to the graphics card using the `gl_Position` reserved word. Since our vertices, which are saved in the `aVertexPosition` value, are 2D points, we add a third `0.0` value for 3D, and a fourth `1.0` value for math applications to be seen later.

These vertices are then sent to the **fragment shader**, which draws the dots between the vertices. The actual color of each dot is saved to `gl_FragColor`, which is another reserved word. The values are specified as (red, green, blue, 1.0); so, with the color (1.0, 1.0, 1.0, 1.0), this color is white, as presented in the following code:

```
<script id="shader-fs" type="x-shader/x-fragment">
void main(void) {
    gl_FragColor = vec4(1.0, 1.0, 1.0, 1.0);
}
</script>

<script id="shader-vs" type="x-shader/x-vertex">
attribute vec2 aVertexPosition;
void main(void) {
    gl_Position = vec4(aVertexPosition, 0.0, 1.0);
}
</script>
```

The next block of initialization code sets up the link between the code on this web page and the graphics card. Two useful lines in the following code are those specifying the dimensions of these windows on the screen: `gl.viewportWidth = canvas.width;` and `gl.viewportHeight = canvas.height;`, which will help us in later examples when we determine where the mouse is clicked in our 3D scene:

```
<script type="text/javascript">
var gl;
function initGL(canvas) {
    try {
        gl = canvas.getContext("experimental-webgl");
        gl.viewportWidth = canvas.width;
        gl.viewportHeight = canvas.height;
    } catch (e) { }
    if (!gl) {
        alert("Could not initialize WebGL, sorry :-(");
    }
}

var shaderProgram;
    function initShaders() {
    var fragmentShader = getShader(gl, "shader-fs");
    var vertexShader = getShader(gl, "shader-vs");

    shaderProgram = gl.createProgram();
    gl.attachShader(shaderProgram, vertexShader);
    gl.attachShader(shaderProgram, fragmentShader);
    gl.linkProgram(shaderProgram);

    if (!gl.getProgramParameter(shaderProgram,
    gl.LINK_STATUS)) {
        alert("Could not initialize shaders");
    }
}

gl.useProgram(shaderProgram);
shaderProgram.vertexPositionAttribute =
gl.getAttribLocation(shaderProgram,
"aVertexPosition");
gl.enableVertexAttribArray(
shaderProgram.vertexPositionAttribute);
}
```

Every 3D mesh is made up of a set of vertices; these are loaded into a buffer, which is simply a memory area. The three vertices making up the triangle are (-0.75, 0.5), (0.4, -0.4), and (-0.5, -0.6), which are saved in a block of memory along with `numItems = 3;`, each item being assigned an item size of `2`, as shown in the following code:

```
var vertexBuffer;
function initBuffers() {
    vertexBuffer = gl.createBuffer();
    gl.bindBuffer(gl.ARRAY_BUFFER, vertexBuffer);
    vertices = [ -0.75,   0.5,
    0.4,  -0.4,
    -0.5,  -0.6 ];
    gl.bufferData(gl.ARRAY_BUFFER,
    new Float32Array(vertices), gl.STATIC_DRAW);
    vertexBuffer.itemSize = 2;
    vertexBuffer.numItems = 3;
}
```

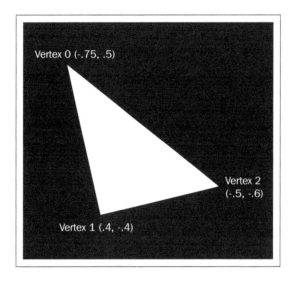

The last phase in our first WebGL program calls `drawScene()`, which sets up the dimensions for the scene's window and clears the buffers where our image is drawn and the depth buffer (the depth buffer saves the distance of a pixel from the camera). When a 3D mesh is rendered, the distance of each pixel to the camera is saved. When another 3D mesh is drawn that overlaps with the previous object, the depth buffer determines which pixel is closer—the saved pixel, in which case, nothing happens; or the pixel from the overlapping 3D mesh, in which case, the pixel is replaced and the distance of this new pixel is now saved in the depth buffer.

Finally, we make our `vertexBuffer` object from above the active buffer (later, we will have multiple buffers and each will become active, one at a time). We connect the `vertexBuffer` object to the vertex shader's `aVertexPosition` value and give the `draw` command, as shown in the following code:

```
function drawScene() {
    gl.viewport(0, 0, gl.viewportWidth, gl.viewportHeight);
    gl.clear(gl.COLOR_BUFFER_BIT | gl.DEPTH_BUFFER_BIT);

    gl.bindBuffer(gl.ARRAY_BUFFER, vertexBuffer);
    gl.vertexAttribPointer(
    shaderProgram.vertexPositionAttribute,
    vertexBuffer.itemSize,
    gl.FLOAT, false, 0, 0);
    gl.drawArrays(gl.TRIANGLES, 0, vertexBuffer.numItems);
}
```

We finally get to the code that initiates the program. In the HTML `<body>` tag, we call `webGLStart()` that makes several `init` (initialization) calls, makes the background black with the `gl.clearColor(0.0, 0.0, 0.0, 1.0);` the red, green, and blue values are all set to `0.0`, and then draws the scene, as shown in the following code:

```
function webGLStart() {
    var canvas = document.getElementById("myCanvas");
    initGL(canvas);
    initShaders();
    initBuffers();
    gl.clearColor(0.0, 0.0, 0.0, 1.0);
    drawScene();
}
</script>

</head>
<body onload="webGLStart();">
<canvas id="myCanvas" style="border: none;" width="256"
height="256"></canvas>
</body>
</html>
```

Objective complete – mini debriefing

We have drawn a 2D triangle, but this has also been a great introduction to WebGL's components. A WebGL program begins just like any typical web page within the `<body>` tag with the `onload="WebGLStart()` call. A canvas is created to draw both 2D and 3D objects. The call to `initShaders()` serves two main purposes: as a link to the program's shader functions and the vertices passed by the `drawScene()` function to those shaders. Currently, there are two shaders, a `shader-vs` vertex shader and a `shader-fs` fragment shader. There will be only one value sent to these shaders: `aVertexPosition`, which represents each vertex in this triangle.

Next, we initialize the buffers. A buffer is simply a block of memory sent to the graphics chip. The buffer contains vertices; the size of each vertex is set to 2 because this is a 2D triangle and the number of vertices that create our triangle is set to 3.

Finally, we get to `drawScene()`; here, the last three lines of the preceding code tell the graphics card where data is located on it.

The `glDrawArrays()` command tells the graphics card to draw the triangle. The graphics card then sends every vertex through the vertex shader. The fragment shader then draws the pixels between the vertices.

WebGL 3D with Perspective View

Now let's convert this 2D triangle to a 3D triangle and see some interesting modifications. A third value is added to each vertex, which is set to -2.0. Note that no position is specified for the camera and therefore, it defaults to the origin (0, 0, 0), with the camera lens pointing down the negative *z* axis.

Engage thrusters

We specify the vertices in 3D just as we did in 2D, using a vertices array, but now each vertex is made up of (x, y, z) values. In WebGL, negative *z* values are further away and the positive direction is towards the user's location. Not all 3D coordinate systems specify negative values as away from the user. Classical geometry sometimes presents the negative values as towards the user. Still, other coordinate systems swap the *y* and *z* axis. No one system is better than another—this serves to show us that there are multiple ways to define the 3D coordinate system, but throughout this book, we will follow the convention that traveling along the negative *z* axis will be away from us. This is presented in the following code:

```
vertices = [
    -0.75,  0.5, -2.0,
     0.4, -0.4, -2.0,
    -0.5, -0.6, -2.0   ];
```

The rest of the code in `initBuffers()` stays the same as in the previous demonstration with just one change: since there are now three values for each vertex, we now have the `vertexBuffer.itemSize = 3;` call instead of 2 to account for the new *z* coordinate. Another change is the addition of a Perspective View matrix. Without the Perspective View matrix, we would have an orthogonal view similar to architectural blueprints, where all objects remain the same size, regardless of how distant the object is. With the Perspective matrix, it causes objects that are further away to appear smaller and objects that are closer to appear larger. Have a look at the following line of code:

```
var pMatrix = mat4.create();
```

Create the perspective view, which is a 4 x 4 matrix with the `mat4.create()` command (you might recall the inclusion of the `glMatrix-0.9.5.min.js` file at the top of the code. This is where these matrix commands are located). Within `drawScene()`, set the perspective view to a 45 degree field of view, followed by the aspect ratio that adjusts the scene when the screen width and height are not the same. The next two values are the near and far clipping planes; if the polygon is closer than 0.1 units or further than 100.0 units, it will be cut off since we don't want to render items too far away or so close to block the camera view. All these values go into `pMatrix`, which is the perspective matrix. The following code snippet sets these perspective matrix values on the graphics card:

```
mat4.perspective(45, gl.viewportWidth / gl.viewportHeight, 0.1,
    100.0, pMatrix);
gl.uniformMatrix4fv(shaderProgram.pMatrixUniform, false, pMatrix);
```

The `shaderProgram.pMatrixUniform` value links to the graphics card memory in the `initShaders()` program, binding `pMatrix` on the CPU with `uPMatrix` on the GPU, as shown in the following code:

```
shaderProgram.pMatrixUniform =
    gl.getUniformLocation(shaderProgram, "uPMatrix");
```

The vertex shader receives the perspective matrix value by first declaring the `uniform mat4 uPMatrix` matrix and then by multiplying each vertex by the perspective matrix as follows:

```
gl_Position = uPMatrix * vec4(aVertexPosition, 1.0);
```

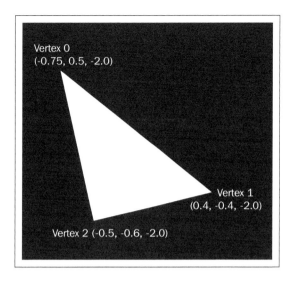

Objective complete – mini debriefing

If we were to reduce any of the *z* values of this triangle from -2.0, the triangle would get smaller. If the value is -0.1 (negative one-tenth), the triangle will not be visible because it's too close to the camera; this is known as the **near-clipping plane**. If the *z* coordinate is positive, the vertex will be behind the camera and not visible. A final point regarding the vertex shader is that the variables are called **attributes**, which means the value is passed in the variable on a per-vertex basis, or they're defined as **uniform**, which means it stays the same for all vertices. For example, the Perspective View matrix, pMatrix, is the same for every vertex and thus defined as uniform. However, there are many vertices sent to the vertex shader (in our example, there were three vertices) so the value of the vertices is defined as an attribute. This does not mean our perspective view can never change, but when drawing a single frame, the perspective view remains constant.

WebGL texture mapping and animation

Next, we include texture coordinates, enabling us to send the vertices with a texture map to the shader. Texture mapping is just pasting an image onto a 3D mesh, which is similar to pasting wallpaper onto a wall. Nearly all 3D objects are drawn using texture maps because you can achieve a higher level of realism instead of just solid colors.

Engage thrusters

In `initShaders()`, a new code passes an array that contains texture coordinates (which are in pairs for the vertical and horizontal directions) and there is one texture coordinate for every vertex. The texture map image is passed to the shader as a sampler, as presented in the following code:

```
shaderProgram.textureCoordAttribute =
    gl.getAttribLocation(shaderProgram, "aTextureCoord");
gl.enableVertexAttribArray(shaderProgram.textureCoordAttribute);
shaderProgram.mvMatrixUniform =
    gl.getUniformLocation(shaderProgram, "uMVMatrix");
shaderProgram.samplerUniform =
    gl.getUniformLocation(shaderProgram, "uSampler");
```

The first two lines of the previous code establish `aTextureCoord` as the variable in the shader that will receive the array of texture coordinates. The third line links the shader's Model View matrix, `uMVMatrix`, with the CPU's `mvMatrixUniform`, which is a 4 x 4 matrix. This matrix contains the 3D object's transformation (rotation, translation/position, and scaling) multiplied by the camera transformation. At this moment, we are not setting any camera transformations, so only the object's transformation is represented in the Model View matrix. Later, we will include the loaction of the camera and the direction in which it is pointing. Finally, the texture map, when sent to Fragment Shader as a sampler, is referenced by an integer rather than its filename. In later examples, we will have multiple texture maps per 3D mesh and each texture map will have a unique identifier, but for now, every texture map will be assigned the value `0`. Have a look at the following screenshot:

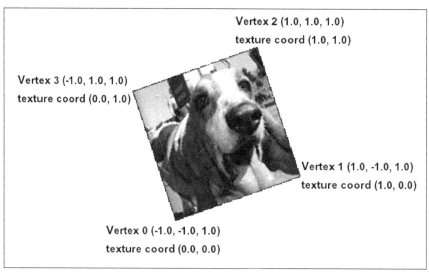

A 3D mesh with a texture map, slightly rotated

The initBuffers() function adds the data for the vertices just as before, but now includes texture coordinates and Indexed Face Set buffers, which are concepts previously discussed in *Project 1*, *Building Great Web3D*, when we discussed texture coordinates for X3D objects. There are two values that make up each texture coordinate and four texture coordinates, one coordinate per vertex.

The initTexture() function creates an image object. The difference is that the texture map must be loaded as a background process. HTML loads images progressively as fast as they can be downloaded over the Internet and displays them as they are loaded. WebGL isn't different from HTML, but WebGL needs to set texture map parameters and generate **mipmaps**, which are additional texture maps with dimensions divisible by 2. Mipmaps is Latin *multum in parvo* meaning "many things in small places". These are lower-resolution images of the same texture map. Since a 3D mesh can be very far away, the texture map, which may have originally been 128 pixels x 128 pixels, may be drawn as only 20 pixels by 14 pixels on the screen. We don't want to downsize the original texture map of each frame to fit the screen image. So, instead, we preprocess the images upon download and create smaller versions that look better at further distances than if we used the original image, as follows:

```
bassetHoundTexture.image.onload = function () {
    handleLoadedTexture(bassetHoundTexture)
}
bassetHoundTexture.image.src = "./textureMaps/bassethound.jpg";
```

The previous lines of code locate the image (which is currently in the textureMaps subdirectory) and then, once the image is loaded, call the handleLoadedTexture() function to set a number of parameters in an advanced process reviewed later and beyond *Project 5*, *Social Media Meets Its Destiny*.

The last function called from webGLStart() is tick(), which sets up a callback to the same function after each frame is rendered for the animation, and then drawScene() is called, as follows:

```
function webGLStart() {
    . . .
    tick();
}

function tick() {
    requestAnimFrame(tick);
    drawScene();
}
```

Within `drawScene()`, the values for the Model View matrix, `mvMatrix`, are set. Much of this process requires you to have a background in matrix math and linear algebra, but the following code shows an overview:

```
mat4.identity(mvMatrix);
mat4.translate(mvMatrix, [0.0, 0.0, -5.0]);
mat4.rotate(mvMatrix, angle, [0, 0, 1]);
angle += .002;
gl.uniformMatrix4fv(shaderProgram.mvMatrixUniform,
    false, mvMatrix);
```

The identity matrix resets the matrix; otherwise, these rotations and translations would accumulate with every frame. First, we translate five units further away in the *z* or depth direction, then increasingly rotate counterclockwise around the *z*-axis by 0.002 radians per frame. The Model View matrix is then passed to the shader. Finally, we bind the texture map to the texture sampler, as follows, so we can access the texture in the shader:

```
gl.activeTexture(gl.TEXTURE0);
gl.bindTexture(gl.TEXTURE_2D, bassetHoundTexture);
gl.uniform1i(shaderProgram.samplerUniform, 0);
```

The list of texture maps begins with zero. This code gets more involved and the rationale behind passing everything to the shader per frame will be revealed when we render more than one object.

The vertex shader now receives texture coordinates, since these are set on a per-vertex basis. Later, we will perform calculations, such as tiling a brick wall from a single brick, but for now, we just pass the texture coordinate value—`aTextureCoord` (which begins with `a` since it is an attribute value that changes per vertex)—to `vTextureCoord` (which begins with `v` since the value is varying for each vertex). The vertex shader has just the following two lines of code:

```
gl_Position = uPMatrix * uMVMatrix * vec4(aVertexPosition, 1.0);
vTextureCoord = aTextureCoord;
```

The vertex position, `aVertexPosition`, is multiplied by the Perspective and Model-View matrices. There are no modifications to the texture coordinates, so they are passed on to the Fragment Shader.

The Fragment Shader receives the texture map bound to the sampler2D and the texture coordinates, as follows:

```
gl_FragColor =
    texture2D(uSampler, vec2(vTextureCoord.s, vTextureCoord.t));
```

This single line gets the pixel from the texture map that is bound to the sampler based on its UV coordinates (which are also called *s* and *t* coordinates. Since there is one-to-one correspondence between vertex and texture map coordinates, some 3D graphics programs group them together as [x, y, z, u, v] and thus you will see *u* and *v* used to distinguish vertex values from texture coordinates).

Objective complete – mini debriefing

Once we specify the texture map, texture coordinates, and vertices of the polygon, the shader, or more specifically, the graphics card, applies its own algorithms to select the specific pixel to draw in our scene.

Classified intel

It is really wonderful that the graphics card calculates which pixel to apply to the texture map for us. Not only does the fragment shader get the right pixels from the correct mipmap, but there are corrections for perspective view. Looking internally at the work of the graphics card, suppose the final image to be drawn on the screen is 16 pixels wide and 12 pixels high, yet the original texture map is 64 x 64 pixels. The mipmap command, which was discussed earlier, has already created smaller copies of the original image in the sizes 32 x 32, 16 x 16, and so on by sampling neighboring pixels to ensure some image details of the original image are not lost. This is quite similar to how Photoshop would create a reduced-size image. Instead of drawing a 3D object rendered on the screen as 16 pixels x 12 pixels, from a texture map of size 64 x 64, we start with the 16 x 16 mipmap, and then the graphics card skips every fourth vertical pixel for the 16 x 12 rendered image.

Loading a 3D modeled object, normals, and lighting

Ultimately, we want to display 3D objects that look like regular characters and objects. Generally, these are 3D meshes designed by professional artists in 3D modeling programs such as 3D Studio Max, Maya, and Blender. There is no single standard file format, but the `.obj` format is a common file format to export from those 3D modeling tools. Barring some exceptions, we only want to export triangles—for the 3D artist, this is just a checkbox on the file/export user interface of 3D modeling programs. For the programmer, however, to accept polygons other than three-vertex triangles requires a lot of programming. There are other issues too with exporting polygons with four or more vertices from a 3D modeling program, as all the vertices must be located on a flat plane. The polygon can be angled, but it has to stay on a planar surface. Another way to think of this is that a three-legged table will not wobble, but a table with four legs may have one leg that is of a different length than the others and so the table will wobble. So, in summation, work with only three-vertex polygons.

If we want these 3D objects to appear 3D such that the shading is a little darker around the edges, then we need to include lighting and another very important attribute of 3D objects—**normals**. In *Project 1*, *Building Great Web3D*, we discussed normals, but now we will use them in calculations. If we did not calculate lighting using normals, every object would look 2D and flat, as shown in the following screenshot:

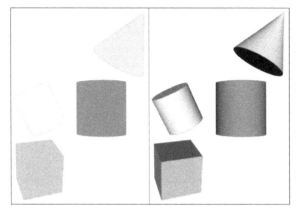

Flat shaded on the right and with normals on the left

Engage thrusters

This demonstration uses a prebuilt JavaScript library, `'mesh3dObject.js'`, to read 3D meshes, material properties, and texture maps from the server. Because these 3D meshes often have a file size of 10,000 to 100,000 bytes or larger, we use the **AJAX** technology to download the meshes off the server and then tell us once the entire files have been downloaded and are ready to be displayed. AJAX enables the server and the user's computer to communicate the progress of the downloading `.obj` files without having to wait for all the 3D meshes to download. Our current example calls the `'AddMeshObject()'` function, as presented in the following code:

```
AddMeshObject("sphere", "./3dmeshes/sphere.obj",
[3, 1.0, -10.0], [1, 1, 1], [.7, 1.3, 0], false );
AddMeshObject("teapot", "./3dmeshes/teapot.obj",
[0, -3, -20.0], [1, 1, 1], [.3, -2.8, 0], false );
AddMeshObject("texturedPlane", "./3dmeshes/texturedPlane.obj",
[-8, 3.0, -20.0], [1, 1, 1], [0, .9, 0], false );
```

The first value gives the object a name so that we can later refer to it to add interactivity. The second value is the location of the file containing the 3D mesh. The next three sets of values are translation, scaling, and rotation around the *x*, *y*, and *z* axes. The final true/false Boolean value is used for environment mapping, which is something we will cover later. Additionally, note that `initBuffers()` and `initTextures()` are gone as they are handled in the `AddMeshObject()` function.

The `InitShaders()` code now handles sending an array of normals produced by the 3D modeling program to the GPU and the object's rotation matrix, which is saved in `uNMatrix`. This matrix seems like it should be the same as the Transformation matrix for the object—after all, as the object moves, scales, and rotates, shouldn't the normal do the same? The answer is no, because a normal is a vector, which has direction and a magnitude of 1 unit, so if we move the object, the normal still points in the same direction. Since we don't need the fourth transformation column (or row), we can use just a 3 x 3 matrix to save us some computation, as presented in the following code:

```
shaderProgram.vertexNormalAttribute =
    gl.getAttribLocation(shaderProgram, "aVertexNormal");
    gl.enableVertexAttribArray(shaderProgram.vertexNormal
    Attribute);

shaderProgram.nMatrixUniform =
    gl.getUniformLocation(shaderProgram, "uNMatrix");
```

Moving on to `drawScene()`, all the vertex attributes for each object are in the `meshObjectArray[]` array. This example has three objects and the `for` loop in `drawScene()` will pass that data on to the GPU. There is some new code to handle the normals, which is similar to that used to calculate other matrices and vertex arrays. Have a look at the following screenshot:

Three 3D mesh files with texture maps read by the WebGL program

The most interesting code is in the shaders. The vertex shader adds a new line to transform each vertex normal by the Normal matrix:

```
vTransformedNormal = uNMatrix * vec3(aVertexNormal);
```

The Normal matrix only has rotations. Normals are vectors and are not affected by the translation or movement of the 3D mesh. However, rotating the mesh requires the Normal vector to be similarly rotated.

Fragment shaders are exciting because we calculate the lighting here and the GPU does a much better job of calculating the effect of lighting on a pixel-by-pixel basis. Lighting is calculated based on the angle between the direction of the light and the normal. The light's direction is reversed to create an angle between the two-unit vectors (each having a length of 1 unit), and then we find the dot product by *Nx * Lx + Ny * Ly + Nz * Lz* where the normal is *(Nx, Ny, Nz)* and the light's direction is *(Lx, Ly, Lz)*. This dot product is also equal to the cosine of the angle between the two vectors, which is also known as Lambert's Cosine Law. This is presented in the following code:

```
void main(void) {
    vec3 lightDirection = normalize(vec3( 0, 0, -1 ));
    vec3 normal = normalize(vTransformedNormal);
    float lightAngleToVertex = dot(-lightDirection, normal );
    if (lightAngleToVertex < 0.0) lightAngleToVertex = 0.0;
    vec4 fragmentColor =
        texture2D(uSampler, vec2(vTextureCoord.s,
        vTextureCoord.t));
    gl_FragColor =
    vec4(fragmentColor.rgb * lightAngleToVertex, 1.0);
}
```

If the angle between the normal and the light is greater than 90 degrees, no light shines on this vertex and then we set `lightAngleToVertex` to `0.0`. The initial light is pointed directly down the z-axis, so the edges of the teapot or sphere are darker, which creates a 3D look. Finally, the `lightAngleToVertex` value is a number between 0.0 and 1.0—the smaller the number, the greater the angle between the direction of the light and the normal, resulting in less light on that pixel. This `lightAngleToVertex` value between 0.0 and 1.0 is multiplied by the red, green, and blue values of the pixel to obtain the final color. Less light for the pixel results in a darker pixel.

Objective complete – mini debriefing

Now would be a good time to experiment with the light's direction to test and familiarize yourself with lighting in shaders.

One final point is to ensure your server will indeed download `.obj` files. Some servers will need their MIME types set to allow these files to be downloaded by end users. If your 3D meshes load by running on your hard drive with the Firefox browser but not when they are uploaded to a server, you may want to check with your server's administrator regarding MIME types and downloading `.obj` files.

Using the mouse for interactivity

We are almost ready to build e-commerce websites. However, if we are going to buy products, we need to click on them. This is a bit more complex than the traditional 2D website where each product can use HTML and JavaScript to indicate whether or not it has been clicked. In 3D space, a mouse click, which is a 2D device, produces an *x* and *y* value. That *x* and *y* value must be converted into 3D space, which generates a ray from the camera (our point of view) to the (x, y, z) location. We then determine whether or not the ray passes through any 3D meshes along the way. However, unlike with 2D web pages where only one item—either text or an image—occupies the same space, in 3D, that ray could intersect multiple objects. Therefore, if the ray intersects multiple products, we must determine which object is closest to the camera. This is indeed a daunting task.

This demonstration has three additional slider bars that control the red, green, and blue lights. The WebGL code now checks for the mouse over dragging the three bars. If the red, green, and blue values are decreased all the way down to 0, then no objects will be visible, like a room with no lights on. However, this would also cause some problems for our three new red, green, and blue slider bars, because if the bars are completely dark, we could never see the bars to turn the lights back on. Therefore, some light will be added to just those three slider bars, and the way to accomplish this is by adding another shader. So, the objects, such as the teapot, will be controlled by one shader which reacts to the light settings, and another shader will be used to keep the slider bars visible. Just to be fancy, the shader bars become dim as they are dragged to their lowest positions, but never completely black. Thus, this demonstration adds interactivity via the mouse, showing us how we can control properties in the shader, such as the light color, and demonstrates using multiple shaders. Have a look at the following screenshot:

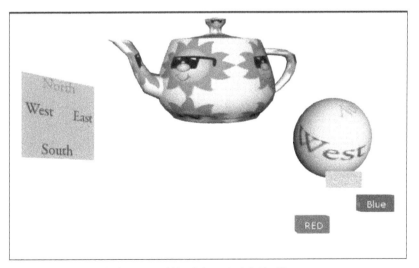

Red, green, and blue light controls in the 3D scene

Controlling objects in 3D involves clicking on them with the mouse. It seems that we could just ask the computer if we clicked on the object it just drew. Unfortunately, interactivity with the mouse in 3D is not so simple. It is often calculated using **ray picking**. Ray picking is just one method.

Prepare for lift off

Picking shoots an infinite ray from our camera into 3D space. The *x* and *y* axes values are derived from the point where the mouse is clicked. But what *z* value do we use? The *z* value is based on the field of view, using the following equation:

1 / Math.tan(fieldOfView / 2)

This value is also the distance from the view plane. Objects closer than this distance will appear larger due to Perspective View. Objects further than the distance to the view plane will appear smaller. Using some common field-of-view values, such as 30 degrees, the distance from the view plane is 3.73; at 45 degrees, we get 2.41; and at 60 degrees, we get 1.73. So, at 60 degrees, any object (vertex) closer than 1.73 units appears larger due to Perspective View, which is similar to the effect that occurs when you hold an object really close to your face. Objects further than 1.73 units away will appear smaller in perspective view. Thus, the infinite ray originates from our camera at (0, 0, 0) and passes through the *x* and *y* coordinates of the location of the mouse click. We still have to convert our *x* and *y* 2D mouse coordinates to 3D space, but that is just a conversion from screen coordinates (mouseX, mouseY) to world coordinates, as follows:

```
xWorld = (mouseX - width/2) * (2/width)
yWorld = -(mouseY - height/2) * (2/height)
```

The width and height values are the dimensions of the WebGL window. For example, let's have a window that is 800 units wide and 600 units tall, noting that (0, 0) is the location of upper-left corner of this window. Suppose the user clicks on the pixel (200, 525), which is 200 pixels from the left and lower vertically, then the conversion to world coordinates would be as follows:

```
xWorld = (200 - 800/2) * (2/800) = -0.5
yWorld = -(525 - 600/2) * (2/600) = -0.75
```

Note that many graphics cards number their pixels down in screen space, but world coordinates count up and thus, the *y* equation has a negative sign. Using a 45 degree field of view, the screen coordinates (200, 525) would convert to the 3D world coordinates (-0.5, -0.75, -2.41).

A 3D mesh is often made up of thousands of polygons. So, do we check whether or not the ray has intersected each polygon? In making our decision, we should remember that this could be rather time consuming. We have to detect every ray-polygon intersection in one-thirtieth of a second to maintain a smooth animation running at 30 frames per second. Instead, we test whether or not the ray intersects a bounding box or bounding sphere. A bounding box or bounding sphere encompasses the 3D mesh. If the ray goes through this bounding volume, it's considered to be an intersection. The math is not too bad either. We just have to create an invisible box to fit our 3D mesh. Since we read the vertices of each 3D mesh when we load the WebGL scene, just record the maximum and minimum sizes to create the bounding box. We search for two values—tMin and tMax—with t as the intersection point. We begin with creating the minimum and maximum points of the bounding boxes, using the following code:

```
tMin = ( BBxMin/xWorld,   BByMin/yWorld, BBzMin/zWorld)
tMax = ( BBxMax/xWorld,   BByMax/yWorld, BBzMax/zWorld)
```

If the largest tMin value is greater than the smallest tMax value, we have an intersection.

Previously, we found that the (xWorld, yWorld, zWorld) coordinates are (-0.5, -0.75, -2.41). However, to keep our example simple, we are going to use a field of view of 11.4 degrees, which would cover the zWorld value -10. Suppose the minimum and maximum values of our bounding box were (1, 0, -6) and (3, 2, -8) respectively and there was a teapot within it. After converting the 2D mouse click into 3D world coordinates, we had two rays: (6, 4, -10) and (3, 2, -10). The tMin and tMax values for the first ray would be the following:

```
tMin = ( 1/6,   0/4,  -6/-10) = (.167, 0, .6)
tMax = ( 3/6,   2/4,  -8/-10) = (.5,  .5,  .8)
```

The maximum tMin value is 0.6 and the minimum tMax value is 0.5. Since 0.6 is not less than 0.5, we do not have an intersection.

Using the second ray, the maximum tMin value is 0.6 and the minimum tMax value is 0.8, as follows:

```
tMin = ( 1/3,   0/2,  -6/-10) = ( .333, 0,  .6)
tMax = ( 3/3,   2/2,  -8/-10) = ( 1, 1,  .8)
```

Since 0.6 is less than 0.8, we have an intersection, which is demonstrated in the following figure:

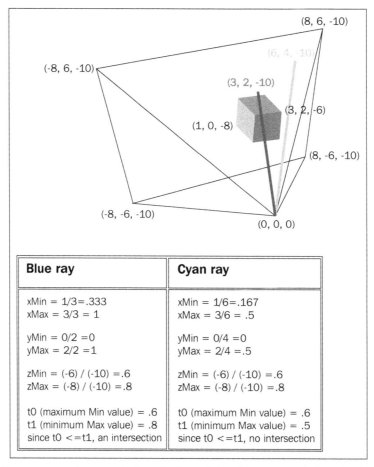

Blue ray	Cyan ray
xMin = 1/3=.333 xMax = 3/3 = 1 yMin = 0/2 =0 yMax = 2/2 =1 zMin = (-6) / (-10) =.6 zMax = (-8) / (-10) =.8 t0 (maximum Min value) = .6 t1 (minimum Max value) = .8 since t0 <=t1, an intersection	xMin = 1/6=.167 xMax = 3/6 = .5 yMin = 0/4 =0 yMax = 2/4 =.5 zMin = (-6) / (-10) =.6 zMax = (-8) / (-10) =.8 t0 (maximum Min value) = .6 t1 (minimum Max value) = .5 since t0 <=t1, no intersection

Two rays; one ray intersects the bounding box and the other ray misses the bounding box

A follow-up point to this is that since our `tMin` value is 0.6, if we multiply it by the value of our ray (3, 2, -10), we can determine the actual point of intersection: *0.6 * (3, 2, -10) = (1.8, 1.2, -6)*. Additionally, if we have a ray that intersects multiple objects, the object with the smallest `tMin` value is the closest.

Don't bounding boxes contain excess area? For example, a box around the teapot would have some empty space around the spout, but it would still register as an intersection; the answer is yes. Bounding boxes are imperfect. They can be tailored to be smaller than the object, such as by excluding the spout or handle from its parameters, but that would mean the user might click on the spout, and it won't register a hit. This is something video game players are familiar with; they may have shot at a character in the game and nothing would have registered even though the player knew it was a near-perfect shot. Sometimes, we can put a bounding box around a character and if clicking on that registers a hit, have smaller boxes that contain a character's head, torso, arms, and legs. This increases the accuracy, but it is still imperfect. In the end, when the decision comes down to perfect ray-polygon intersection versus ray-bounding box intersection, choosing one over the other has various trade-offs in 3D.

Engage thrusters

This program uses two shaders: `shaderLightingFX` for lighting effects and `shaderLightingCtrl` for the slider bars controlling the lights. The `initShaders()` function calls `createShaderProgram()`, which reads the vertex and fragment shader for each shader program; this is shown as follows:

```
function initShaders() {
    shaderLightingFX = createShaderProgram(
        "shaderLightingFX-fs", "shaderLightingFX-vs");
    shaderLightingCtrl = createShaderProgram(
        "shaderLightingCtrl-fs", "shaderLightingCtrl-vs");
}
```

Within `createShaderProgram()`, there is just one new line of code:

```
shaderProgram.lightColorUniform =
gl.getUniformLocation(shaderProgram, "uLightColor");
```

This is our first opportunity to set a variable in the CPU to control the GPU. We set `lightColorUniform`, which is an array of three values—red, green, and blue—and pass that information per frame to the GPU's variable `uLightColor`, which is used in the `shaderLightingFX` fragment shader.

In `drawScene()`, we now choose the shader based on the object. The red, green, and blue slider buttons use the `shaderLightingCtrl` fragment shader, while all other objects use the `shaderLightingFX` shader, shown as follows:

```
if ( (meshObjectArray[i].name == "lightCtrlRed") ||
(meshObjectArray[i].name == "lightCtrlGrn") ||
(meshObjectArray[i].name == "lightCtrlBlu"))
{
```

```
        shaderProgram = shaderLightingCtrl;
    }
    else {
        shaderProgram = shaderLightingFX;
    }
    gl.useProgram(shaderProgram);

    gl.uniform3f(shaderProgram.lightColorUniform,
    lightColor[0],  lightColor[1], lightColor[2] );
```

The final line links the `lightColor` array data containing the colors red, green, and blue to the shader program's `lightColorUniform` variable in the GPU. There is also a transformation of the bounding box using the same transform matrix as the object itself:

```
    mat4.set(mvMatrix, meshObjectArray[i].boundingBoxMatrix);
```

Within each of the two fragment shaders, a variable is declared using `code uniform vec3 uLightColor`. Recall that `uniform` just establishes that the variable is the same for all pixels. In the `shaderLightingFX-fs` fragment shader, the value of the light color is multiplied by the pixels generated from the texture map:

```
gl_FragColor =
    vec4(fragmentColor.rgb * uLightColor * lightAngleToVertex,
    1.0);
```

In light, in the material color and texture map color calculation, we multiply the red pixels together, the green pixels, and the blue pixels. In the `shaderLightingCtrl-fs` function, it was not necessary to include the data from the slider bars controlling the colors, but it looked better when the slider bars were darker when that color was reduced in the scene:

```
gl_FragColor =
    vec4(fragmentColor.rgb * ((uLightColor + 0.6)/2.0), 1.0);
```

Objective complete – mini debriefing

A final note on this functional demonstration is that the preceding code was added to have the cursor change over the objects that are controlled using the mouse. This uses the same code as that for ray-bounding box intersection and provides a good visual cue to the user.

E-commerce using existing assets

It would surely be nice to have an unlimited budget with a staff of 3D modelers, artists, programmers, and web developers. However, rarely do we inherit a blank cheque in development. An even bigger consideration is that we are applying a new communications medium. Deploying a new technology and user interface must be done smartly. The design must be intuitive and subtle, rather than 3D in your face. Technology should not call attention to itself; rather, it serves the user, making web activities such as searching and shopping easier.

Some wonderful applications have been created using WebGL, such as navigating public transportation systems and luxury cars with reflective surfaces that can be spun 360 degrees. Here, however, the emphasis will be on applying Web3D in building user interfaces with existing assets from common applications; we begin with a 3D shopping cart, as shown in the following screenshot:

Engage thrusters

Our first demonstration makes use of existing assets and uses 3D similar to some of the advanced features of Flash or HTML5. On a retail store website, I want users to see and compare products and make informed purchases, but do so simply. The developer may be asked to design a Web3D site with little increment in budget. Meanwhile, the customer wants to see a range of comparative products without extensive search and feel confident in the purchase. Thus, this first design reuses existing images. No additional assets other than the WebGL are deployed. The opening screen merges several different sections of this camera store website into one, as shown in the following screenshot:

Canon EOS 5D Mark III - Body Only - Black

The opening screen shows the products to the left, angled to show that there are many products to choose from. They are also organized by product: cameras, lenses, and flashes. Grabbing a product highlights the image using shader languages and describes the product at the bottom. Products can be placed back in the stack and reordered (but those features are not included with the code in order to streamline the demonstration). Depending on the object, there are four shaders: two for the products—highlighted and unselected—and two for the shopping cart and the logo behind, as presented in the following code:

```
if ( meshObjectArray[i] == shoppingCartObject)
    shaderProgram = shaderShoppingCart;
else if ( meshObjectArray[i] == storeLogoObject)
    shaderProgram = shaderStoreLogo;
else if ( meshObjectArray[i] == meshObjectPicked)
    shaderProgram = shaderHighlighted;
else   shaderProgram = shaderNonSelected;
gl.useProgram(shaderProgram);
```

In the `drawScene()` function in the preceding code, the appropriate shader is selected for each object. In the `shaderNonSelected` and `shaderHighlighted` vertex and fragment shaders, a border is used around each image to separate it from the others and the background:

```
if ( abs(vVertexPosition.x) > 0.95)
    gl_FragColor = vec4( 0.7, 0.66, 0.3, 1.0);
else if ( abs(vVertexPosition.y) > 0.95)
    gl_FragColor = vec4( 0.7, 0.66, 0.3, 1.0);
else gl_FragColor =
vec4(fragmentColor.rgb * 0.7 * lightAngleToVertex, 1.0);
```

A light border color is applied when the *x* or *y* values of any pixel are set to `+0.95` or `-0.95` units. The plane is a 2 x 2 square that extends from -1 to 1 in both the *x* and *y* directions, so just the edges will have a border. The unselected object's color is also multiplied by 0.7.

The shopping cart is see through, just like an actual shopping cart has a wire mesh. The original image is gray against a white background—you can't use the transparency portions of `.gif` images on a web page. Instead, the shader will set the alpha value to `0` where any pixel has a green value greater than 0.95. This would be the case where a pixel is white. Once we detect that the alpha value is not 1, we discard the white pixel:

```
if (fragmentColor.g > .95)
    discard;
else gl_FragColor =
    vec4(fragmentColor.rgb * lightAngleToVertex, 1.0);
```

Objective complete – mini debriefing

We place the objects we want to purchase into the shopping cart. In a real example, clicking on the shopping cart would take us to the check-out stand. Another feature in the example provides a description of the product at the left-bottom corner. The demonstration gets more products before the user in the same space like a typical website would, dividing products into categories, allowing users to scroll through them all on one page and over multiple pages. Web3D for e-commerce is more convenient, consumes less time, provides more information, and better serves the customer. Simply put, it is a more effective communication tool. This is demonstrated in the following screenshot:

E-commerce with 3D modeling

A 3D website naturally has the ability to include 3D models. There are a variety of tools to create 3D models, including Maya, 3D Studio Max, and Blender. These are similar products used for animation in movies and video games. Seeing a product in 3D and trying out its features and options creates a more knowledgeable, confident, and eager consumer. 3D product views also have advantages over a user manual as you can really see the product in action rather than reading about it. The consumer is better informed and more satisfied while spending more time enjoying their new purchase and less time frustrated with some confusing manual. The following screenshot demonstrates the 3D model of a chainsaw:

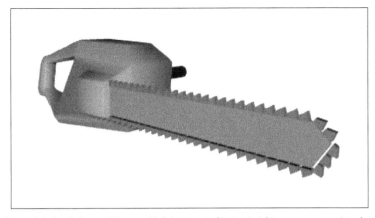

The 3D model of a chainsaw. Who wouldn't be tempted to try it right now on some virtual wood?

Viewing and interacting with products on a 3D website can be a very effective way to communicate with customers. Web3D educates users in less time and space while providing more information and perhaps in a more fun way. However, it is unlikely that we can use existing models from the manufacturer. Those engineering models are, typically, far too detailed, which isn't a bad thing, except the download size becomes impractical. The original chainsaw shown in the preceding screenshot is 5 megabytes—that's larger than many audio files, except unlike music, there is no streaming; the 3D mesh must be downloaded completely before any scene can be drawn. There are other bottlenecks such as limitations to the number of vertices, which can vary with the end user's graphics card. In the end, be sensitive to the customer's time and know that they could be viewing WebGL on a mobile device.

Prepare for lift off

3D modeling programs are capable of reducing the number of polygons, and we can reduce their precision values, which are typically five decimal places by default, to just two decimal places—it will not be noticeable onscreen. So, perhaps we can occasionally use existing 3D models from mechanical engineers and product designers, but in all likelihood, their objects will need polygon reduction or complete remodeling to be rebuilt for Web3D. When I first got into Web3D programming, my benchmark for the total download (3D meshes, texture maps plus the code) was based on CNN's home page. Back in the 1990s, the size of CNN's home page was between 100 kb and 200 kb. With more images and banner ads, excluding streaming media such as video files, CNN's home page is now just over 2 MB. However, much of that content is toward the bottom of the page and cannot be seen until we scroll down, so the page seems to download fast. Contrast this with WebGL: by the time we include a few highly detailed 3D models plus texture maps, we can exceed that 2 MB benchmark. With the AJAX technology, we can download texture maps and 3D meshes in the background and have control over which 3D models begin downloading first. So, we can begin downloading the smaller file sizes or closer objects first, but be careful about modeling the world in detail.

Engage thrusters

The chainsaw example added a camera since the model was not positioned towards the center. First, we set up the parameters of the camera: the eye or location of the camera; the target, which is essentially what the camera is pointed towards; and the up vector, which almost always points in the positive direction on the *y* axis:

```
var eye    = [ 140, 0, -180, 1 ];
var target = [ 0, 0, -60.0, 1 ];
var up = [ 0, 1, 0, 1 ];
var camera = mat4.create();
```

The up vector is at (0, 1, 0), which is pointing upwards. The up vector will generally continue to point straight upwards, except when we're maybe simulating bank turns in a car race or on a roller coaster. The eye is set to (140, 0, -180) and the camera is pointing towards (0, 0, -60) in 3D space. In drawScene(), we set up the camera matrix using the lookAt() method. The lookAt() method builds the 4 x 4 matrix based on the three parameters (eye, camera, and up vectors) and builds a 4 x 4 matrix that contains the camera's position and rotation similar to previous 3D object matrices. However, this camera matrix is the inverse of the original. If an object were to move 2 units to the left, one would get the same result as if the camera did the opposite and moved 2 units to the right. The camera matrix is then multiplied by the model's Transformation matrix, as shown in the following code snippet:

```
mat4.identity(mvMatrix);
mat4.lookAt( eye, target, up, camera );
mat4.multiply( mvMatrix, camera );
```

Later, we will animate and give the user control over the camera, which gives 3D applications their first-person point of view. The characters in such video games are often referred to as first-person shooters.

Objective complete – mini debriefing

There is more that we can include in Web3D online shopping, such as some enjoyment! After all, if you had a chainsaw in a store full of wood products, wouldn't you want to do a little harmless destruction? What better way to test out a few chainsaws than to ravage the store. This would also invite the audience to come back for more, merging shopping with fun. Maybe destroying a store isn't your idea of fun until you try it. A female art colleague once said "Women like to create things, and men like to destroy things". I'll leave it at that.

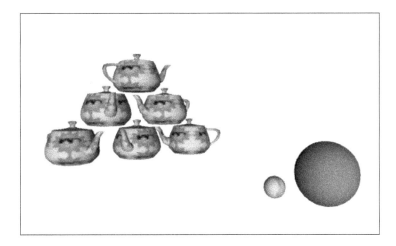

The final demonstration is an example of interacting with objects to turn the online shopping experience into a game. Using existing objects from 3D modeling programs, I thought of a sporting goods store with baseballs, basketballs, and sports equipment. As far as 3D objects go, there is not much to demonstrate—just a selection of basketballs, prices, and maybe a word or two about which professional league uses a brand, and what famous player endorses it. Of course, we could include a hoop in the scene and take some shots, but throwing the basketball or baseball at some objects would be more fun. Would that entertain audiences? It certainly would not be boring.

Since we previously saw how to click on an object with our mouse, and change an object's position per frame by incrementing the *x*, *y*, or *z* values, we can create a simple animation with that to knock over some teapots. Once the basketball hits near the teapots it triggers an animation of random movements and rotations to send them flying, as shown in the following screenshot. In the upcoming projects, we shall look at interactivity, animation, and collision detection.

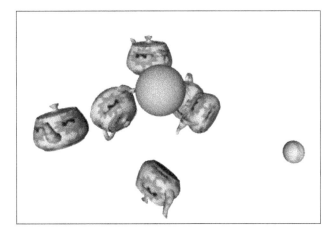

This gets to the heart of advertising. Many commercials are about imagery. Soft drink advertisements are about fun, friends, good times, relationships, and parties. They certainly don't mention the syrup, water, or show highlights of how Coke or Pepsi are manufactured. Car commercials are much the same, featuring ruggedness for trucks, or freedom, the intelligent buyer, and quality for high-end models. WebGL enables imagery, transforming a website from an online advertisement of products to a personal expression of that business—an opportunity to engage the customer.

Mission accomplished

This project covered the groundwork in WebGL: shader languages, reading 3D models by artists, the math behind ray-bounding box detection and matrices, and examples of how WebGL can transform the world of e-commerce. Along the way, we covered the fundamentals: 3D meshes built from a set of vertices connected three-somes to form triangles; the normals at each vertex, used to calculate the light; and cameras, so we can render a scene from any location. We then applied texture maps to 3D meshes that apply a virtual wallpaper to our 3D structures. Finally, we included interactivity to manipulate objects in the 3D scene.

A factor for WebGL as a tool for e-commerce will be transitioning from the current catalog design of 2D websites, listing products as if we were reading a newspaper advertisement. This style for e-commerce is certainly functional, but we rarely get to try out the products, experience its features, and configure its options, and we are hardly engaged in a shopping experience. For this, WebGL offers a breakthrough in e-commerce.

Project 3

User Experience, Story, Character, Visual Design, and Interactivity

"It's worth it to pay a little more for a better Whiskey."

– Artist Bob Schuchman

We often think of a *story* as a feature film or a novel where characters are developed for audiences to identify, sympathize, or detest. The aim of a story is to evoke an emotion, to frighten, embrace, or ponder difficult questions or understand them better. A *story* is not just a dialogue though, and it includes the design of the characters, scenery, music, and the balance of each of these elements. A *story* is not related to duration either. We know that movies and poems are stories and so is an advertisement, especially a web advertisement. On radio and television, an advertisement usually has 30 seconds to inform, educate, entertain, build brand loyalty, and be memorable. Web banner advertisements often lack this. Banner ads are informative, targeted, and measureable, but devoid of a story. Maybe that is why, according to Wikipedia, banner ad click-through rates (the ratio of banner ads clicked on divided by the number of times the advertisement is displayed) have declined from the Web's early days of 5 per cent down to about 0.2 percent today. This is happening even in an era of targeted marketing, where advertisements are contoured towards the audiences' interests based on web searches and surf results that are recorded or stored in cookies.

There is a feeling that banner ads now say, "You were just surfing the Web for hotels in Chicago, and here is one last additional advertisement in case you closed your browser early." In essence, banner advertisements today seem like someone just left the store, and the salesperson is trying to get your attention well after you turned your back and walked out.

The challenge, even for WebGL, is to grab the audience's attention. Web3D may have the best chance to do this since people are attracted to 3D art and graphics—one validation of this is the success of 3D graphics in movies and games. Nowadays, web advertising feels outdated. We've seen these banner advertisements before—they're hardly fresh. Web ads are little more than a graphic with a link. That's not to say that there aren't a lot of cool websites out there. In addition, many websites are very creative and make effective use of HTML5, but often, the banner advertisements seem like dull wall posters. The next few sections are going to highlight the features of WebGL and Web3D in general, including immersion, shader languages, and interactivity. The art design is intended to demonstrate WebGL's features and have you say, "I can apply these concepts creatively." The brands are fictitious, but the messages are similar to what advertisers would use to sell their product or brand.

Mission briefing

Web advertisements must download fast. That's a concern because artists like to build nice 3D models where the file size is hardly a consideration. At the same time, we want to show off the best features of interactive Web3D that will grab the viewer's attention. The features that best highlight 3D are often found in lighting and immersive environments. The technology behind much of this is shader languages—pixel-by-pixel calculations in the graphics card. We will first program a shader language to animate textures and 3D meshes in order to create waving flags, waterfalls, and change sand to greenery. Next, we will animate lights and cameras to demonstrate fascinating scenes with neon and light bulbs. Finally, we will enable the user to navigate through the scene, allowing the user to move the camera with the mouse and keyboard, and then solve some of the difficult issues of lighting in foggy or nighttime scenes.

Why is it awesome?

If you are an advertiser or designer, you are always looking for ways to grab a user's attention. You will want to be edgy, avant-garde, apart from the crowd, distinct, and most of all, capable of delivering a message. While *traditional* web advertising may be concerned with clicking on the banners, Web3D can tell us which objects the user clicked on within the 3D scene and features products with engaging animations.

Your Hotshot objectives

The major tasks required to complete our project are as follows:

- ▸ Refreshment with shader languages
- ▸ Lighting 3D depths
- ▸ Visual design and interactivity
- ▸ Full navigation
- ▸ Order of transparencies
- ▸ Scene lighting

Refreshment with shader languages

The design here is simple—a can of **X Y Z** brand of soft drink on concrete with a flag in the breeze texture-mapped with **Thirst**. Everything here was made with Adobe Photoshop. 3D Studio Max was used only to create primitives such as the cylinder for the soda can. When the mouse is over the can, the can is highlighted and the cursor changes to grab the viewer's attention. We respect that the audience comes to a website for a specific reason, but if the cursor hovers over the banner advertisement, we may just catch their attention. Since the scene is animated, this banner ad will likely be more inviting than other advertisements. The fictitious advertisement opens up to a dry, asphalt environment with an animated flag waving **Thirst** and a can of our **X Y Z Soft Drink** as shown in the following screenshot:

Engage thrusters

The flag waving in the wind is achieved entirely by using shader languages. There are two effects used here: the waving of the flag and the slight changes in the shading of the flag. These changes involve the *z* value of each vertex moving back and forth in a sine wave, and the shading changes are created by manipulating the vertex normals. Since these changes involve the vertices, we naturally start with the flag's vertex shader that now includes the time variable, `uniform float uTime;`, as a parameter inside the sine wave to animate the flag.

The time is sent to the vertex shader to create the animation from `drawScene()`. We get the computer clock time in milliseconds and then pick an equation that creates a repeating wave every half second:

```
var time = new Date();
var currentTime = time.getTime();

currentTime = ((currentTime % 2000) / 500.0) * Math.PI;
gl.uniform1f(shaderProgram.timeUniform, currentTime );
```

Since we use `currentTime` for other animations, we perform the *modulo* function later in the `drawScene()` function. The `currentTime % 2000` code snippet (pronounced as currentTime *modulo* 2000, or just *mod* for short) returns the remainder of a division, and thus returns a result between 0 and 1999. In case you were wondering, the `getTime()` function returns the number of milliseconds (thousandths of a second, 1000 milliseconds = 1 second) since January 01, 1970. Dividing the result by 500 gives us a value between 0 and 4, and multiplying with π gives us two loops around a circle per second, or one rotation per half second which represents the wave of the flag back to its original position. This code hooks up the `currentTime` CPU time variable to the `uTime` shader variable, so we can use the time in our shader code as follows:

```
shaderProgram.timeUniform = gl.getUniformLocation
    (shaderProgram, "uTime");
```

Now that we have discussed time, let us return to the rest of the code that creates the waving of the flag. There are two elements here: the flag's back and forth movement in the direction of the *z* axis, and changing the *x* and *y* axis values of the normals to add a slight shading to give the illusion that the flag is waving, explained as follows:

> ▸ The first line positions the flag; the *x* and *y* values don't change, but the *z* value causes the flag to move in and out. In order to create the wind effect, the *x* value is added to the time so that the end of the flag that has the largest *x* value furthest from the flagpole has the most flutter.

- ▶ We take `cosine(aVertexPosition.x + uTime)` to obtain a value between -1 and 1. Recall that the original *z* value for each vertex was zero, so now, the flag will flutter.

- ▶ Next, we calculated the *x* component of the vertex normal, which is used to calculate the shading based on the angle between the vertex normal and the direction of the light. Changing the *x* value of the normal alters the angle between the light and vertex normal, reinforcing the impression that the flag is waving.

In the next line, we first calculate `vTransformedNormal`, the value passed on to the fragment shader. Initially, we get a runtime error until `vTransformedNormal = uNMatrix * vec3(aVertexNormal);` is inserted. Array values sent to the vertex shader, such as `aVertexNormal`, must be referenced akin to C or Java giving a compiler warning if a variable was declared but not used. The value of `vTransformedNormal` will be between (-1, 0, 0.5) and (1, 0, 0.5), which will give us enough variation in the vertex normals to have changes in the shading to add to our waving flag simulation in the vertex shader. After the flag-position's *z* value and the vertex normals' *x* value has been modified to wave the flag, we transform (multiply) the vertices and the vertex normals according to the flag's location in the 3D scene and camera (`uMVMatrix`) and then convert to perspective view by multiplying it with `uPMatrix`:

```
void main(void) {
    vec3 flagPosition = vec3(aVertexPosition.x,
      aVertexPosition.y, cos(aVertexPosition.x + uTime) );
  float xNormal = sin(aVertexPosition.x + uTime);
  vTransformedNormal = uNMatrix * vec3(aVertexNormal);
  vTransformedNormal = uNMatrix *
    normalize(vec3(xNormal, 0.0, 0.5));
  vTextureCoord = aTextureCoord;
  vVertexPosition = flagPosition;
  gl_Position = uPMatrix * uMVMatrix * vec4(flagPosition, 1.0);
}
```

In the fragment shader, the key feature is the transition from one texture map to another. This eye-catching effect demonstrates how shaders can be used in multitexturing as we transition from the **Thirst** flag to the **Refreshment** flag. We use a similar effect on the transition from yellow sand to green grass. Thus far, all our texture maps have had a one-to-one correspondence with 3D meshes.

Now we have two texture maps for the same 3D mesh. To read in the second texture map, we use a similar code from `meshObject.js`, one of our JavaScript utilities.

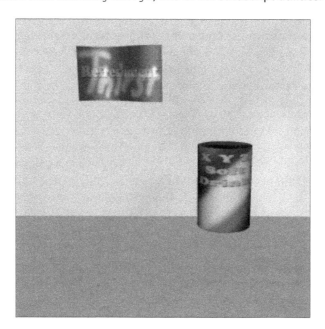

In `webGLStart()`, the same place where we download our `.obj` 3D mesh files, we also get the alternative texture map, `refreshment.jpg`. The code creates a new `gl.textureMap` object with an image property link to a new `image` object and then uses AJAX technology to download the texture map in the background. This is similar to how we loaded texture maps when we first called `AddMeshObject()` in `mesh3dObject.js`:

```
flagAltTextureMap = gl.createTexture();
flagAltTextureMap.image = new Image();
flagAltTextureMap.image.onload = function () {
  handleLoadedTexture( flagAltTextureMap );
}
flagAltTextureMap.image.src = "refreshment.jpg";
```

When we are done, the new `flagAltTextureMap` variable will be passed to the flag fragment shader for our second texture map. The `thirst.jpg` texture map is downloaded with the original flag file.

In `createShaderProgram()`, we do the customary link between the JavaScript and the shaders, which essentially bridges our CPU variables with the shader variables. In the following code, we are informing the shader program of a link to the alternative texture map:

```
shaderProgram.samplerAltUniform =
  gl.getUniformLocation(shaderProgram, "uSamplerAlt");
```

We bind the second texture map, `flagAltTextureMap`, with the fragment shader's `samplerAltUniform` in `drawScene()`. Texture maps are referenced by an ID number, starting with 0. We don't actually pass the texture map in each frame. That would be highly inefficient as texture memory is shared by the CPU and GPU.

```
if ( flagAltTextureMap != null ) {
  gl.activeTexture(gl.TEXTURE1);
  gl.bindTexture(gl.TEXTURE_2D, flagAltTextureMap);
  gl.uniform1i(shaderProgram.samplerAltUniform, 1);
}
```

The fragment shader has a single directional light parallel to the negative *z* axis. The `thirst.jpg` texture map is `gl.TEXTURE0` in `drawScene()` and is bound to `uSampler` in the shader. The `refreshment.jpg` texture map is `gl.TEXTURE1` in `drawScene()` and is bound to `uSamplerAlt` in the fragment shader. The blending of the two texture maps as we transition from `thirsty.jpg` to `refreshment.jpg` is controlled by the `uTextureTransitionTime` variable:

```
void main(void) {
  vec3 lightDirection = normalize(vec3( 0, 0, -1 ));
  vec3 normal = normalize(vTransformedNormal);
  float lightAngleToVertex = dot(-lightDirection, normal );
  if (lightAngleToVertex < 0.0) lightAngleToVertex = 0.0;
  vec4 fragmentColor =
    texture2D(uSampler, vec2(vTextureCoord.s, vTextureCoord.t))
      - uTextureTransitionTime) + texture2D(uSamplerAlt,
      vec2(vTextureCoord.s, vTextureCoord.t)) *
      uTextureTransitionTime;
  gl_FragColor = vec4(fragmentColor.rgb * lightAngleToVertex, 1.0);
}
```

The `uTextureTransitionTime` is initialized to 0. When the soda can is clicked on, a floating point number counts to 1 over 4 seconds. To change the texture from sand to green grass, we animate the colors, reducing red and blue to 20 percent of their original color, leaving mostly green. The value of `uTextureAnimatedColor` in the fragment shader is bound to `sandTextureColorAnimated` in `drawScene()`, which animates from white to green in order to change sand to grass. At the beginning of the animation, when `uTextureTransitionTime` is 0, `uTextureAnimatedColor` is (1, 1, 1), and at the end of the four-second animation, `uTextureAnimatedColor` is (0.2, 1, 0.2):

```
vec4 fragmentColor = texture2D(uSampler, vec2(vTextureCoord.s *
  uTextureScaling.s, vTextureCoord.t * uTextureScaling.t));
gl_FragColor = vec4(fragmentColor.r*uTextureAnimatedColor.r,
  fragmentColor.g*uTextureAnimatedColor.g,
  fragmentColor.b*uTextureAnimatedColor.b, 1.0);
```

The third blending animates the texture map coordinates to create a moving waterfall. The `TextureTranslation` value in the `shaderWaterfall-fs` fragment shader is bound to `waterfallTextureTranslation` in the JavaScript code. The `waterfallTextureTranslation` value is initialized to (0, 0.5), but its second value is incremented by 0.005 for every frame in `drawScene()`. Since `uTextureTranslation.t` increments in every frame, adding this to the `vTextureCoord.t` texture coordinate creates the animated waterfall effect. As with the other two animations, `uTextrueTranslationTime` starts at 0 and increments to 1 over 4 seconds to blend in the animated waterfall once we click on the soda can:

```
vec4 fragmentColor = vec4(0.68, 0.96, 0.976, 1.0) *
   (1.0 - uTextureTransitionTime) +
   texture2D(uSampler, vec2(vTextureCoord.s,
   vTextureCoord.t + uTextureTranslation.t)) *
   uTextureTransitionTime;
```

Objective complete – mini debriefing

A story involves action. In this demonstration, we included the activity of clicking on the soda can, which invoked three animations: vertex and normal animations to create the waving flag, color animation to progress from sand to green grass, and texture map animation to create the waterfall. We also demonstrated blending between the two texture maps. Texture map animations can also be scaled or rotated for nice effects, such as clouds drifting in the sky, pinwheels, barber shop poles, car tires, and so on. If you are a video game player, you may notice some of these subtle techniques. Most importantly, these techniques were all done primarily using shader languages.

Lighting 3D depths

You can think of 3D as the objects in a scene, but there are also unseen objects such as the lights and camera. This next web advertisement animates a camera while deploying two different light sources: neon lights and spotlights. To add a little character, the spotlights flicker and the neon sign turns on in a sequence.

Engage thrusters

The advertisement begins with the camera animation and the lights randomly turning on in order to catch the viewers' attention. This also emphasizes the features of 3D that cannot be emulated in a 2D animation without a heavy download. The camera points to a fixed target while slowly animating from the left of the 3D scene towards the center by changing the camera's `eye` value. This is shown in the following screenshot:

We begin by defining the start and end positions for the camera:

```
var eyeStart = [ -10, 5, -2, 1 ];
var eyeEnd   = [ -6, 3, 6, 1 ];
var eye      = [ eyeStart[0], eyeStart[1], eyeStart[2], 1 ];
```

Within the `drawScene()` function, the per frame animation simply increments the eye object's current value:

```
if ( eye[0] < eyeEnd[0] ) eye[0] += .003;
if ( eye[1] > eyeEnd[1] ) eye[1] -= .0015;
if ( eye[2] < eyeEnd[2] ) eye[2] += .006;
```

The art style was to capture an old-time signage look using neon and a traditionally lit sign using spotlights. The lights flicker to add character, as if there was an electrical problem. The neon lights are on an 8-second timer to blink off and on. In the `drawScene()` function, `neonTimer` will have a value from 0 to 7:

```
var time = new Date();
var currentTime = time.getTime();
var neonTimer = parseInt((currentTime % 8000) / 1000);
```

A bit later in the code, the color is set to either neon or off-color. For example, **Schuchman's** is red (red, green, and blue = (1, 0, 0)) or its off-color is a faint red (0.2, 0, 0):

```
if (meshObjectArray[i] == schuchmansObject) {
  shaderProgram = shaderNeon;
  if ( (neonTimer == 1) || (neonTimer >= 4) )
    lightColor = [ 1, 0, 0 ];
  else lightColor = [ .2, 0, 0 ];
}
else if (meshObjectArray[i] == americanObject) {
  shaderProgram = shaderNeon;
  if ( (neonTimer == 2) || (neonTimer >= 5) )
    lightColor = [ 1, 1, 1 ];
  else lightColor = [ .1, .1, .1 ];
}
else if (meshObjectArray[i] == whiskeyObject) {
  shaderProgram = shaderNeon;
  if ( (neonTimer == 3) || (neonTimer >= 6) )
    lightColor = [ 0, 0, 1 ];
  else lightColor = [ 0, 0, .2 ];
}
```

The shader code is simply a single line in the fragment shader that receives the `lightColor` value. The text models were developed in 3ds Max. The text models are shown in the following screenshot:

The spotlights are made up of two components: the 3D model of a cone and the actual light itself. The cones use a texture map and shader from an example in *Project 2*, *WebGL for E-Commerce*. There is also a point light in the scene. Often, it is wise to throw in some ambient light so that the scene is not pitch black.

Every spotlight has a location, direction, and variables to turn the spotlights on or off. The spotlights are numbered 0 to 2, but the initial settings of spotlight number 0 are shown in the following code; it is located at (3, 0.5, -1) and points at (4, -0.5, -1):

```
var sL0Loc = [ 3,   .5, -1 ];   //spotlight #0 Location
var sL0Dir = [ 4, -.5, -1 ];   //spotlight #0 Direction
var sL0on = false;
var SL0enableOn = false;
```

Within `drawScene()`, each spotlight sends its location (`sL0LoC`), direction (`sL0Dir`), and on/off value (`sL0on`) to the shader:

```
gl.uniform3f(shaderProgram.spotLt0LocUniform,
  sL0Loc[0], sL0Loc[1], sL0Loc[2] );
gl.uniform3f(shaderProgram.spotLt0DirUniform,
  sL0Dir[0], sL0Dir[1], sL0Dir[2] );
if ( (currentTime % 13000) < 300) {
  sL0on = false;
  SL0enableOn = true;
}
else if ( SL0enableOn ) sL0on = true;
  gl.uniform1i(shaderProgram.spotLt0onUniform, sL0on );
```

We added `if ( (currentTime % 13000) < 300)` to flicker the spotlight off for about 0.3 seconds out of every 13 seconds. The `SL0enableOn` variable initializes the scene with the spotlight off and then turns the spotlight on while the camera is animating within the first 13 seconds at a random time for an interesting effect. The `sL0on` Boolean informs the shader whether the light is on or off.

In the spotlight's fragment shader, the `main()` function, we can see the amount of light that the three spotlights contribute to each individual pixel. A point light is also added as an ambient light so that nothing is pitch black.

```
void main(void) {
  float lightWeighting = 0.0;
  if ( uSpotLight0on ) lightWeighting +=
    calcLtContribution (uSpotLight0Loc, uSpotLight0Dir, false);
  if ( uSpotLight1on ) lightWeighting +=
    calcLtContribution(uSpotLight1Loc, uSpotLight1Dir, false);
  if ( uSpotLight2on ) lightWeighting +=
    calcLtContribution (uSpotLight2Loc, uSpotLight2Dir, false);
  lightWeighting += calcLtContribution
    (uPointLightLoc,uPointLightLoc, true);
  if (lightWeighting > 1.0) lightWeighting = 1.0;

    vec4 fragmentColor = texture2D(uSampler,
      vec2(vTextureCoord.s, vTextureCoord.t));
  gl_FragColor = vec4(fragmentColor.rgb * lightWeighting, 1.0);
}
```

The combined weight of the lights cannot exceed 1. If any of the color components—red, green, or blue—were to exceed 1, it is up to the graphics card to determine how to handle that. The graphics card can clamp the red, green, or blue values to 1, or it can reduce the three colors by a percentage so that the largest value is reduced to 1. We add `if (lightWeighting > 1.0) lightWeighting = 1.0;` to clamp the value at 1. This is the first time that we have the `main()` function calling another function, `calcLtContribution()`. Since we perform the same calculations for all three spotlights, it's simpler to define this new function and call it three times.

The first line of the `calcLtContribution()` function calculates the distance from each pixel position, `vPosition.xyz`, to the light's location, `lightLoc`, and then normalizes the value to a unit vector:

```
vec3 vectorLightPosToPixel = normalize(vPosition.xyz - lightLoc);
```

Looking at the example, it's clear that spotlight #0 is located at (3, 0.5, -1), the value for `lightLoc`. To keep the math simple, let's use the center pixel of the *Bob's Market* advertisement at (5, 0, 0) for `vPosition.xyz`. This subtraction is (5, 0, 0) - (3, 0.5, -1), or the x, y, and z values, $(5-3, 0-.5, 0-(-1)) = (2, .5, 1)$. We normalize (2, -0.5, 1), meaning that we make it a unit value of the length 1 such that $x^2 + y^2 + z^2 = 1$. To convert a unit value, divide the x, y, and z values by the squareroot of $x^2 + y^2 + z^2$ or use the formula $(x, y, z) / Square-root(x^2 + y^2 + z^2)$. Using the numbers mentioned previously, (2, -0.5, 1) as a unit vector is as follows:

```
( 2, -.5, 1 ) / Square-root( 2² + (-.5)2 + 12 ) =
 ( 2, -.5, 1 ) / Square-root( 4 + .25 + 1) =
 ( 2, -.5, 1 ) / Square-root( 5.25 ) =
 ( 2, -.5, 1 ) / 2.29 = ( 2/2.29, -.5/2.29, 1/2.29 ) =
 ( .87, -.22, .436 )
```

The amount of light emitted from a source on an individual pixel is based on the angle between the two vectors; the two vectors are the light's location to the pixel and the pixel's normal (not to be confused with the term *normalize*, which means making a vector into a length of 1). The dot product of these two vectors (light-location-to-pixel and pixel-normal) equals the cosine of the angle between these two vectors.

To demonstrate lighting calculations, let us place the spotlight at (-5, 0, 0) and calculate the amount of light on the three different pixels located at (-5, 0, -10), (0, 0, -10), and (5, 0, -10). The vectors from the spotlight to each respective pixel would be (-5-(-5), 0-0, 0-(-10)); (-5-0, 0-0, 0-(-10)); and (-5-5, 0-0, 0-(-10)). Simplifying the equations, the vectors from the spotlight to each pixel would be (0, 0, 10); (-5, 0, 10); and (-10, 0, 10). Normalizing these three light-to-pixel vectors for a unit length of 1: (0, 0, 1); (-0.447, 0, 0.894); and (-0.707, 0, 0.707).

The normal vertex for the entire plane is (0, 0, 1). We use the dot product to calculate the angle between the light-to-pixel vector L and the normal N. The dot product multiples the x values, y values, and z values of the two vectors; *dot product = $N_x * L_x + N_y * L_y + N_z * L_z$.* This is equal to the cosine of the angle between the vectors:

1st pixel = (0, 0, 1)·(0, 0, 1) = 0*0 + 0*0 + 1*1 = 1

2nd pixel = (-0.447, 0, 0.894)·(0, 0, 1) = -0.447*0 + 0*0 + 0.894*1 = 0.894

3rd pixel = (-0.707, 0, 0.707)·(0, 0, 1) = -0.707*0 + 0*0 + 0.707*1 = 0.707

We calculate the angle from the light to each pixel using the arc-cosine of these numbers: first pixel, $\cos^{-1}(1)$ = 0 degrees; second pixel, $\cos^{-1}(0.894)$ = 26.6 degrees; and third pixel, $\cos^{-1}(0.707)$ = 45 degrees. These degrees are important because spotlights have a cut-off angle, where beyond this angle, no light shines. For example, if the cut-off angle is 30 degrees, then the third pixel at a 45-degree angle to the spotlight receives no light.

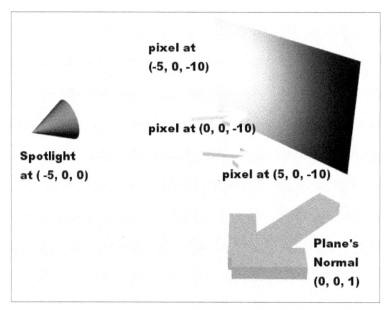

Spotlight with three pixels centered at the far left (-5, 0, -10), middle (0, 0, -10), and far right (5, 0, -10)

The next line calculates the cosine of the angle between the two vectors using the dot product:

```
float lightAngleToPixel = dot(vectorLightPosToPixel,
    normalize(lightDir) );
```

The light direction (lightDir) for spotlight 0 is (4, -0.5, -1), initialized in JavaScript:

```
var sL0Dir = [ 4, -.5, -1 ];  // spotlight #0 Direction
```

Since vectors need to be unit values, we normalize spotlight #0's direction. Note that we could improve performance by calculating this just once in advance, but it's easier to understand the spotlight's direction given an actual location to point towards rather than a vector. Normalizing (4, -0.5, -1) to a unit value becomes (0.96, -0.12, -0.24).

The dot product between `VectorLightPosToPixel` and the normalized `lightDir` is as follows:

```
( .87, -.22, .436 ) · ( .96, -.12, -.24 ) =
( .87 *.96 + (-.22)*(-.12) + .436 * (-.24) ) = .835 + .026 - .104
= .757
```

Thus, about 75.7 percent of the light from spotlight #0 comes to the pixel in the center of the **Bob's Market** sign.

The spotlight's beam width is set to 0.25 radians (about 14 degrees). Outside this 14 degree radius, the light diminishes until finally it cuts off at 0.5 radians (about a 28 degree radius):

```
float cutOffAngle = .878; // equal to cosine(0.5);
float beamWidth = .97; // equals cosine(.25);
```

Previously, we determined the cosine of the angle between spotlight #0's direction and the center of the **Bob's Market** sign at 0.757. The inverse cosine of (0.757) is 40.8 degrees or 0.71 radians, which is beyond the 28 degree radius of spotlight #0. Thus, no light shines from spotlight #0 to the center of the sign at the pixel (5, 0, 0).

The following block of code checks whether the angle from the light to the pixel is within the cut-off angle, and if so, the amount of light is a ratio between the cut-off angle and the beam width. If the light is inside the beam width, then we use the light's full intensity. Often, a light's intensity is set to 1, but here we set the intensity to 0.6 (60 percent) as intensities above 60 percent appeared too bright in this scene:

```
if ( pointLight ) spotLightWeighting = 0.3;
else {
  if ( lightAngleToPixel > cutOffAngle ) {
    //note, these are cosines of the angles, not actual angles
    spotLightWeighting = (lightAngleToPixel - cutOffAngle) /
      (beamWidth - cutOffAngle) * .6;
}
  if ( lightAngleToPixel >= beamWidth ) {
    //note, these are cosines of the angles, not actual angles
    spotLightWeighting = 0.6;
  }
}
return spotLightWeighting;
```

Objective complete

This example included two types of light used with objects: **emissive light** and **reflective light**. Emissive lights include objects such as the sun, a light bulb, neon lights, or a television or computer screen. Emissive lights will not have any shading around the edges. The other type of lighting is reflective, which calculates its color based on the lights shone upon it. Reflective lights are more complex to calculate, requiring the dot product between the light's direction and the pixel's normal. For a point light or spotlight, we also have to calculate the normalized vector from the light's location to each pixel, unlike a directional light such as the sun. In addition, for spotlights, we also determine if the angle from the light to a specific pixel is within the spotlight's beam width or cut-off angle.

Prior to advanced graphics cards, we could not perform precise lighting calculations on a pixel-by-pixel basis in real time. However, with GPU programming, video games and WebGL can create effects such as flashlights, streetlights, car headlights, and great scenes with spotlights.

Visual design and interactivity

3D graphics, by themselves, do not create a story; music also does not create a story, but it can set the mood. From the opening sequence of a small town on a sunny day to a dark mystery in a gritty big city, the design of the scene contributes to the dialogue, acting, and director's staging. This next demonstration introduces a street in daylight that transitions to night in a 24-second cycle. We control the camera to move from left to right, forward and back with the arrow keys. Since we can navigate anywhere in the scene, some 3D meshes such as signs and light posts reach the far-clipping plane and are chopped off. The far-clipping plane ensures that we do not waste computing power by rendering 3D meshes very far away. However, clipping looks unnatural. To prevent 3D meshes from just disappearing, we add fog so that these 3D meshes will fade off into the depths. Fog also adds character to the scene—the charm of London or San Francisco is its fog. In addition, at night, a black fog creates realism by making distant objects appear darker.

Engage thrusters

Video games typically use the arrow keys or the *W*, *A*, *S*, and *D* keys to move the camera. The setup inside `webGLStart()` tells the operating system on a key down or key up event to call the `handleKeyDown()` and `handleKeyUp()` functions, respectively. When the browser's built-in function detects a key down or key up event within the document, the browser is instructed to call the `handleKeyDown()` and `handleKeyUp()` functions in our WebGL page:

```
document.onkeydown = handleKeyDown;
document.onkeyup = handleKeyUp;
```

The key down and key up events are saved in the `currentlyPressedKeys` array for processing on a per-frame basis. A value for every key is saved in an array of Boolean (`true` or `false`) values, which are used to inform which key was pressed:

```
var currentlyPressedKeys = {};
function handleKeyDown(event) {
  currentlyPressedKeys[event.keyCode] = true;
}
function handleKeyUp(event) {
  currentlyPressedKeys[event.keyCode] = false;
}
```

The `tick()` function used for animation now calls `handleKeys();`. Since this code can be used for any keyboard keys, a source for the ID numbers for each key is the World Wide Web Consortium, or W3C, at `http://www.w3.org/2002/09/tests/keys.html`. For example, key ID 38 is the up arrow key:

```
function handleKeys() {
  if (currentlyPressedKeys[38]) {
    // up arrow, camera forward along negative z-axis
    eye[2] -= .1; target[2] -= .1;
  }
  else if (currentlyPressedKeys[40]) {
    // down arrow, camera backward along positive z-axis
    eye[2] += .1; target[2] += .1;
  }
  else if (currentlyPressedKeys[37]) {
    // left arrow, camera moves along negative x-axis
    eye[0] -= .1; target[0] -= .1;
  }
  else if (currentlyPressedKeys[39]) {
    // right arrow, camera moves along positive x-axis
    eye[0] += .1; target[0] += .1;
  }
}
```

Recall that in the previous examples, we set the camera's `eye`, `target`, and `up` vectors and used `mat4.lookAt( eye, target, up, camera );` to set up the camera matrix. If the `target` and `eye` values do not move in unison, then we would revolve around a single point.

This scene has two streets, Beach Avenue and Pier Avenue, plus a black fog to emulate the night. Much of the work is performed inside the fragment shader. For adding the fog, we need to determine the distance of the camera from our location to each pixel inside the fragment shader. We can either obscure the pixel by the fog if it is beyond `fogDepth` of 60.0 or blend in the fog based on the pixel's depth:

```
void main(void) {
  float distanceCameraToPixel = length(vVertexPosition.xyz);
  float fogDepth = 60.0;
  vec4 fragmentColor = texture2D(uSampler,
    vec2(vTextureCoord.s, vTextureCoord.t*10.0));
  if ( distanceCameraToPixel < fogDepth ) {
    fragmentColor =
      vec4(fragmentColor.rgb * ( 1.0 -
      distanceCameraToPixel/fogDepth) +
      uFogColor.rgb*(distanceCameraToPixel/fogDepth), 1.0 );
  }
  else {
    fragmentColor = vec4(uFogColor, 1.0);
  }
  gl_FragColor = vec4(fragmentColor.rgb, 1.0);
}
```

The extent to which the fog obscures the street is based on how far each pixel is from the camera. Therefore, the first line calculates the distance of the camera to each pixel. If the distance is greater than `fogDepth`, then all we should see is fog. However, if the distance is less than `fogDepth`, the color of the pixel will be a blend of the texture map pixel and the fog—the greater the distance, the thicker the fog. The `fogDepth` value can be programmed to be denser for night scenes. For example, with `fogDepth` set to 60.0, a pixel that is 45 units away will be 25 percent of its color (1 − 45/60), and the remaining 75 percent will be the fog color. For example, for the yellow line in the center of the street, the color (1.0, 1.0, 0.0) with a gray fog (0.5, 0.5, 0.5) 45 units away would be calculated as *(1.0, 0.0, 1.0)*(1-45/60) + (0.5, 0.5, 0.5) * 45/60 = (1.0, 1.0, 0.0)*1/4 + (0.5, 0.5, 0.5)*3/4 = (0.5, 0.5, 0.375)*. Note that true atmospheric conditions such as fog are not linear but exponential, meaning that if you double the distance, the fog is four times thicker. In physics, this is known as the *Inverse-square law*. However, linear depth—where one fourth of the distance to the maximum fog depth is one fourth the fog color, and half the distance is half the fog color—appears more realistic than actual atmospheric conditions. It does not hurt that linear fog is easier to calculate than inverse-square fog.

The most complex parts of this demonstration are the cones representing the light cast by the streetlights. In computer graphics, this is known as volumetric rendering where you can slice into a 3D mesh and see the two parts, as if you were slicing an apple. However, in the world of fast 3D graphics, we often emulate effects such as volumetric rendering. Here, we can see the light shafts coming from the streetlights in the fog, but we are simulating the effect using the partially transparent cones.

To simulate the transparent effect of light shafts, translucent cones were added to our array of 3D meshes in `webGLStart()`, furthest cone first. This scene has four streetlights, each 25 units apart along the *z* axis at -40 units, -15 units, 10 units, and finally the fourth streetlight is 35 units along the *z* axis. Transparencies must be drawn after all the other objects are drawn, with the furthest transparent object drawn first and the closest transparent object drawn last. The calculation of transparencies must blend the background with the color of the transparent object; thus, backgrounds must be calculated before foregrounds. Generic 3D graphic engines can handle transparencies in any order, but it is a tedious process for the renderer. Without ordering the transparent 3D meshes in advance, the renderer has to examine the depth of every pixel for all the transparent 3D meshes to see which is the furthest, calculate the color for that pixel, and then follow the process again for the next closest pixel until we have accounted for every transparent pixel at that location. Later, we will have to do this process ourselves, but for now, our scene renders our four cone-shaped shafts of light in the order of furthest first and closest last.

Near the top of `drawScene()`, we disable blending, `gl.disable(gl.BLEND);`, and then enable blending *after* we render all the other opaque objects. When we encounter our first transparent cone, we enable blending as follows:

```
shaderProgram = shaderTransparency;
gl.enable(gl.BLEND);
gl.blendFunc(gl.SRC_ALPHA, gl.ONE);
```

The blend values are just the default, and most of the work will occur here in the fragment shader. We calculated the values for a black fog, which is a night scene, and checked if the pixel is closer than the fog depth, and if so, we blended the pixel with the fog:

```
void main(void) {
  float distanceCameraToPixel = length(vVertexPosition.xyz);
  float fogDepth = 60.0;
  vec3 lightColor = vec3(0.1, 0.1, 0.1);
  vec4 fragmentColor = vec4( 0.0, 0.0, 0.0, 1.0 );
  if ( distanceCameraToPixel < fogDepth ) {
    fragmentColor = vec4( lightColor * ( 1.0 -
    distanceCameraToPixel/fogDepth), 1.0 );
  }
  gl_FragColor = vec4(fragmentColor.rgb, 1.0);
}
```

As in the previous examples, we calculate the distance to each pixel. The `fogDepth` value that is chosen is 60.0, and thus the fog will hide any 3D mesh beyond 60 units. Since the streetlight cone blends with the background, we only brighten the cone area slightly by 10 percent with red, green, and blue set to (0.1, 0.1, 0.1)—we want the streetlight effect, not some brilliant light. If the cone is closer than the fog depth of 60.0, we calculate a ratio of light to add to the scene—the closer the cone, the greater the value of `fragmentColor`. For example, a streetlight just 15 units away would create `fragmentColor = (0.1, 0.1, 0.1) * ( 1.0 - 15.0/60.0) = (0.075, 0.075, 0.075)`. A streetlight 40 units away results in `fragmentColor = (0.1, 0.1, 0.1) * ( 1.0 - 40.0/60.0) = (0.033, 0.033, 0.033)`.

Objective complete

We made some significant additions to our WebGL scenes, allowing us to now walk down the street and strafe to the left or right. We also included fog for both day and night scenes. However, this implores us to want to do more, such as turn around and view the scene from any location. This means that we have to address the transparency issue when we do not have 3D meshes in a predetermined order.

Full navigation

The 3D user experience includes the freedom to roam anywhere and look in all directions. Instead of the left and right arrow keys allowing us to move along the *x* axis, users in 3D environments prefer to navigate anywhere, including rotate left and right around the *y* axis.

Engage thrusters

To enable us to turn in any direction, we added a new `cameraRotation` variable initialized to 0. Our new code responding to the arrow keys allows us to rotate around the *y* axis to look left and right:

```
function handleKeys() {
  if (currentlyPressedKeys[38]) { // up arrow, camera forward
    eye[0] += Math.sin( cameraRotation ) * .1;
    eye[2] -= Math.cos( cameraRotation ) * .1;
  }
  else if (currentlyPressedKeys[40]) { // down arrow, cam. back
    eye[0] -= Math.sin( cameraRotation ) * .1;
    eye[2] += Math.cos( cameraRotation ) * .1;
  }
```

```
    else if (currentlyPressedKeys[37]) {
      // left arrow, camera  looks left
      cameraRotation -= .008;
    }
    else if (currentlyPressedKeys[39]) {
      // right arrow, camera looks right
      cameraRotation += .008;
    }
  }
```

The camera's `eye` that provides our location is still handled in the `handleKeys()` function. However, we moved the calculation of the camera's `target` property inside the `drawScene()` function. The `targetDistance` value was set to 10, which means that our camera will always aim 10 units directly in front, regardless of the direction in which we are looking. It's much like the hands on a clock where the `eye` is the center of the clock and the `target` represents where the clock's hour and minute hands are pointing.

```
target[0] = eye[0] + Math.sin( cameraRotation ) * targetDistance;
target[2] = eye[2] - Math.cos( cameraRotation ) * targetDistance;
mat4.lookAt( eye, target, up, camera );
```

Objective complete

The left and right arrow keys now increase or decrease the camera rotation of 0.008 radians. This gives a fairly smooth rotation around the y axis, but will likely be adjusted for the particular application. Finally, readers looking for a good source of three-dimensional rotations can visit `http://mathworld.wolfram.com/RotationMatrix.html`.

It's really great to create worlds where we can go anywhere. However, we left one artifact that needs to be addressed: transparency.

Order of transparencies

The flexibility of being able to navigate anywhere has also created a new problem—the transparent cones that represent the light shafts from the streetlights will no longer be ordered furthest to closest. We can walk to the other side of the scene, turn around, and see the spotlight cones overlapping in the wrong order. We have to render the scene so that with each frame, we test the stacking order of the transparent objects. This is a tedious bit of coding, but it also demonstrates the issue. The following screenshot shows the same scene from the opposite side. Notice that the closest spotlight cone obscures the furthest cone where the two overlap. We cannot ignore the issue, so let's devise a program to fix this.

Engage thrusters

The solution is to restack the order with which the items are rendered. Currently, the 3D meshes are rendered in the order that they are added in webGLStart(). There is an array, meshObjectArray, of the 3D meshes in this scene. The ten items are numbered 0 to 9. If we have a new array that tells us the order in which the 3D meshes should be rendered, then that would fix the problem. Earlier, the items were rendered in a numerical order: 0, 1, 2, 3, 4, 5, 6, 7, 8, and 9. Now, we will have a new objectIndex array that will stack the last four spotlight cones in the order of distance, from furthest to closest, or in a numerical order: 0, 1, 2, 3, 4, 5, 9, 8, 7, 6.

All the work takes place in drawScene() beginning with the code that puts objects in their default order:

```
var objectIndex = [];
for ( var i = 0; i < totalMeshObjects; i++ ) objectIndex[i] = i;
```

A checkbox was added above the WebGL window on the web page so that we can demonstrate the principle of stacking the spotlight cone order. The first step is to determine whether the checkbox is checked:

```
indexOrdering =
document.getElementById("orderIndexCkBox").checked;
```

If `indexOrdering` is true, calculate the distance from the camera to each object and restack the order in several steps:

▶ Find the distance from the camera to each spotlight

▶ Search our list for the longest distance, save it in the ordered list, and mark the order once found

▶ Overwrite the list of spotlights into our `objectIndexed` list, which has the order of objects to be rendered

First, we declare and initialize the arrays: `distanceSpotLight` to save the distance from each of the four spotlights to the camera, and `spotLightOrdered`, which is initialized to false until they are placed in our last array, `distanceSpotLightOrdered`, in the order of furthest from the camera to closest.

```
if ( indexOrdering )
{
// order the transparent objects from furthest to closest
  var distanceSpotLight = [];
  var spotLightOrdered = [false, false, false, false];
  var distanceSpotLightOrdered = [0, 0, 0, 0];
```

Find the distance from each streetlight to the camera's `eye`, which is our location. We call the `distanceToSpotLt()` function, which uses basic algebra for the distance between two 3D points—the streetlight's position and the camera's `eye`:

```
// get the distances from the camera to each spotlight cone
if (streetLightObject0.meshLoaded) distanceSpotLight[0] =
  distanceToSpotLt( streetLightObject0.translation, eye );
if (streetLightObject1.meshLoaded) distanceSpotLight[1] =
  distanceToSpotLt( streetLightObject1.translation, eye );
if (streetLightObject2.meshLoaded) distanceSpotLight[2] =
  distanceToSpotLt( streetLightObject2.translation, eye );
if (streetLightObject3.meshLoaded) distanceSpotLight[3] =
  distanceToSpotLt( streetLightObject3.translation, eye );
```

Next, we sort our list by finding the furthest streetlight, saving this in our `distanceSpotLightOrdered[]` array, and marking it as found (`true`) in the `spotLightOrdered[]` array. Then, we determine the next furthest streetlight until the four streetlights are in order: furthest to closest. This is a basic sorting algorithm from computer science, and Wikipedia has more detailed information and comparisons at `http://en.wikipedia.org/wiki/Sorting_algorithm`:

```
// order the lists, largest distance first
for (var i = 0; i < distanceSpotLight.length; i++ )
{
  // find the first spotlight in the remaining list
  var largestIndex = 0;
  while ( spotLightOrdered[largestIndex] ) {
    largestIndex++;
  }
  // compare the distances of the remaining spotlights
  // check if there are distances larger than the first
  // item in the list
  for (var j = 0; j < distanceSpotLight.length; j++ ) {
    if ( !spotLightOrdered[j] &&
      (distanceSpotLight[largestIndex] <
      distanceSpotLight[j]) )
    {
      largestIndex = j;
    }
  }

  // After finding the largest, insert it next into
  // the ordered list, and mark it found so we exclude
  // it from checking again.
  distanceSpotLightOrdered[i] = largestIndex;
  spotLightOrdered[largestIndex] = true;
}
```

The last step is to copy the ordered list of these four streetlights into the `objectIndex[]` array—our complete list of all the 3D meshes to be rendered in order.

```
// rewrite the ordered list of spotlights furthest to closest
for ( var i = 0; i < 4; i++ ) {
  objectIndex[totalMeshObjects - 4 + i] =
    distanceSpotLightOrdered[i] + totalMeshObjects - 4;
}
```

We are finally ready to render each 3D mesh in our `for` loop. Our 3D meshes were added in `webGLStart()` with the `meshObjectArray[0]` first item, the `meshObjectArry[1]` second item, and so forth. If the camera never moved in our 3D scene, the `objectIndex[]` array would be `[0, 1, 2, 3, 4, 5, 6, 7, 8, 9 , 10]`, and thus would render `meshObjectArray[0]` first, then `meshObjectArray[1]`, and so on. However, by reordering the objects due to transparencies and viewing the scene from the other side as shown in the next screenshot, the `objectIndex[]` array will be `[0, 1, 2, 3, 4, 5, 6, 10, 9, 8, 7]`. We still first render `meshObjectArray[0]`, then `meshObjectArray[1]`, and so forth, but now, we render the last four streetlights in order of furthest from the camera to closest: `meshObjectArray[10]`, `meshObjectArray[9]`, `meshObjectArray[8]`, and finally, `meshObjectArray[6]`.

```
for ( var index = 0; index < totalMeshObjects; index++ ) {
if ( meshObjectArray[index].meshLoaded )
  {
    // get the object number from the ordered array
    var i = objectIndex[index];
    // --- rest of the code as before ----
  }
}
```

Objective complete

The final scene shows that we have walked down to the end of our virtual street, turned around, and seen the transparent cones representing the light shafts:

Clearly, a lot of code! The rendering of transparent meshes can be computationally expensive. If we know the order of the objects, we can design our renderer to draw the transparencies in order. For example, in video games, a first person player may be wearing sunglasses, driving a car, and looking through a tinted windshield while staring into a windowed building for a total of three transparencies. However, we know the backward order of the transparencies to render the scene in advance: the windowed building, followed by the car's windshield, and then the sunglasses. We should be cautious when designing scenes with intersecting transparent 3D meshes. The following screenshot shows three 3D meshes intersecting and overlapping with each other. Two of the 3D mesh planes are rotated such that each 3D mesh has sections in the foreground and background. We cannot simply determine from these three planes which 3D mesh is furthest. Instead, we need to test the order of the rendering on a pixel-by-pixel basis. Such calculations should be avoided as they decrease performance.

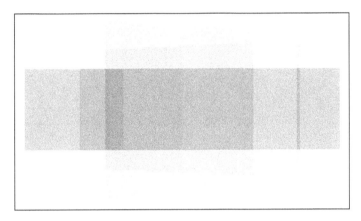

Scene lighting

This capstone scene advances lighting to create the story. The streetlights continue to use spotlights to create the circles on the street and the transparent cones for volume lighting.

The neon **X Y Z** display on the left turns on in a red, green, and blue sequence, and glows onto the street with a red, green, and blue tinge using point lights. The following example makes use of the neon shader we used in our second example of this project:

Engage thrusters

To create the neon light tinge on the street, the location and color of each neon light is passed to the `shaderScene-fs` fragment shader. Following the streetlight calculations, the lights from each neon letter use the same `calculateLightContribution()` code:

```
fragmentColor.rgb +=
    (calculateLightContribution(uXYZsodaXLoc,
    uSpotLightDir, true)*uXYZsodaXColor) +
    (calculateLightContribution(uXYZsodaYLoc,
    uSpotLightDir, true)*uXYZsodaYColor) +
    (calculateLightContribution(uXYZsodaZLoc,
    uSpotLightDir, true)*uXYZsodaZColor);
```

The key difference in the three calls to `calculateLightContribution()` is that these neon signs are point lights, similar to light bulbs casting light in all directions. Thus, the third parameter for `calculateLightContribution()` is `true`, indicating a point light. As point lights, the spotlight's direction value (`uSpotLightDir`) is not used—point lights have no direction and instead shine in all directions. Beyond this, the calculation of point lights and spotlights have much in common, so they call the same `calculateLightContribution( lightLoc, lightDir, pointLight)` function.

In the `calculateLightContribution()` function, we first find the distance from the light to each pixel on the street. This sounds like a lot of work for the shader, but note that shader languages are calculated in parallel on the GPU, so this is computed for many pixels simultaneously:

```
vec3 distance = vec3(vPosition.xyz - lightLoc);
```

The maximum distance for which the point light will shine is 25 units, and it linearly decreases over distance. For example, if the pixel is 10 units away, then 60 percent (`1 - 10.0/25.0`) of the neon light shines on this pixel. For the three neon lights, which use point lights, we calculate the distance to the pixel, determine if the distance is less than the maximum of 25 units, and use the percentage for the neon light's effect:

```
if ( pointLight )
{
  float maxDist = 25.0;
  float pointLighttDistanceToPixel = length(distance);
  if (pointLighttDistanceToPixel < maxDist ) {
    lightAmt = 0.9 * ((maxDist -
    pointLighttDistanceToPixel)/maxDist);
    }
}
```

The point light's intensity is set to 0.9, so `lightAmt` is multiplied by 0.9. Ambient light is just added to ensure that no part of the scene is completely black. Upon returning `lightAmt` to the main program, we do one final check to ensure that the red, green, or blue color values are less than or equal to 1.0, which can happen when adding multiple lights in a scene, as shown in the following piece of code:

```
fragmentColor.r = min(fragmentColor.r, 1.0);
fragmentColor.g = min(fragmentColor.g, 1.0);
fragmentColor.b = min(fragmentColor.b, 1.0);
```

Objective complete

This final example removed the fog to simplify and condense the code, but fog would add a nice nighttime noir design.

Scene lighting is very critical in design. One can chronicle the progression of video games just by comparing lighting. Original 3D video games used ambient light, where there was no shading. We then expanded to directional lights, such as sunlight, giving objects more of a 3D appearance instead of a flat look. However, with the arrival of shader languages, we can calculate the precise lighting per pixel for point lights and spotlights. As we have seen, once we code the fragment shaders for a single spotlight, the code can be shared for point lights.

Mission accomplished

This project followed the old Hollywood saying "lights, camera, action." We deployed the most complex lighting in spot and point lights. Point lights are similar to lightbulbs; they shine in all directions, whereas spotlights have a direction with a beam-width radius of high intensity and a wider cut-off angle radius where the light fades out. Other lighting parameters include attenuation, where the light fades out over distance.

Night scenes deploy a black fog, also known as depth cueing, where objects that are more distant appear darker and thus give users a visual cue of depth. Dark scenes have intriguing designs because they focus our attention on key scene objects in the foreground. Fog is useful too because distant objects blend into the background rather than just disappearing past the far-clipping plane that cuts off the rendering of objects.

We also rendered partially transparent objects. The order of drawing partially transparent overlapping objects must be stacked from furthest to closest, after the opaque objects have been drawn.

We added keyboard arrow keys to navigate our camera anywhere in the scene, which is a key component of interactive 3D worlds allowing users to go anywhere they wish.

Perhaps the most impressive accomplishment is how all these features were enabled with shader languages—with the help of the processing capabilities of the GPU—to create flags blowing in the wind, animated texture maps for waterfalls, and scenes with neon signs and streetlights.

Project 4

Mobile and Web3D Gaming

"Compared with games, reality is too easy. Games challenge us with voluntary obstacles and help us put our personal strengths to better use."

– Jane McGonigal, Reality is Broken, Fix #1 for reality

"Fun and games" sounds unstructured, leisurely, unpredictable, and unscripted, which is not something to be studied, researched, and engineered. Yet, there is an art and science in fun—a method to making something more challenging and engaging to the audience. Ironically, the pleasure of games is not derived from winning. A perfect example of this is *Tetris*, one of the most popular games in the world—the game continues dropping more pieces, faster, until the player finally loses. This game is an ideal example of the elements of a good game—a progressive challenge, a simple concept, and an easy user interface. Building on these elements, video games have great visuals, entertaining music plus Sound FX, and engaging characters that we either sympathize with, or hate and want to defeat. We certainly don't want to discount the pleasure we get from winning at video games. But that just tempts us to take on greater challenges.

Screen sizes tend to dictate the complexity and the playing time of the games. Console games such as *Call of Duty* and *Grand Theft Auto* come on several DVDs, which allow for large environments to play where one can roam the entire city. These games are priced above $60 and provide hours of entertainment. Mobile and WebGL games are a bit more modest. They are often completed in a matter of a few minutes, but played over and over with new random challenges. While console games offer virtually unlimited worlds to roam, mobile and web games often play within the confines of the device's screen. Some mobile games, particularly those adapted from the larger console versions, can have multiple locations and places to roam, but most are 2D.

Mobile and the Web have been dominated by 2D games that have a much broader demographic than console games typically played by teenagers and early 20s males. *Angry Birds*, *Candy Crush*, and others have a wide appeal with men and women from teenagers to the elderly.

The first 3D-capable phones have been commercially available since 2007. For some time, Mobile 3D suffered from battery drain and heat, but those issues are being addressed with impressive improvements annually. Game engines such as Unity 3D are now available for mobile devices, playing the same role that game engines perform for console games—handling the lower-level math algorithms, rendering, and cross-platform issues between iPhone, Android, and Windows mobile phones. Yet, within these operating systems, there are many devices with varying capabilities and screen dimensions. Despite this product fragmentation, Mobile 3D has a bright future. In 2013, we crossed the threshold of 1 billion devices sold with 3D GPUs.

One problem with developing for mobile devices is that we still leave out a very large audience—people still on PCs. Despite the growth of mobile devices, desktops and notebook PCs are still the tools used for business. Fortunately, WebGL is the real cross-platform game environment. If your device has a web browser, which mobile devices and PCs do, then WebGL can be used for video games on practically any Internet-connected device.

Mission briefing

These demonstrations exhibit common programming techniques found in video games: 2D user interfaces inside a 3D graphics world; allowing movement of the camera in 3D space; interactivity, including controlling lighting in a room; basic gravitational physics; and collision detection between two objects. From these examples, you can extrapolate to make full-fledged video games such as traversing 3D mazes or shooting projectiles. From here, just add imagination.

Why is it awesome?

Video games are one of the most pervasive applications of 3D graphics. Yet, most 3D games are limited to console devices such as Xbox and PlayStation, or PCs. At the same time, many people have access to a 3D-graphics-chip-capable device, either a smartphone, tablet, or a web browser on their desktop. This is a large audience, the type that likes to play a quick, enjoyable, artistic game—the kind of games produced with WebGL.

WebGL is cross platform, so we don't have to be concerned with Android versus iPhone, or the brand—Samsung or Nokia—used by our end users. JavaScript programming is all you need, so if you are not a Java or objective-C programmer, do not worry. You can program a 3D game faster in WebGL than a programmer can for an iPhone. There is one area of common development, though: shader language programming, used in WebGL, iPhone, iPad, or Android devices. If you get a chance to compare shader language programming on Android and iPhone, you will notice it is similar to WebGL. So, the skills we will learn here apply to any smartphone. WebGL just has an easier learning curve.

Your Hotshot objectives

- ▸ Creating user interfaces in the 3D environment
- ▸ Designing a game
- ▸ Fun with physics and collisions

Mission checklist

In the final demonstration, we will discuss the equations for gravity. However, it is not necessary to know the precise equation—just its fundamental concept.

Creating user interfaces in the 3D environment

One of the three components of a great game is the user interface, with the others being a challenge and an intuitive concept. Console games come with their own controllers, which now include motion sensors such as in the Wii. Some games have their own controllers, such as the guitar for *Guitar Hero*. Smart phones beginning with the iPhone introduced the touch screen, leaving only a few simple buttons on the sides and the bottom. With few external buttons, the user interface will reside inside the game—this is an ideal scenario for WebGL.

Prepare for lift off

There are two basic types of user interfaces inside 3D environments: **Head-Mounted Display** (**HMD**) and **billboarding**. HMD is often depicted as glasses or helmets with LCD screens. This may become more commonplace with Google Glass and Oculus Rift VR glasses. In our example, the user interface will be a virtual HMD, where the controls are overlaid onto the 3D scene. Billboarding is the other interface where the 3D object is positioned inside the 3D scene but is always rotated to face us.

Our first example is a simple math game where the goal of the player—presumably a child learning about 2D and 3D coordinate systems and multiplication—is to get to the golden teapot. The *x*, *y*, and *z* coordinates of the current position of the camera and teapot are shown at the top. Clicking on the **X**, **Y**, or **Z** buttons increment those values and updates the camera position. To subtract for any coordinate, click on the **+** or **-** button below each **X**, **Y**, or **Z** value. On the left side, there are multiplier buttons that will move us two, three, or four times the single movement. These buttons can be combined, so clicking on **2** and **4** moves us eight spaces in the corresponding distance, as shown in the following screenshot:

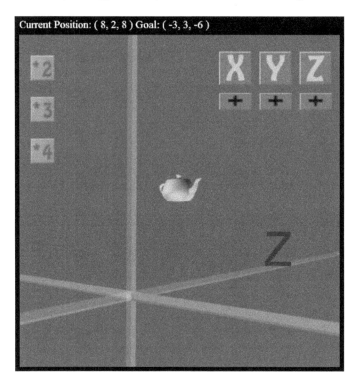

Engage thrusters

The position of the buttons will be relative to the camera. In *Project 2, WebGL for E-Commerce*, we discussed ray intersection with a figure of the view frustum, which is the area viewable by the camera and rendered onscreen. The frustum begins as a single point at the camera and then expands out like a sideways pyramid that extends infinitely (though there is usually a far-clipping plane that cuts off any 3D objects beyond a certain distance). The frustum passes through the four corners, where *x* and *y* are (-1, -1, -z), (-1, 1, -z), (1, -1, -z), and (1, 1, -z). For example, the upper-right corner is (1, 1, -z) and the lower-left corner is (-1, -1, -z). The following *z* coordinate, also known as the viewing plane, is based on the field of view:

$$distanceToViewPlane=1/Math.tan(fieldOfView/2).$$

When we render a 3D mesh, we typically rotate and translate (move) it using matrix math, and then move it into camera space. Think of it like placing a lamp in a room where the center of the room is at the origin (0, 0, 0). Then place a camera in that room to take a picture of the lamp. The scene's origin is transformed from (0, 0, 0) to the location of the camera. But now, our menu featuring the **X**, **Y**, and **Z** buttons will always be in the upper-right corner in front of our camera. Regardless of where we move in that room, the menu will appear in the upper-right corner. Since we always render the scene from the camera's view, the only transformation for our menu is the offset in front of the camera. For example, the **X** button will always be a fixed position in front of our camera, specified by the following line of code:

```
var buttonXOffset = [.35, .8, -distanceToViewPlane];
```

Each **X**, **Y**, or **Z** button has an accompanying **+** or **-** button below it, so its location is offset 0.2 units below its button, presented in the following code snippet:

```
var buttonXOffset = [ .35, .8, -distanceToViewPlane  ];
var buttonPlusMinusXOffset =
    [buttonXOffset[0], (buttonXOffset[1] - .2), buttonXOffset[2]];
```

Inside the `drawScene()` function, we set the `shaderProgram = shaderButton` shader for buttons. We also set other variables passed to the shader. One of these is the button location, that is, whether it is in the "down" state, so the shader knows whether to display the button-up or button-down texture map, and the alternate button-pressed texture map if the button is depressed. Each button has two texture maps: one that appears unclicked, and the other texture map with a pushed-in depressed look, similar to when user interface buttons in Google Chrome or Microsoft Word are clicked on, presented in the following code:

```
else if (meshObjectArray[i] == buttonXObject) {
    shaderProgram = shaderButton;
    gl.useProgram(shaderProgram);
    vec3.set(buttonXOffset,  buttonLocation);
    buttonDown = buttonXdown;
    if ( buttonXAltTextureMap != null ) {
        gl.activeTexture(gl.TEXTURE1);
        gl.bindTexture(gl.TEXTURE_2D, buttonXAltTextureMap);
        gl.uniform1i(shaderProgram.samplerAltUniform, 1);
    }
}
```

Inside the `shaderButton` vertex shader, this line adds the button location to the vertices. For example, the X, Y, and Z buttons have the vertices (-0.1, 0.1, 0), (-0.1, -0.1, 0), (0.1, 0.1, 0), and (0.1, -0.1, 0). The `buttonXOffset` value (0.35 0.8 -`distanceToViewPlane`) is set to `uButtonLocation` in the GPU and adds it to each vertex, as shown in the following code snippet:

```
gl_Position = uPMatrix *
    vec4(uButtonLocation + aVertexPosition, 1.0);
```

Unlike past shader language programming, we are not multiplying the button's vertices by its transformation matrix, `uMMatrix`, or the combined viewpoint and model transformation, `uMVMatrix`. Remember, the user interface button's location is relative to the camera's location only. We still multiply by the Perspective matrix, `uPMatrix`, which may seem odd since the button will be a fixed size and its location is on the viewing plane, but the Perspective matrix also contains information about the width-height ratio of our WebGL window. Finally, inside the button shader's fragment shader, we select the appropriate texture map depending on whether the button is unclicked or pressed down, as shown in the following code:

```
if ( uButtonDown ) gl_FragColor = texture2D(uSamplerAlt,
    vec2(vTextureCoord.s, vTextureCoord.t));
else gl_FragColor = texture2D(uSampler,
    vec2(vTextureCoord.s, vTextureCoord.t));
```

Have a look at the following screenshot:

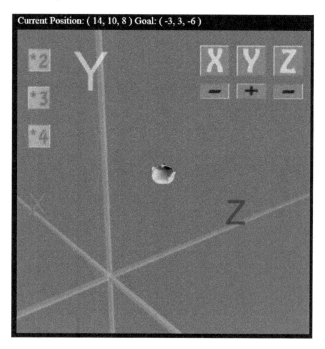

Have a look at the preceding screenshot. Checking for the mouse clicking on a menu button does not require the ray-bounding box detection seen in previous examples. We just need to check if the mouse clicked anywhere between the *x* and *y* bounding box values of the button. For example, the **X** button's *x* and *y* center is at (0.35, 0.8), shown in the following line of code:

```
var buttonXOffset = [ .35, .8,
    -distanceToViewPlane ];
```

Since the dimensions of the button are -0.1 to 0.1 in both the *x* and *y* dimensions, check if the mouse clicked between 0.25 and 0.45 in the *x* direction, and 0.7 and 0.9 in the *y* direction. The mouse over (to change the cursor) and mouse down (to change the camera's position) share the same function. We still use the bounding box values, and convert the mouse's *x* and *y* screen coordinates into 3D world coordinates. The mouse's 3D location is saved in the `rayMouseDown[x,y,z]` array, as shown in the following code:

```
function mouseOverObject(buttonObject, buttonOffset ) {
isMouseOverObject = false;
    if (
        // check if mouse is inside the button's left edge
        ((buttonOffset[0] + buttonObject.boundingBoxMin[0]) <=
        rayMouseDown[0]) &&
        // mouse inside the right edge
        (rayMouseDown[0] <=
        (buttonOffset[0] + buttonObject.boundingBoxMax[0])) &&
        // mouse above the bottom edge
        ((buttonOffset[1] + buttonObject.boundingBoxMin[1]) <=
        rayMouseDown[1])   &&
        // mouse below the menu button's top edge
        (rayMouseDown[1] <=
        (buttonOffset[1] + buttonObject.boundingBoxMax[1]))
    )
    {
        isMouseOverObject = true;
    }
    return isMouseOverObject;
}
```

Clicking on the **X** button as an example, the camera eye's *x* value will be incremented (or decremented if the - (minus) button was previously clicked). The `buttonXdown` value sets the shader's `uButtonDown` value to use the alternate pushed-down texture map, as shown in the following code snippet:

```
if ( mouseOverObject(buttonXObject, buttonXOffset) )
{
    // button X button clicked. Increment/decrement the
    // camera x value, eye[0].
    if ( buttonPlusMinusXdown ) eye[0]-= multiplicationFactor;
    else eye[0] += multiplicationFactor;
    buttonXdown = true;
}
```

The other user interface concept is billboarding—the technique of having the 3D mesh always face the camera. In this scene, the *X*, *Y*, and *Z* labels along their respective axes always point toward the camera. Billboarding sets each *X*, *Y*, and *Z* label's transformation matrix to the inverse of the camera's transformation matrix. To envision billboarding, imagine standing directly across another person. For that person to continue standing across from you, they would take the inverse movement. If you were to move two steps to the right, the person across you would take two steps left, as shown in the following screenshot:

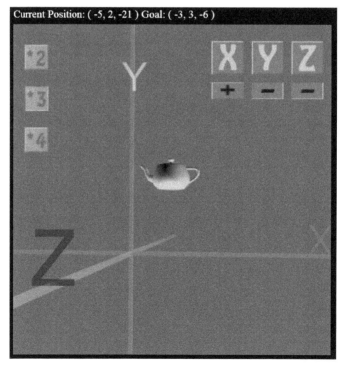

X, Y, and Z axes labels using billboarding to always face the camera

After calculating the camera matrix based on the `lookAt()` function, which builds a 4 x 4 matrix using `eye` (location of the camera), `target` (set to the teapot's location, `winLocation = [-3, 3, -6]`), and `up` (0, 1, 0). We copy the `camera` matrix into `cameraRotationMatrix`. Since the X, Y, and Z labels are only rotating for the billboarding effect and not moving (translating), we use the `toRotationMat()` command to copy the camera's rotation into `cameraRotationMatrix`. Then we inverse that matrix since the labels undergo the opposite rotation of the camera. The previous figure shows the X, Y, and Z labels facing the camera:

```
mat4.lookAt( eye, target, up, camera );
mat4.toRotationMat(camera, cameraRotationMatrix);
mat4.inverse(cameraRotationMatrix);
```

Have a look at the preceding code. Inside the `shaderLabel-vs` vertex shader, we multiply the vertices of the X, Y, and Z labels by `cameraRotationMatrix` to support billboarding. Although the labels are a single color and there are no light calculations, `vTransformedNormals`, the vertex normals, will still be rotated in case we performed lighting calculations later. Finally, the rotated vertices are multiplied by the usual Perspective matrix, `uPMatrix`, and the Model-View matrix, `uMVMatrix`, to account for the X, Y, and Z labels' positions along their respective axes, and the camera transformation matrix. The `uMVMatrix` function places the X, Y, and Z labels in the correct location along their respective axes, and the `uCamRotMatrix` function creates the billboarding effect, as presented in the following code:

```
vec4 vRotatedPosition = uCamRotMatrix *
    vec4(aVertexPosition, 1.0);
vTransformedNormal = uNMatrix *
    vec3(uCamRotMatrix * vec4(normalize(aVertexNormal), 1.0) );
vTextureCoord = aTextureCoord;
gl_Position = uPMatrix * uMVMatrix * vRotatedPosition;
```

Objective complete – mini debriefing

The goal was to create a user interface inside the 3D scene. Intriguing that much of the user interface such as the buttons and X, Y, and Z billboarding were based on the camera transformation, and that these 3D mesh placements were implemented inside the vertex shader. While we often think of user interface controls as the mouse and keyboard, we took an important step building the menu inside 3D space and applying billboarding techniques to keep elements facing the user. Now, with our understanding of menus, we can add some fun elements into our game.

Designing a game

A number of elements are involved with game design: characters both endearing and despiteful, in-depth detailed environments, audio—both sound effects and musical score—and a real challenge. Note that neither realism nor winning are components necessary to a great game. Since we are concerned here with interactivity and shader languages, we will look at how lighting, implemented in shader languages, can be used in game design.

Several years ago, before the introduction of the first iPhone, 3D graphics applications were already being written for mobile phones that had 3D graphics hardware. One of the first games was *A Teenager's Bedroom*. Its goal was to find your keys, wallet, feed the fish in the tank, and any other critical elements of a teenager's day. In the bedroom, every object could be thrown while looking for your keys and wallet, including couches, tables, the bed, pizza boxes, a case of beer, or a bag of potato chips. The fun was actually destroying the room, not finding the keys. In this example, I rebuilt some of that game using lighting as part of the challenge and misdirection. We have moonlight coming through the window, a lava lamp, and a dimmer switch on the back wall. The wallet and keys are not here, but the design concepts remain.

Engage thrusters

To help guide the player, we begin with a few visual cues, such as the poster on the wall, a few objects on the ground, and two faint light sources—the lava lamp and the moonlight—to assist in navigation. The lava lamp is a cylinder with an animated textured map. To find the wallet and keys, we need to turn on the lights. But just like entering a strange room, we have to first look for the light switch.

The Moon and lava lamp, our two initial light sources, are emissive lights and thus have very simple fragment and vertex shaders. The lava lamp's animated texture map plays a key role in keeping the scene from appearing stagnant. In video games, it's always good to provide some fidget animation so the user knows the game is not frozen. In the original *Teenager's Bedroom* game, the lava lamp sat upon a table, but for our programming purposes, it is just floating in space (though I do like games that break the laws of physics—it allows for more creative design), as presented in the following screenshot:

The scene begins rather dark with the animated lava lamp on the right

We have animated texture maps previously, but it's a simple technique worth repeating. Inside `drawScene()`, for every frame to be drawn (hopefully at least 30 times or more per second for a smooth animation), we increment the `s` and `t` parameters of the texture map placement as follows:

```
lavaLampTextureTranslation[0] += .001;
lavaLampTextureTranslation[1] -= .005;
```

We pass this set of two floating point values from the JavaScript program to the `LavaLamp` fragment shader—essentially passing values from the CPU to the GPU graphics card. Have a look at the following line of code:

```
gl.uniform2f(shaderProgram.lavaLampTextureTranslationUniform,
    lavaLampTextureTranslation[0],  lavaLampTextureTranslation[1]
    );
```

Upon initialization, in the shader program setup `createShaderProgram()`, which is called from `WebGLSteup()`, we set up the `uLavaLampTextureTranslation` shader variable to hold the texture translation values, as follows:

```
shaderProgram.lavaLampTextureTranslationUniform =
    gl.getUniformLocation(shaderProgram,
    "uLavaLampTextureTranslation");
```

Finally, inside the `lavaLamp` fragment shader, which requires its own shader to support the texture map animation, we pass the `uLavaLampTextureTranslation` value in as a `uniform` value since the texture transform values are constant for each pixel of the lava lamp. It contains two values for the `s` and `t` dimensions: `uniform vec2 uLavaLampTextureTranslation`.

Within the fragment shader, we increment the texture map's `s` and `t` coordinates, as shown in the following code snippet:

```
gl_FragColor = texture2D( uSampler,
    vec2 (vTextureCoord.s + uLavaLampTextureTranslation[0],
    vTextureCoord.t + uLavaLampTextureTranslation[1] ) );
```

The other light source is the Moon, whose light is coming through the bedroom window. The Moon's shader is similar to the lava lamp's shader without the animation. The Moon's light can be seen on the carpet and far walls coming through the window. This worked well because there was just enough light to see the posters on the walls.

The lighting calculations are performed in the fragment shader for the lava lamp, moonlight, and the light bulb hanging from the ceiling. Illumination for the reflective (non-light emitting) objects in the scene occur in the `shaderRoomLight-fs` fragment shader.

So that no area in the scene is black, we begin by adding a bit of ambient light before adding the Moonlight, lava lamp, and the light bulb controlled by the dimmer switch:

```
float ambientLight = 0.1;
vec3 roomLight = vec3(ambientLight, ambientLight, ambientLight);
```

The Moon seen through the window, with the yellow dimmer switch to its left

The moonlight shines through the rectangular window with a night sky behind it. This wall was 3D modeled with the window cut out. For casting the moonlight, we need to specify the dimensions of the window in the fragment shaders, `uniform vec2 uBackWallWindowMin;` and `uniform vec2 uBackWallWindowMax;`. Another critical variable is the location of the Moon, `uniform vec3 uMoonLightLoc;`. The actual location of the moonlight is not the same location as where the Moon's 3D mesh is rendered. The Moon's 3D mesh is set in `WebGLStart()` when the object is constructed and positioned at `[0, 70, -100]`. But to simulate the moonlight shining through the window, the light's location is far away, given by the following line of code:

```
var moonLightLoc = [ 0, 120, -200]
```

To get the dimensions of the moonlight coming through the window, draw imaginary lines from the Moon's light location at (0, 120, -200) to each corner of the window and beyond till it reaches the carpet or any other objects. The following code is basic algebra, but it's worth going through as we want to learn new programming techniques:

```
vec3 lineLength = vec3(vPosition.xyz - uMoonLightLoc);
float wallZpct = (uWallBackLocation.z - uMoonLightLoc.z) /
    lineLength.z;
vec2 passThruBackWindow = vec2(lineLength.xy) * wallZpct +
    vec2(uMoonLightLoc.xy);
if ( (uBackWallWindowMin.x <= passThruBackWindow.x) &&
    (uBackWallWindowMax.x >= passThruBackWindow.x ) &&
    (uBackWallWindowMin.y <= passThruBackWindow.y ) &&
    (uBackWallWindowMax.y >= passThruBackWindow.y )
) {
    roomLight += vec3(0.1, 0.1, 0.1);
}
```

In the first line of the preceding code, `lineLength` determines the (x, y, z) distance from each pixel in the scene to the moonlight location. The `wallZpct` value is just a percentage of where the line crosses the window divided by the length of the line. For example, suppose the pixel in the scene is 200 units from the moonlight, and the window is 150 units away from the moonlight, then `wallZpct` is *150/200=0.75*. We then determine the *x* and *y* values of this line as it passes through the open window. For example, if the *x* and *y* values for `lineLength` are (40, 100), then at 0.75, the line passes through the window at *(40, 100)*0.75=(30, 75)*, the `passThruBackWindow` value. We then check if the `passThruBackWindow` value is within the minimum and maximum window dimensions, in which case the moonlight reaches this pixel, so add (0.1, 0.1, 0.1) to `roomLight`, the cumulative light at this pixel. The window's dimensions are a minimum of (-42.5, -13) to a maximum of (42.5, 37) based on the actual 3D model. Since (30, 75) is not within the window's dimensions, no additional room light from the Moon is added to this pixel.

Next, add in the light from the lava lamp. The lava lamp is a point light (similar to a light bulb), using only red and blue (no green) to give a pink glow matching the texture map. Lava lamps do not give off a lot of light, so we reduced its maximum distance by coding this: `float lavaLampCutOffDistance = 60.0;`

The next two lines calculate the angle between the light from the lava lamp to each pixel, and that pixel's normal. We first normalize both the vector from the lava lamp to the pixel, and the pixel's normal (making each pixel's normal a unit vector of length 1 unit). The dot product—equal to the cosine of the angle between the two vectors—calculates the amount of light from the lava lamp reaching this pixel, as shown in the following code:

```
vec3 pixelToLavaLampDistanceVector =
    vec3(vPosition.xyz - uLavaLampLocation);
float lavaLampContribution =
dot( -normalize(pixelToLavaLampDistanceVector),
normalize(vTransformedNormal) );
```

It is critical to normalize both the light and normal vectors. The fragment shader interpolates the normals at each pixel between two vertices. In the sample polygon shown in the following figure, the normal at vertex *a* is (-0.5, 0.4, 0.77) and vertex *b* is (-0.7, -0.4, 0.59):

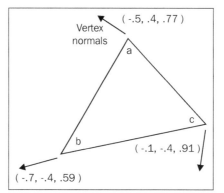

Halfway between these vertices, the fragment shader calculates the normal to be (-0.6, 0, 0.68). If we had a light vector of (0, 0, 1), then the dot product would be *-0.6*0+0*0+0.68*1=0.68*, or the amount of light would be 68 percent of the original.

However, when we normalize the following equation with a light vector of (0, 0, 1), the amount of light would be 0.75, or 75 percent:

(-0.6, 0, 0.68)=(-0.6, 0, 0.68)/sqrt(-0.62+0.2+0.682)=(-0.6, 0, 0.68)/0.907=(-0.66, 0, 0.75)

Now, we calculate attenuation, which is the fall-off of light over distance, with the help of the following code. In real-world physics, light falls off geometrically—double the distance and the light is one quarter as powerful. But a linear fall-off of light—double the distance and the light's effect is halved—is faster to calculate and often looks better.

```
float pixelToLavaLampDistance =
    length(pixelToLavaLampDistanceVector);
if ( pixelToLavaLampDistance > lavaLampCutOffDistance ||
    lavaLampContribution < 0.0) lavaLampContribution = 0.0;
else lavaLampContribution =
    (1.0 - (pixelToLavaLampDistance/lavaLampCutOffDistance))
    *0.35; // multiply by the lava light's intensity
roomLight +=vec3(lavaLampContribution, 0.0, lavaLampContribution);
```

After calculating the distance from the light to the pixel, `length(pixelToLavaLampDistanceVector)`, if the distance is greater than the light's cut-off, then the contribution of light is 0. We also check if the light is behind or facing away from the polygon, `lavaLampContribution < 0.0`, in which case the light does not contribute to the pixel either.

Finally, if the distance from the light to the pixel is within the cut-off distance, then add in the light's contribution based on its proximity. For example, if the pixel is 45 units from the light, then the contribution of light at that pixel is *(1-(45/60))=0.25*. The intensity of the light—a value from 0 to 1—is set to `0.35`. Being a lava lamp, we would not expect a very high intensity from it. Multiply the light contribution by 0.35, and using our 0.25 value calculated previously, the total amount of light from the lava lamp 45 units away is *0.25*0.35=0.0875*.

Now comes the moment to turn on the main light using the dimmer switch. It is always good to provide visual cues to your audience. In this case, the dimmer switch is the only bright object in the room. When the mouse rolls over the dimmer switch, the mouse cursor changes. Another technique used in video games is when the user rolls over an object we want them to click on; we brighten the object to get their attention. Clicking on the dimmer switch and dragging the mouse left and right will increase/decrease the lighting and rotate the dimmer switch.

The dimmer switch is texture mapped with a visible red line to detect its rotation, as shown in the following screenshot:

The `mouseMoveEvent()` function checks if the value of `mouseDownDimmerSwitch` is true or false. If it is false, meaning the dimmer switch has not been clicked on, then we use the previous `RayBoundingBoxIntersection()` function in the `rayIntersection. js` external JavaScript file. If the mouse is over the dimmer switch, we change the mouse cursor as a visual cue for the user. Normally, we are interested in which object the mouse rolled over is closest, for example, if the pizza box were in front of the dimmer switch, then the pizza box is the closest object. But here, we are not too particular, thus if the mouse rolls over the dimmer switch, even if there are other objects in the way, we change the mouse cursor, as presented in the following code:

```
var overDimmerSwitchObject = false;
if ( RayBoundingBoxIntersection(dimmerSwitchObject,
    xWorld, yWorld) ){
    overDimmerSwitchObject = true;
}
var elementToChange = document.getElementsByTagName("body")[0];
if ( overDimmerSwitchObject )
    elementToChange.style.cursor = "pointer";
else elementToChange.style.cursor = "auto";
```

Inside `mouseDownEvent()`, we again check if the mouse is over the dimmer switch, in which case, save the initial *x* position (often when dragging or moving objects, we also track the *y* position, but here only the *x* position is used for turning the dimmer switch), as shown in the following code:

```
if ( RayBoundingBoxIntersection( dimmerSwitchObject,
    xWorld, yWorld ) ) {
    startMouseDownX = event.clientX;
    mouseDownDimmerSwitch = true;
}
```

Once `mouseDownDimmerSwitch` is set to `true`, when we drag the mouse with the button down, `mouseMoveEvent()` rotates the dimmer switch object around the *z* axis. The following code verifies that the rotation is never less than 0 degrees or more than 360 degrees (6.28 radians):

```
if ( mouseDownDimmerSwitch ) {
    dimmerSwitchRotation += (mouseDownX - startMouseDownX) * .005;
    if ( dimmerSwitchRotation < 0) dimmerSwitchRotation = 0;
    else if ( dimmerSwitchRotation > 6.28)
    dimmerSwitchRotation = 6.28;
    dimmerSwitchObject.rotation[2] = - dimmerSwitchRotation;
}
```

As this dimmer switch rotates, the light bulb hanging from the ceiling in the center of the room brightens using the `Emitting Light` shader. Inside the `Room Light` shader, the point light is added to the existing moonlight and lava lamp. In fact, its code is similar to the lava lamp with just a few parameters changed to reflect a whiter, brighter light.

Objective complete – mini debriefing

A lot of this game is now left for you to design. It is clear that lighting plays a major role in the design and interactivity. And the major enabler to lighting games is the capabilities of shader languages. A final interesting phenomenon is how much streamlining of code occurs as the game develops. For example, the lava lamp and light bulb exhibit the same behavior with just a few different parameters. This would be a great candidate for which to write a single function or object class to handle this lighting, which would then make it simpler to add additional lights. For example, the original *Teenager's Bedroom* game had a fish tank with its own source of light that needed to be turned on to see if the wallet and keys were at the bottom of the tank. The fish tank added a nice blue glow to the room, along with some funny characters that liked to hide your wallet.

Fun with physics and collisions

Perhaps the most successful mobile game has been *Angry Birds*—a simple concept of sling-shooting cartoon birds to knock over the frame of a house. Angry Birds has several fundamental elements that make it a successful game, which are mentioned as follows:

- ▸ Identifiable characters that people hold an affinity toward. In Angry Birds, even the pigs playing the role of bad guys are fun and rather adorable.
- ▸ Physics and collision detection.
- ▸ Simple, easy-to-understand concept—one can begin playing in an instant.
- ▸ Easy user interface.
- ▸ Fun challenge.

An interesting fact is that all this applies equally to *Pac-Man* or *Mario*, who himself is now considered one of the most recognized characters in the world, right up there with Mickey Mouse.

The game presented here is the basis for another game under development that takes place in a backyard with a dog chasing squirrels and other creatures running on top of, in front of, behind, and through a fence. Here, we replace the dog with a cannon (though the dog is pictured on the cannon ball). The goal is to aim the cannon and hit the target. The cannon is controlled by the left, right, up, and down arrow keys. We register a hit by bouncing the cannon ball off the target. The cannon ball also bounces off the brick wall. Moonlight was left over to provide some ambient light, as shown in the following screenshot:

Opening to the cannon ball game

Engage thrusters

Since these examples are meant to show you what's happening behind the scenes, the *a* and *b* keys toggle between the game view and a developer view where you can use the arrow keys to walk through the scene.

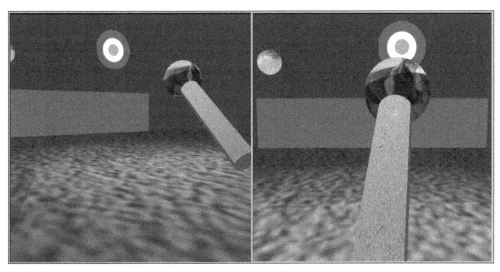

Comparison of the developer mode on the left and game mode on the right

It helps during the programming of the game to walk through the scene to review the lighting and actual position of the objects.

The `cameraControl` Boolean function is set inside the `handlekeys()` function when pressing the *a* or *b* keys, as shown in the following code:

```
// change from game to developer mode
    if (currentlyPressedKeys[65]) {  // lower case 'a'
        cameraControl = false;
        eye = [ eyeStart[0], eyeStart[1], eyeStart[2], 1 ];
        cameraRotation = 0;
    }
    else if (currentlyPressedKeys[66]) {  // lower case 'b'
        // change to game-play mode
        cameraControl = true;
        eye=[eyeStartAlt[0], eyeStartAlt[1], eyeStartAlt[2], 1];
        cameraRotation = cameraAltRotation;
    }
```

Based on the `cameraControl` value, we determine if hitting the arrow keys applies to aiming the cannon. Otherwise, we navigate the camera, setting its `eye` and `cameraRotation` values. Those values are used to calculate the camera's target inside `drawScene()`, as shown in the following code:

```
function handleKeys() {
if ( cameraControl ) {
    //up arrow, move camera forward, changes x, z direction
    if (currentlyPressedKeys[38]) {
        eye[0] += Math.sin( cameraRotation ) * 1.75;
        eye[2] -= Math.cos( cameraRotation ) * 1.75;
    }
    //down arrow, move camera back, changes x, z direction
    else if (currentlyPressedKeys[40]) {
        eye[0] -= Math.sin( cameraRotation ) * 1.75;
        eye[2] += Math.cos( cameraRotation ) * 1.75;
    }
    // left arrow, camera rotates left
    else if (currentlyPressedKeys[37]) {
        cameraRotation -= .018;
    }
    // right arrow, camera rotates right
    else if (currentlyPressedKeys[39]) {
        cameraRotation += .018;
    }
}
```

The camera rotates around the *y* axis by changing the camera's *x* and *z* values. For more in-depth references on 3D rotation matrices, visit `http://mathworld.wolfram.com/RotationMatrix.html`. Multiplication by 1.75 and an increment of the `cameraRotation` value by 0.018 were made to give the right speed for camera movement. These values are often dependent on the scale of your 3D scene. The distance from the cannon to the brick wall is about 200 units. There is no set formula, but moving at 1.75 units per frame would get us to the wall in just over 100 frames—around 3 seconds.

When `cameraControl` is false, the arrow keys rotate the cannon. Most objects rotate around their center, but the cannon rotates at one end where the *z* value of each vertex is 0. At the far end of the cannon, the *z* vertex is 60 units:

```
else { // control the cannon
    // up arrow, cannon aims up
    if (currentlyPressedKeys[38]) {
        if (cannonObject.rotation[0] < 1.5)
        cannonObject.rotation[0] += .002;
    }
    // down arrow, cannon aims down
    else if (currentlyPressedKeys[40]) {
        if (cannonObject.rotation[0] >= 0)
```

```
        cannonObject.rotation[0] -= .002;
    }
    // right arrow, cannon aims right
    else if (currentlyPressedKeys[37]) {
        if (cannonObject.rotation[1] < .5)
        cannonObject.rotation[1] += .002;
    }
    // left arrow, cannon aims left
    else if (currentlyPressedKeys[39]) {
        if (cannonObject.rotation[1] > -.5)
        cannonObject.rotation[1] -= .002;
    }
}
```

The canon rotations are around the x and y axes. Rotation around the x axis raises the cannon, while rotation around the y axis aims the cannon from left to right. The amount of rotation set to 0.002 seemed to be the appropriate speed to make the cannon feel heavy. There are checks to ensure the cannon does not rotate too far in any direction.

One of the more complex issues is firing the cannon ball. The cannon ball uses the same transformation matrix as the cannon. First, the cannonball must be transformed (moved) to the end of the cannon. The cannon ball was oversized so it is apparent that it is ready to be fired from the end of the cannon. Once the cannon ball is launched, the cannon can still be moved by the arrow keys, but the cannon ball must remain on its own trajectory. Thus, it is important we save the cannon's transformation matrix the moment the cannon ball was fired, as presented in the following screenshot:

Cannon ball on the same trajectory as the cannon

Inside `drawScene()`, we determine if the cannon is in flight and thus apply physics to simulate the flight of the cannon ball, including its changing velocity.

If the cannon ball has not been launched, we translate it by 60 units—the length of the cannon—and apply the same rotation as the cannon so the cannon ball appears at the end of the cannon. So, if the cannon were rotated 10 degrees up (around the *x* axis) and 15 degrees right (around the *y* axis), we apply the same transformation to the cannon ball and move it 60 units down the *z* axis to the end of the cannon, as shown in the following code:

```
else if (meshObjectArray[i] == cannonBallObject) {
    shaderProgram = shaderRoomLight;
    gl.useProgram(shaderProgram);

    if ( !cannonBallLaunched )  {
        mat4.identity(cannonBallLocationMatrix);
        mat4.translate(cannonBallLocationMatrix,
        cannonObject.translation);
        mat4.rotate(cannonBallLocationMatrix,
        cannonObject.rotation[0], [1, 0, 0]);
        mat4.rotate(cannonBallLocationMatrix,
        cannonObject.rotation[1], [0, 1, 0]);
        mat4.multiplyVec3(cannonBallLocationMatrix,
        cannonBallPosition, cannonBallObject.translation);
    }
```

The last line in the preceding code translates (moves) the cannon ball to the end of the cannon. We use `cannonBallLocationMatrix` for the trajectory once the cannon ball has been fired.

Once the cannon ball is launched, we increment its *z* value so it travels downfield. We multiply this *z* value by `cannonBallLocationMatrix`, which contains all the cannon's rotations from the moment the cannon ball was launched. Therefore, the cannon ball travels in the direction of the cannon, not straight down the *z* axis. Finally, we apply gravity by reducing the cannon ball's height, that is, its *y* value, `cannonBallObject.translation[1]`. As we know from physics, objects gain velocity while falling. Since gravity causes objects to fall geometrically instead of linearly, the `cannonBallGravity` value is squared. This value is subtracted from the cannon ball's *y* value. Initially, `cannonBallGravity` has little effect, but over time the cannon ball will fall back to Earth, producing the curved path we expect to see from a thrown object.

Once the cannon ball hits the ground, where *y=0*, using `(cannonBallObject.translation[1] + cannonBallObject.boundingBoxMax[1])` < `0.0`, we stop. We also stop if the cannon ball has traveled 400 units. To stop, we set `cannonBallLaunched = false` and reset the cannonball to its original position at the end of the cannon. Incidentally, the brick wall does a nice job of hiding the cannon ball once it disappears out of view, as presented in the following code:

```
    if ( cannonBallLaunched ) {
        // fire the cannon down the z-axis, though it will be
        // transformed by the cannonBallLocationMatrix for aim.
        cannonBallPosition[2] += cannonBallZdirection;
        mat4.multiplyVec3(cannonBallLocationMatrix,
        cannonBallPosition, cannonBallObject.translation);
        cannonBallGravity += .04;
        cannonBallObject.translation[1] -=
            Math.pow(cannonBallGravity, 2);
        // check if the cannon ball's flight is over
        if ( (cannonBallObject.translation[1] +
            cannonBallObject.boundingBoxMax[1]) < 0.0 ||
            cannonBallObject.translation[2] < -400.0)
        {
            cannonBallLaunched = false;
            cannonBallPosition  = [0, 0, -cannonLength, 1.0];
        }
    }
} // end of cannonBallObject transformation
```

The following screenshot shows a cannon ball in the same direction of the cannon:

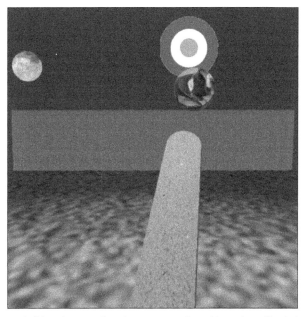

Cannon ball has the same direction as cannon, but with gravity pulling it down

The cannon is fired by a mouse click, captured by mouseDownEvent (event). This function sets up the initial values of the cannon ball, as shown in the following code snippet:

```
function mouseDownEvent(event) {   // fire away
    // used to change direction when it hits an object
    cannonBallZdirection = -1;
    cannonBallGravity = 0;
    cannonBallLaunched = true;
} // end mouseDownEvent
```

One final programming issue is collision detection, when the cannon ball hits either the brick wall or the target. The cannon ball simply reverses direction by negating cannonBallZdirection. To check for a collision on the brick wall, we first check if the cannon ball is crossing the wall using the cannon ball's z value and the wall's z value. If the wall's z value is between the cannon ball's minimum and maximum z value (its depth), we may have a collision, as presented in the following code:

```
function collisionDetection() {
. . .
if (
    // check if the cannon ball's furthest edge past the wall
    brickWallObject.translation[2] <
    (cannonBallObject.boundingBoxMax[2] +
    cannonBallObject.translation[2])   &&
    // and check if the cannon ball's closest edge
    // is before the wall
    brickWallObject.translation[2] >
    (cannonBallObject.boundingBoxMin[2] +
    cannonBallObject.translation[2]) )
    // if both are true, the cannon ball is passing the
    // brick wall.  Now check if it bounces against the
    // brick wall or off the top of the wall
```

If the cannon ball currently has the same depth as the brick wall or target, we perform one last check to see if the bottom of the cannon ball bounces off the top of the wall, or hits the wall or target, in which case it bounces back. To create the effect of bouncing off the top of the wall, we add 0.02 to cannonBallGravity—enough to slightly change the cannon ball's trajectory. Otherwise, the cannon ball squarely hits the wall or target, and thus reverses the cannonBallZdirection direction, as presented in the following code:

```
{
    if ( (brickWallObject.boundingBoxMax[1]
    +brickWallObject.translation[1]) >
    (cannonBallObject.boundingBoxMin[1] +
```

```
        cannonBallObject.translation[1]) )
        {
        if ( (brickWallObject.boundingBoxMax[1]
        +brickWallObject.translation[1]) >
        (cannonBallObject.boundingBoxMin[1]*.75 +
         cannonBallObject.translation[1]) )
            // direct hit, change the cannon's direction
            cannonBallZdirection = -cannonBallZdirection;
            // otherwise bounce off the top of the wall
            else cannonBallGravity -= .02;
        }
    } // end ck for brick wall
```

The circular target that sits above the brick wall uses similar collision detection with the cannon ball. Once the cannon ball travels to the same depth as the target, we check if the distance between the target and the cannon ball is smaller than their combined radii, in which case we have a collision, as shown in the following code:

```
// check for target 1
if ( target1Object.translation[2] <
(cannonBallObject.boundingBoxMax[2] +
cannonBallObject.translation[2]) &&
target1Object.translation[2] >
(cannonBallObject.boundingBoxMin[2] +
 cannonBallObject.translation[2]) )
{
        // cannon ball's depth is at the target
        // Now get the distance the cannon ball is
        // from the target to see if they collide
    var distanceTarget1CannonBall = Math.sqrt(
    Math.pow( (target1Object.translation[0]-
    cannonBallObject.translation[0]), 2) +
    Math.pow( (target1Object.translation[1]-
    cannonBallObject.translation[1]), 2) );
    if ( distanceTarget1CannonBall <=
        Math.abs(cannonBallObject.boundingBoxMin[1])*2 )
        {
        // The cannon ball collides with the target
        // reverse the cannon ball's direction
        cannonBallZdirection = -cannonBallZdirection
    }
    } // end ck for target1
    . . .
} // end collisionDetection
```

Have a look at the following screenshot:

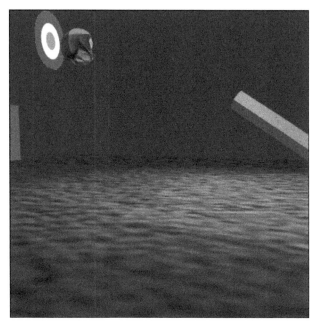

Cannon ball makes a direct hit and will now reverse direction

Objective complete – mini debriefing

Implementing physics can be one of the most difficult programming tasks. Since we already calculated the cannon ball's matrix to position it at the end of the cannon in its ready-to-fire state, it was convenient to continue using this matrix once the cannon was fired. An alternative would be to calculate the actual physics using three direction vectors and three velocities: *x* for the left-right direction, *y* for the up-down direction, and *z* for the forward-back direction.

The direction vectors are constant (unless we collide with another object, such as the cannon ball with the brick wall). In the `mouseDownEvent()` function, the *x*, *y*, and *z* direction vectors would be set as follows:

```
cannonBallLeftRightVector =
    Math.sin(cannonObject.rotation[1]);
    cannonBallUpVector = Math.sin(cannonObject.rotation[0]);
    cannonBallForwardVector = Math.cos(cannonObject.rotation[0]);
```

Velocity is measured as meters per second or miles per hour. Velocity is constant, but we would still compensate for gravity as we did before. For example, if the cannon were pointed at 45 degrees in the upward direction, and 10 degrees to the right, we may have a velocity of 3 meters per second in the *x* direction, and 10 meters per second in the *y* and *z* directions. However, gravity would still bring the cannon ball back to Earth.

True physics gets more complex, beyond just compensating for gravity. There may be wind blowing, and once the cannon ball hits Earth, would we continue bouncing it yet have friction to slow it down? Much of this physics simulation is at the advanced video game level.

Often, a game company will utilize off-the-shelf software such as Havok's physics engine (`http://www.havok.com/`), which allows for real-time collisions and dynamic objects that deform upon collision. Some WebGL physics engines are available as well, such as Three.js (`http://threejs.org/`).

Mission accomplished

Did you really think one project could cover all there is to do in games? Of course not, but we looked at some of the key elements of popular games: user interfaces both overlaid onto the window such as the buttons to move the camera, and controls within the game such as the dimmer switch for the lights. This project reviewed lighting, discussed misdirection to create a challenge, and implemented game physics. Oddly enough, my advice to students is to break the laws of physics. Be creative, be whimsical; there is humor in almost everything. Take game ideas, and then consider what its parody would look like. The spectrum is wide open. Games can be creative, such as *Farmville*, or destructive, such as *Angry Birds*; games can have simple characters like *Pac-Man* or complex characters like *Batman*. The art style can range from the retro-pixelated look of *Minecraft* to the futuristic look of *Bioshock*. So go out and construct in order to destroy.

Project 5

Social Media Meets Its Destiny

"Doc, I'm from the future. I came here in a time machine that you invented."

– Marty McFly (Michael J. Fox) to Dr. Emmett Brown (Christopher Lloyd),
Back to the Future, 1985

The telephone began communication over long distances—in essence, it was the first virtual reality—the ability to have real-time live conversations with persons half a world away. The first digital message was sent about a century later over the **Advanced Research Projects Agency Network** (**ARPANET**), a forerunner to the Internet. About a quarter century later, the Internet was commercialized. The infrastructure to connect to the Internet was in place as personal computers became standard with fax/modems being able to connect through standard phone lines. Early on, there was **BBS** (**Bulletin Board System**)—an online, text-only chat area used primarily for technical topics. In many ways, BBS was similar to the operating systems of their day, such as DOS where just arrow keys can be used to navigate text menus. Netscape Navigator browser and **America Online** (**AOL**) were one of the very first graphical user interfaces to the Internet and the first chat rooms—a place to connect with others, share thoughts and opinions with people you likely will never meet face-to-face. AOL chat rooms enabled about 35 people to post messages in real time. Never since the dawn of the written language had communication been so widespread. Chat rooms were lively, and when one was full, a new one sprung up. It was fun and a fad that gave way to the next generation of Internet connectivity: *social media*.

Today, we think of social media as Facebook, Twitter, YouTube, LinkedIn, Flickr, texting, **Massively Multiplayer Online games** (**MMO**), and a host of mobile applications. Ironically, Twitter, with its maximum of 140 characters, resembles the defunct telegraph services from over 150 years ago. However, most social media includes multimedia—images, video, audio, and interactivity—with one missing component: 3D. There have been 3D social media platforms—*Second Life*, *There*, *Active Worlds*, and others. However, they did not integrate well into our daily lives. Instead, you had to adapt to it. First, you had to download and install plugins. Then, after running the application and logging in, you often found yourself alone. Cities were built, and shopping was added, but these commercial businesses soon went under and these virtual cities resembled ghost towns. Many of these early social 3D web sites were not available on mobile devices either—they failed because they were not convenient and offered few social aspects. However, they were worthy experiments, maybe ahead of their time. Perhaps the public was not ready for purely social interactive 3D worlds. Instead, we needed social media that conveniently integrated into our daily lives. We are a mobile society with cameras, voice, video recording, and texting capabilities in our hands to connect to the world. At the fork in the road where we had to choose between 3D world or mobility, we chose the latter. Now, these roads are about to intersect again.

Mission briefing

Wherever social media meets 3D, we find WebGL. Binding two different technologies such as Facebook and WebGL is a **mashup**—technologies not designed for each other but integrated to work seamlessly. This requires learning the Facebook **API** (**Application Programming Interface**) to acquire pictures that will become texture maps on our 3D objects. This also means grabbing content from Facebook's server for an application hosted on another server. This security issue is the first of many technical challenges. This mission will take us into the future of social media and 3D and a few starting applications, from which we can build the next generation of social media. We will first bridge social media with WebGL by having our own image on Facebook textured onto a 3D mesh, and then build a 3D world of our social media friends that we can navigate and instantly access.

Why is it awesome?

Social media has been one of the most rapidly adopted applications. Facebook has signed over 1.1 billion active users in ten years—90% of the users in the last five years (`http://news.yahoo.com/number-active-users-facebook-over-230449748.html`). Most of the people on social media use a WebGL capable device, namely smartphones and tablets (`https://www.khronos.org/assets/uploads/developers/library/2013-siggraph-opengles-bof/OpenGL-ES-BOF_SIGGRAPH-2013.pdf`). Clearly, we are a social, mobile, and technically savvy society. Now just imagine the potential of an interactive 3D interface. Somewhere in the future, there will be great 3D applications waiting to be developed by designers who can bring their vision to fruition. This is the starting point that lays the foundation of great social media 3D applications to come.

Your Hotshot objectives

In order to build WebGL applications with Facebook, we first need to set up a Facebook application and then grab images from the Facebook's server, which will be used as texture maps in WebGL. We conclude by building a user interface to visit our Facebook friends in 3D space. The major tasks required to complete our project are as follows:

- Bridging Facebook to WebGL
- Visiting Facebook friends in WebGL
- Building a navigable world of Facebook friends

Bridging Facebook with WebGL

This first demonstration is a start-to-finish example of how you can grab your own Facebook image and texture it onto a flat plane with WebGL. Along the way, we will be confronted by several technical issues and solutions that will also be instructive.

Prepare for lift off

To create a Facebook application, we need our own server to host the application and register it with Facebook. It might be rather obvious, but be sure that you are logged in to Facebook first. Begin with Facebook's developer site at `https://developers.facebook.com`. Navigate to **Apps** | **Create a New App**. We will be asked for an app name or website, in which case I simply used my website address. The **Namespace** field is optional, but it is recommended that we select the closest choice from the selection box. Since nothing really matched—after all, Facebook in 3D is ahead of its time—I selected **Communication**. Facebook uses this information to catalog applications written by developers.

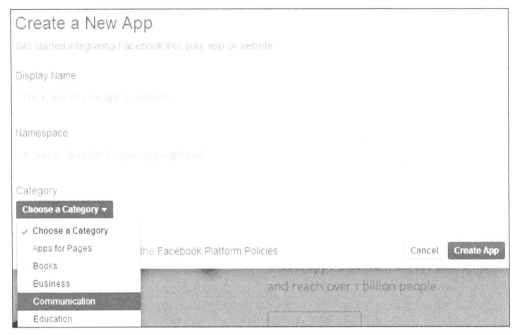

Creating a new application on the Facebook developers network

Creating the app will generate an **App ID/API Key**. You will need this for your Facebook-WebGL program, but don't worry about memorizing it—you can always return to the Facebook developer website and see your app name now listed under the **Apps** menu. Something that may impress or overwhelm you is the number and length of these ID numbers. Everything has an identification number, including photos, postings, home cities, your interests, friends lists, and favorite sports. Another equally impressive fact is that Facebook's apps page will keep statistics on how frequently people use your application. The app dashboard also has a number of options and settings for your app, such as enabling payments and porting to mobile devices. Therefore, when your WebGL Facebook app becomes a hit, you will have metrics from Facebook to prove it.

An app page with the ID information blurred out

Now that our Facebook app is registered, it is time to start development.

Engage thrusters

Facebook requires users to log in to your application. This is not the same as logging in to your Facebook account. However, if you were not previously logged in to your Facebook account, then logging in to your application also logs you in to Facebook. To enable users to log in to your application, Facebook provides a default login button and code given as follows:

```
<fb:login-button show-faces="true" width="200" max-rows="1"></
fb:login-button>
```

Be sure this line of code is in the body of your HTML page. In addition, there is another default code required by Facebook. This handles the interface to Facebook's **JavaScript Software Developers Kit** (**JSSDK**) and other support functions. More information and tutorials can be obtained from the Facebook developers website, `https://developers.facebook.com`. For now, it would be best to just copy and paste these Facebook functions:

```
<script>
// Load the SDK asynchronously
(function(d){
  var js, id = 'facebook-jssdk', ref =
  d.getElementsByTagName('script')[0];
  if (d.getElementById(id)) {return;}
    js = d.createElement('script');
```

```
    js.id = id; js.async = true;
    js.src = "//connect.facebook.net/en_US/all.js";
    ref.parentNode.insertBefore(js, ref);
  }(document));
</script>

<script>
(function(d, s, id) {
  var js, fjs = d.getElementsByTagName(s)[0];
  if (d.getElementById(id)) return;
    js = d.createElement(s); js.id = id;
    js.src =
    "//connect.facebook.net/en_US/all.js#xfbml=
      1&appId=1422842541262514";
    fjs.parentNode.insertBefore(js, fjs);
  }(document, 'script', 'facebook-jssdk'));
</script>
```

Next, we initiate our program. This is invoked automatically by the login button code shown earlier. There are four components to initiate the program:

▸ Connecting to the Facebook application we registered earlier

▸ Initiating our application

▸ Logging in to our application, if we were previously logged in to our Facebook account

▸ Users logging in to both their Facebook account and our application

Commands that begin with FB, such as FB.init, FB.Event, FB.login, or FB.api, are Facebook's own commands. The call to FB.init() will invoke our WebGL application. The appId parameter is currently set to the fictitious value samplenumber_0097, and this will be replaced by the actual application ID that Facebook assigns to us. The FB.Event. subscribe() call invokes our application with a call to facebook3dUI(). If we have not logged in to our Facebook app or the user has not logged in to their Facebook account, then a call to FB.login() is performed first as given in the following code snippet:

```
<script>
  // Called automatically when the Facebook app is invoked
  window.fbAsyncInit = function() {
    FB.init({
      // App ID, generated when we created the
      // Facebook app on developers.Facebook.com
      appId      : 'samplenumbers…0097', // App ID
      // URL of the where the app is stored
      channelUrl : '//www.yourWebSite.com/channel.html',
```

```
      status      : true, // check login status
      // enable cookies to allow the server to
      cookie      : true, // access the session
      xfbml       : true  // parse XFBML
    });

    // Subscribe to the auth.authResponseChange
    // JavaScript event.
    FB.Event.subscribe('auth.authResponseChange',
    function(response) {
      if (response.status === 'connected') {
        // Call to our Facebook 3d app
        facebook3dUI();
        linkToGraphAPIexplorer();
      }
      else if (response.status === 'not_authorized') {
        // Person is logged into Facebook,
        // but not into the app, so we call
        // FB.login() to prompt them to do so.
        FB.login();
      }
      else {
        // Person is not logged into Facebook
        FB.login();
      }
    });
  };
</script>
```

Once a user is logged in to their Facebook account and our application, we call
`facebook3dUI()` to build a flat plane 3D mesh and texture map it with our Facebook
image. In the `facebook3dUI()` function, the call to `FB.api` requests data from Facebook
using their API and saves the information in a `response` object. Here, we request for
information about the `me` property, basically the data that is typed in when you first create
your Facebook account. The rest of the line, `?fields=picture`, informs Facebook to limit
the data returned to just your posted picture. The type of data that Facebook returns should
be limited because each personal account can contain hundreds of images and text postings:

```
function facebook3dUI() {
  FB.api('/me?fields=picture', function(response) {
    fbTextureMap = gl.createTexture();
    fbTextureMap.image = new Image();
    fbTextureMap.image.crossOrigin = "anonymous";
    fbTextureMap.image.src = response.picture.data.url;
```

```
          fbTextureMap.image.onload = function () {
            handleAltLoadedTexture( fbTextureMap );
          }
      });
    }
```

The next two lines, `fbTextureMap = gl.createTexture();` and `fbTextureMap.image = new Image();`, create buffer space for a texture map sent to the graphics card, which we have programmed in previous WebGL demonstrations (see the `mesh3dObject.js` file, and the `AddMeshObject()` function). The next line, `fbTextureMap.image.crossOrigin = "anonymous";`, enables us to download a picture from the Facebook server onto an application running from a different server. This is part of a standard known as **Cross-Origin Resource Sharing (CORS)**. In the last decade, it was recognized that web pages may wish to grab data that did not originate from its own server. For example, data from the stock market can be integrated into another website that performs investment analysis. Developers had to write various hacks to enable requests across domain boundaries. CORS became a **W3C (World Wide Web Consortium)** standard to allow servers to share this information and for applications to receive it. Thankfully, Facebook has enabled application writers to integrate their data into other applications. Additional information on CORS can be found at `http://www.w3.org/TR/cors/`.

Finally, we get to the location of the image, `fbTextureMap.image.src = response.picture.data.url;`. How did we know this would be the location of the image or find any other data on Facebook? On Facebook's Developer page, `https://developers.facebook.com`, navigate to **Tools | Graph Explorer**. Assuming that you are logged in to Facebook, the page refreshes with your **id** and **name**, with checked boxes on the left-hand side next to **id** and **name**. Uncheck these options and click on **Submit**. The entire list of data about you appears such as employers, favorite sports teams, education, and much more. The plus sign (**+**) on the left, where **id** and **name** were checked, has a roll-out menu of more data, such as your friends, photos you've posted, photos that friends have posted of you, and so on.

Select the **picture** checkbox, and then click on **Submit** as shown in the following screenshot. You will see the data regarding your Facebook photo. Included in this data structure is the `url` of your picture. We submitted `me?fields=picture` to the Facebook API, so we received the `picture` object containing a data object, which contains the URL. Thus, the link to the image is `response.picture.data.url`. After reading this introduction, you might be tempted to explore the *Facebook Graph API Explorer*:

The Facebook Graph Explorer with the picture field selected

Now that we know the location of our image, we will download it in the background. One additional technical issue with Facebook images is that we have no control over the dimensions. The texture mapping of images needs the width and height in powers of two, such as 32 pixels (width) by 64 pixels (height). When you choose an image as your Facebook photo, a copy of that image is saved in dimensions of 50 x 50, which is clearly not a power of two. Yet, even if Facebook did not make a copy of your image, it is unlikely that Facebook users would post images with dimensions in powers of two. Therefore, we have to overcome these dimension issues. Fortunately, WebGL allows us to use images of different dimensions; however, there is a trade off—the images will not look crisp and instead will appear blurry. In the `handleAltLoadedTexture()` function, we set parameters for the image to be used as a texture map. Previous texture maps set the **mipmap** function, where we replicate the image several times, each being half the dimensions of the previous image. For example, if the original image were 128 x 64, the first mipmap image would be 64 x 32, then 32 x 16, and so on.

The mipmap process works as follows: we replicate the original image into a quarter-size image (dimensions are halved both horizontally and vertically). The new pixels of the quarter-sized image blend into the neighboring pixels so that these smaller versions of the image do not lose any color from the original texture map. For example, a single pixel blends its color with the eight surrounding pixels to form a new pixel. We then repeat the blending process on every other pixel. The result is an image that is one-fourth the size of the original, but with the original colors saved. We then repeat this image-blending process to create one-fourth sized images from the previous image. Thus, a 128 x 64 size image creates smaller images of the size 64 x 32, 32 x 16, and so forth. When we display these images as texture maps in 3D, if the texture-mapped object is far away, one of the smaller mipmap images will be used closest to the size of the object in 3D. The mipmap process retains much of the original picture despite the texture map being rendered on to rotated objects with varied dimensions.

Since Facebook images do not start with dimensions in powers of two (8, 16, 32, 64, and so on), we cannot use the mipmap process, and thus, we do not call the `gl.generateMipmap(gl.TEXTURE_2D);` command used in the previous examples.

Two additional commands inside the `handleAltLoadedTexture()` function clamp the image to the edges of our 3D mesh. This stretches or squashes the image from edge to edge and prevents the image from tiling or duplicating onto a non-square 3D mesh.

```
gl.texParameteri(gl.TEXTURE_2D, gl.TEXTURE_WRAP_S,
gl.CLAMP_TO_EDGE);
gl.texParameteri(gl.TEXTURE_2D, gl.TEXTURE_WRAP_T,
gl.CLAMP_TO_EDGE);
```

An image from my dog's Facebook page textured onto a plane in WebGL is shown in the following screenshot. The plane is angled rather than facing the camera to emphasize the 3D aspect:

In the `drawScene()` function, we test if our Facebook image—`fbTextureMap`—is available, and if so, we send this image to the shader:

```
if ( fbTextureMap != null ) {
  gl.activeTexture(gl.TEXTURE1);
  gl.bindTexture(gl.TEXTURE_2D, fbTextureMap);
  gl.uniform1i(shaderProgram.samplerAltUniform, 1);
}
```

The fragment shader is quite simple. There are no lighting calculations. We simply use the Facebook texture map referenced by uSampleAlt that was linked to sampleAltUniform, binded to fbTextureMap:

```
vec4 fragmentColor = texture2D(uSamplerAlt,
  vec2(vTextureCoord.s, vTextureCoord.t));
gl_FragColor = vec4(fragmentColor.rgb, 1.0);
```

We added one last feature to assist in our Facebook development; after calling facebook3dUI(), we also called linkToGraphAPIexplorer(). This demonstrates that we can call the FB.api() function more than once in an application. For example, facebook3dUI() only fetches a single image. If we want to get more data, such as educational background, we can make additional FB.api() calls to download other information.

This function creates a link to Facebook's Graph API Explorer. By passing the value /me, we can get basic information about ourselves such as our hometown, educational background, everything we typed about ourselves on Facebook. Clicking on the personal Graph API Explorer link was included in order to assist you to get data about yourself listed on Facebook's Graph API:

```
function linkToGraphAPIexplorer() {
  FB.api('/me', function(response) {
    var graphAPIexplorerMssg =
    document.getElementById('graphAPIexplorerLink');
    graphAPIexplorerMssg.innerHTML = '<A
      HREF="https://developers.facebook.com/tools/explorer?
    method=GET&path=" + response.id +
      " target="_blank">Personal Graph API Explorer</A>';
  });
}
```

Objective complete – mini debriefing

Facebook is becoming a great survey and data mining resource. With over 1 billion users, Facebook can provide instant demographic information by programming the Facebook API. That was certainly a bit of work just to post a single image of ourselves in WebGL. However, it is an important start, a proof-of-concept, to open the door for more applications to come.

Classified intel

We noted that the majority of Facebook images will likely not be in dimensions of two, and thus, we will not be able to access the features of mipmapping. To change the dimensions of an image so that it is a power of two requires an image-editing tool such as Adobe Photoshop. We can write our own program to perform this conversion, but this requires a high-level programming language such as Java or C++. JavaScript is too slow for the job. Resizing the image would also add a lengthy task before our WebGL Facebook application runs.

However, there is another way to use a graphics card for this image processing. Currently, we are writing shader programs running on the graphics card to perform pixel-by-pixel calculations for lighting and texture maps. Inside the graphics card, these pixel calculations run in parallel. The processing power of graphics cards can also be used for other tasks running in parallel. The technology is known as **OpenCL** and is often used in image manipulation. In addition, just as WebGL is the web browser-based version of OpenGL, **WebCL** is the web browser-based version of OpenCL. WebCL is an ideal technology for processing images in order to transform texture maps to have dimensions in powers of two. Moreover, since it runs on the graphics card, WebCL won't demand resources from the CPU. WebCL is new but is likely to play a role in future WebGL development.

Visiting Facebook friends in WebGL

Now that we have built our first application by acquiring a Facebook image and displayed it in WebGL, it is time to create a 3D user interface of our Facebook friends.

Prepare for lift off

As it often happens in programming when we are just grabbing a single item, such as an image, there is not a great deal of complexity. However, once we want to access two or more of our Facebook friends' images, we have additional issues, in particular, downloading multiple images simultaneously in the background. We begin by building on the previous example that focused on just the critical interfacing with Facebook. In this example, we will create the 2D flat plane for the texture images by specifying the vertices instead of importing a 3D mesh. Texture mapping our Facebook friends onto a 3D mesh such as a dog or cow would be fun, but let's leave the creativity to you—the designers.

Engage thrusters

Similar to the previous example, once Facebook verifies that the user is logged in to both their Facebook account and our application, we begin by calling `facebook3dUI()`. However, this time we are acquiring the pictures of our friends using the Facebook API. The `/me/friends?fields=picture&limit='+photosListed` line of code tells the Facebook API to retrieve pictures from my friends and to limit the number of friends to the `photosListed` value, which is set to 6. I chose this number for this demonstration. We specify the only field we want as `picture`. Facebook has a lot of data about each of us, and thus, it helps to improve the performance if we retrieve only what we need:

```
<SCRIPT>
  function facebook3dUI() {
    var photosListed = 6; // number of photos in the application
    FB.api('/me/friends?fields=picture&limit='+photosListed,
    function(response) {
```

We now have an array of data including the web address (URL) of our friends' pictures. For each Facebook image, we call `createObject(name, translation, scale, rotation)`, which creates a flat plane composed of four vertices. The `name` field is just a default place holder, `fbObj`, but the `translation` and `rotation` fields are set to where the image will be placed in our 3D scene. The `scale` is set to its default, `[1, 1, 1]`.

Next, we will create a texture object that contains an image object. The texture and image objects may seem like the same thing, but textures can be made up of more than just images, such as equations or cube images. We assign our texture map's image source (`image.src`) to the URL of our Facebook image, `facebookTextureMap[totalFBobj].image.src = response.data[i].picture.data.url;`, and then call `GetFacebookTexture( facebookTextureMap[totalFBobj] );` to download the actual image:

```
for (var i = 0; i < photosListed; i++) {
  createObject( "fbObj", [ facebookObjLoc[0],
    facebookObjLoc[1], facebookObjLoc[2]],
    [1, 1, 1], [0, facebookObjYrotation, 0] );
  facebookTextureMap[totalFBobj] =
    gl.createTexture();
  facebookTextureMap[totalFBobj].image =
    new Image();
  facebookTextureMap[totalFBobj].image.
    crossOrigin = "anonymous";
  facebookTextureMap[totalFBobj].image.src =
    response.data[i].picture.data.url;
  GetFacebookTexture(facebookTextureMap[totalFBobj])
```

Before examining the call to GetFacebookTexture(), the last few lines of the facebook3dUI() function set the (*x, y, z*) location of the next Facebook image so that they are spaced out in our 3D world into the upper, lower, left, and right quadrants of the screen. After every 4th image, the next set of 3D meshes are placed further back by four units and slightly closer to the center:

```
facebookObjLoc[0] = -facebookObjLoc[0];
facebookObjYrotation = -facebookObjYrotation;
if ( (totalFBobj %2) == 0) {
  facebookObjLoc[1] = -facebookObjLoc[1];
}
totalFBobj++;
if ( (totalFBobj % 4) == 0) {
  facebookObjLoc[0] += 1.5;
  facebookObjLoc[1] -= .5;
  facebookObjLoc[2] -=4;
}
} // end for loop
});
}
</script>
```

Our first example retrieved a single image, so there was no concern whether the correct image was assigned to the correct 3D mesh, since there was only one of each. Now, we are downloading multiple images textured onto multiple 3D meshes; therefore, we need to manage the downloading process. Once again, we will deploy the **AJAX (Asynchronous JavaScript and XML)** technology and its XMLHTTPRequest() function. AJAX connects to the Facebook server and informs us when an image has been downloaded. We previously used AJAX to download the .obj files, which contained the 3D mesh plus the .mtl material file that specified the image used for texture mapping. Therefore, we have had a lot of practice with AJAX. Here, we use AJAX's XMLHttpRequest() method to load the Facebook images that will be used as texture maps in our WebGL scene. The texture map will be applied to a flat plane built from four vertices inside the createObject() function, similar to what we first learned about creating 3D objects in the *WebGL Texture Mapping and Animation* section of *Project 2*, *WebGL for E-Commerce*, with the demonstration of the rotating image of the basset hound.

We begin `GetFacebookTexture()` by first creating the `requestFBImage` object, which manages the connection to the Facebook server, and then use a `GET` command, `requestFBImage.open("GET", facebookTextureMap.image.src)`, to acquire the Facebook image. The value `facebookTextureMap.image.src` is the web address of our friend's Facebook image. We use the `send()` function to send this request over to Facebook using the `requestFBImage.send()` command. The `requestFBImage.onreadystatechange = function()` line receives the status from Facebook. AJAX technology provides support for this handshaking between our application and the Facebook server. When the value of `requestFBImage.readyState` is 4, the downloading of the image is complete and we are now ready to create a texture map object.

The remainder of this code creates a texture map as in the previous example. As before, this image will not be in the dimensions that are powers of 2, and thus, we will not use mipmaps:

```
<SCRIPT>
  function GetFacebookTexture(facebookTextureMap) {
    var requestFBImage = new XMLHttpRequest();
    requestFBImage.onreadystatechange = function() {
      if (requestFBImage.readyState == 4) {
        gl.pixelStorei(gl.UNPACK_FLIP_Y_WEBGL, true);
        gl.bindTexture(gl.TEXTURE_2D, facebookTextureMap);

        gl.texImage2D(gl.TEXTURE_2D, 0, gl.RGBA,
          gl.RGBA, gl.UNSIGNED_BYTE,
          facebookTextureMap.image);

        gl.texParameteri(gl.TEXTURE_2D,
          gl.TEXTURE_MIN_FILTER, gl.LINEAR);
        gl.texParameteri(gl.TEXTURE_2D,
          gl.TEXTURE_WRAP_S, gl.CLAMP_TO_EDGE);
        gl.texParameteri(gl.TEXTURE_2D,
          gl.TEXTURE_WRAP_T, gl.CLAMP_TO_EDGE);
        gl.bindTexture(gl.TEXTURE_2D, null);
      }
    }
    requestFBImage.open("GET", facebookTextureMap.image.src);
```

```
        requestFBImage.send();
    }  // end GetFacebookTexture
</SCRIPT>
```

Dee Dee Williams uses
Virtualbeachtest05.

Your Facebook friends in a 3D world

Objective complete – mini debriefing

As is often the case, an application downloading a single image is not too complex. Once you get to two or more images, we have to manage how the images are downloaded. However, at the same time, once the code is developed, simply changing the value of `photosListed = 6` to a larger number can expand the example from just a few Facebook friends to a few hundred.

We also began to explore and use the Facebook API. Once we master this, we will have access to a large number of good images that in turn will be the basis for some very creative applications.

One concern is that the images begin with 50 x 50 pixels and might end up several times this size in our 3D world, resulting in blurry images. In addition, there are quite a few out-of-focus images on Facebook already. As developers, we always have the final say in how close a close-up can be. We can restrict the camera from being too close to any 3D mesh so that the image quality looks good. Remember that this demonstration is working with the smallest thumbnail images on Facebook. Beyond our thumbnail profile pictures, we, Facebook users, may have posted many images with far larger width and height dimensions. Moreover, with spectacular *selfies* becoming the new art style, we will have many great-looking images to choose from.

Building a navigable world of Facebook friends

The previous example programmed some pretty critical fundamentals of grabbing multiple Facebook images and pasting them into a 3D environment. We have yet to exploit the capabilities of interactive 3D worlds. Now, we shall add the ability to walk through our 3D Facebook world using the arrow keys and the mouse to navigate through Facebook pages. From here, we will use our imagination to create what a 3D social media world can become.

Engage thrusters

We continue to retrieve images using the `facebook3dUI()` function as in the previous example, but now we also call a new `facebookFriendsNames()` function that returns our friends' name and a link to their Facebook page and saves them in the `facebookName` and `facebookLink` arrays. The key coding change is in the data we request from the Facebook API, `FB.api('/me/friends?fields=name,link...)`, which tells Facebook to return the names and web addresses of our friends. Note that we are hardly limited by just this data. Many of us must have posted information about the towns where we grew up, our educational background, favorite musicians, or sports teams on Facebook. In addition, our birthday, relationship status, current residence, and hobbies are also accessible. However, our demonstration keeps things simple—just friends' name and a link to their Facebook page:

```
function facebookFriendsNames() {
  FB.api('/me/friends?fields=name,link&limit='+friendsListed,
    function(response) {
    for (var i = 0; i < friendsListed; i++) {
      // name Facebook friends and URL link to their image
```

```
         facebookName[i] = response.data[i].name;
         facebookLink[i] = response.data[i].link;
      } // end for loop
   });
}
```

Your Facebook friend's name will appear in a pop-up box hovering next to their image when the mouse rolls over it. Down in the <BODY> tag of this HTML page, we add a <DIV> tag that will be used to display our friend's name. Note that visibility is initialized to hidden, so we will not see the box when the page opens (we will only see the box when the mouse rolls over the image):

```
<div id="table" style="border: solid; padding:4px;
   position:absolute;top:60px;left:40px;
   background-color: LightGray; visibility:hidden" >
   Facebook 3d demo</div>
```

We navigate the scene using the arrow keys, and use the mouse to rollover and click on the images. Note that we may have used the mouse exclusively for navigation, but I chose to use the keyboard/mouse combination found in many video games. The setup code is in the webGLStart() function, given as follows:

```
function webGLStart() {
...
   document.onkeydown = handleKeyDown;
   document.onkeyup = handleKeyUp;
   document.onmousemove = mouseMoveEvent;
   document.onmousedown = mouseDownEvent;
...
}
```

Reacting to the arrow keys with document.onkeydown and document.onkeyup for camera navigation was also covered in *Project 3, User Experience, Story, Character, Visual Design, and Interactivity*, in the *Full navigation* section.

The createObject() function was expanded to include a Bounding Box around each flat plane textured with a Facebook image. A Bounding Box is an invisible box that encapsulates the 3D mesh and is used to test if the ray from our camera location to the mouse intersects the 3D mesh, indicating that we clicked on this object. This was also covered in *Project 3, User Experience, Story, Character, Visual Design, and Interactivity*, and was included in the mesh3dObject.js code. Since we are creating our own 3D meshes in the createObject() code, Bounding Boxes were added there. How to check for this intersection was explained in *Project 3, User Experience, Story, Character, Visual Design, and Interactivity*, and the code is a part of the rayIntersection.js file.

When the mouse is moved, the `mouseMoveEvent()` function is called, which provides us with the mouse's *x* and *y* positions:

```
function mouseMoveEvent(event) {
    mouseMoveX = event.clientX;
    mouseMoveY = event.clientY;
```

We convert the 2D screen's *x* and *y* positions into 3D positions. Since the 2D *x* and *y* positions are relative to the top-left corner of the HTML web page, we have to subtract the top-left position coordinates of the WebGL window inside the HTML page. After taking into account this offset of the top-left position of the WebGL window from the web page's top and left, the equation is as follows:

$$X_{3d} = (X_{2d} - Width_{2d} / 2) * (2 / Width_{2d})$$

$$Y_{3d} = -(Y_{2d} - Height_{2d} / 2) * (2 / Height_{2d})$$

For example, if the dimensions of the 2D window are 640 (width) by 480 (height), then clicking in that window at the location (160, 240) will be one fourth of the window's width from the left and centered vertically. The X_{3d} point will be *(160 - 640/2)*(2/640) = -160*(1/320) = -0.5*. The Y_{3d} point will be *-(240 - 480/2)*(2/480) = 0*(1/240) = 0*. Thus, the conversion of 2D screen coordinates (160, 240) to 3D world coordinates is (-0.5, 0, z). The *z* value, distance to the view plane, is fixed at *1 / Math.tan((fieldOfView) / 2)*.

Note that `yWorld` has a leading negative sign because the screen coordinate values increase as we move down the page, while in 3D space, `yworld` coordinates increase as we navigate up the *y* axis. Here is the code for the conversion of 2D screen coordinates to 3D world coordinates:

```
var xWorld = ( (mouseMoveX - windowLeft) - gl.viewportWidth/2)
    * ( 2.0 / gl.viewportWidth);
var yWorld = -( (mouseMoveY - windowTop) -
    gl.viewportHeight/2) * ( 2.0 / gl.viewportHeight);
rayMouseDown = [ xWorld, yWorld, -distanceToViewPlane, 1 ];
```

Next, we check if the mouse rolled over a 3D mesh representing a Facebook friend. We check the furthest 3D meshes first, in case we have two Facebook friend images overlapping in our 3D scene. Thus, the `for` loop counts down, checking our closest objects last, `for (var i = (totalMeshObjects-1); i >= 0; i--)`. We can validate the closest objects mathematically since the calculation for determining a ray-box intersection also provides us with how far the intersection occurred; but for now, we will keep it simple and just check backwards. The call to the `RayBoundingBoxIntersection()` function found in the `rayIntersection.js` file returns true if the mouse is over this 3D mesh.

If the mouse did roll over our Facebook friend's image, we use the name previously saved in the `facebookName[]` array and insert it into the `<DIV>` tag with `id=table: table. innerHTML = facebookName[i];`. Finally, we offset the text that is 15 pixels to the right and 15 pixels below the mouse click so that it won't cover our friend's image:

```
var overObject = false;
var table = document.getElementById('table');
for (var i = (totalMeshObjects-1); i >= 0; i-- )
{
  if ( RayBoundingBoxIntersection( meshObjectArray[ i ],
      xWorld, yWorld ) ) {
    table.innerHTML = facebookName[i];
    overObject = true;
    table.style.left = mouseMoveX + 15;
    table.style.top = mouseMoveY + 15;
    table.style.visibility = 'visible';
  }
}
```

Mouse rolled over the image of me, your humble author, using my dog's Facebook page

If the mouse rolls over empty space and not over any 3D mesh, we hide the `<DIV>` tag by setting its `visibility` property to `hidden`:

```
    if ( !overObject ) {
      table.style.visibility = 'hidden';
    }
  } // end mouseMoveEvent
```

The code to handle `mouseDownEvent()` is similar to `mouseMoveEvent()`. The code for checking if the mouse rolled over a 3D mesh is similar to the code for checking if the mouse clicked on a 3D mesh. We still convert the mouse's 2D screen point to a 3D point and then test if there was a ray-bounding box intersection. However, now if the mouse did click on a 3D mesh, we open our friend's Facebook page. We previously saved the web address of our Facebook friends in the `facebookLink[]` array. Now we use the HTML command `window.open()` to open that web page. The `_target` attribute is included to open a new browser page rather than replace our current web page running our WebGL Facebook app.

```
  function mouseDownEvent(event) {
    mouseMoveX = event.clientX;
    mouseMoveY = event.clientY;

    var xWorld = ( (mouseMoveX - windowLeft) - gl.viewportWidth/2)
      * ( 2.0 / gl.viewportWidth);
    var yWorld = -( (mouseMoveY - windowTop) -
      gl.viewportHeight/2) * ( 2.0 / gl.viewportHeight);
    rayMouseDown = [ xWorld, yWorld, -distanceToViewPlane, 1 ];

    for (var i = (totalMeshObjects-1); i >= 0; i-- ) {
      if ( RayBoundingBoxIntersection( meshObjectArray[ i ],
        xWorld, yWorld ) ) {
        // open a new web page
        window.open(facebookLink[i], "_target");
      }
    }
  } // end mouseDownEvent
```

Objective complete – mini debriefing

In demonstrating this application, the reaction from many was instant amazement. People get it right away; no explanations needed. It is small, simple, and cool. Yet, we have just begun to transform social media from 2D to 3D. We sometimes say *think outside the box*. Now let's *think outside the cube*.

Many applications in this book can be run on your desktop. However, Facebook with WebGL must run on a server. You are invited to try it at:

```
http://www.virtualbeach.com/facebook/friendsNames.htm
```

Mission accomplished

We successfully mashed up Facebook to a WebGL 3D interface. In addition, this has opened the door to creating 3D worlds with over one billion social media users and growing. There are a number of areas that we can continue to pursue through the Facebook API. New applications and content would require additional registrations, application permissions, and an understanding of the Facebook API. In addition, there will likely be new social media applications to build upon what we today might think of as very advanced.

Connecting with people remotely has been happening since the first telephone call. Since then, communication has gone through many iterations. Technology changes; the typewriter, fax, and possibly even the telephone are seeing their last days. However, media expands in sync with our ever-broadening means of communicating with others.

3D and social media are a little more now than a small open door, with a little sunlight shining in. A number of past attempts have failed; all well intended. However, we could not have arrived at this destination without those past efforts. I hope this presents you—designers and developers—with an opportunity to take social media with 3D into the future and to take another step towards its fulfillment.

Project 6

3D Reveals More Information

"You're gonna need a bigger boat."

– Sheriff Martin Brody (Roy Scheider), Jaws, 1975

The information age supplies more data at our fingertips than ever before, literally at the speed of light. In addition, with mobile devices and Wi-Fi, we can get this data from nearly any location. We are receiving more data, yet we are using the same medium of text and two-dimensional images to comprehend this data. However, can 3D reveal more information? Can viewing data in three dimensions add to our comprehension, reveal more information, and enhance our understanding? Will three dimensions reveal hidden information in data mining excavations? As tasks get more complex, detailed, and collaborative, communicating effectively has never been more important, and WebGL just might be the way we meet these challenges.

Mission briefing

We have long used charts and graphs to represent data. Graphs enable us to gather information quickly, spot trends, identify comparisons among demographics, make decisions for financial analysis, or make a medical diagnosis. The goal in visualizing data is to distinguish information, enhance understanding, and communicate more effectively. Two-dimensional charts are ideal for newspapers and now for web pages. However, as the amount of data grows, we need new tools to visualize this data. With 3D, we can walk through the data, zoom in and out of it, and view it from above or straight on. The following examples will bring together how data is shared using common industry formats, how to parse the data, and how to represent it in 3D.

Why is it awesome?

We are inundated with data, and maybe with less time to analyze it. Despite all the advents in communications and instant access to information, we still view data in pretty much the same way as we did at the turn of the previous century over 100 years ago. 3D may provide the key to not only view more information in a single screen, but also to view more connections and relationships that 2D may never have revealed.

Your Hotshot objectives

We will perform the following tasks:

- Linking 3D to data
- Comparing multiple stocks in 3D
- Displaying historical stock data
- Presenting comparative data
- Zooming into the data – the level of detail

Mission checklist

These examples use live demonstrations from the stock market. The data can, however, be from any source such as live sports or Twitter feeds. We also use non-real-time historical data, such as stock performance from the past year. Both live and historical data are equally interesting and demonstrate how WebGL can be used to represent large amounts of data. We will focus primarily on the NASDAQ stock exchange because they provide this information for free. Since information has value, most of the world's stock exchanges charge a fee to receive the real-time feeds. Expanding this demonstration may require a subscription fee from the providers of this stock data.

Linking 3D to data

Sharing data presents both an opportunity as well as a problem. How do separate entities share data in an agreed upon fashion? How can organizations from different industries share common related information? The answer is **XML**, the **Extensible Markup Language**. We saw XML back in *Project 1*, *Building Great Web3D*, with X3D, which used XML to define a 3D graphics file format. In the vast world of news, the XML standard is **RSS (Really Simple Syndication)**. RSS can be any news item—print media, *People* magazine, stock prices, sports reporting, and press releases. Look at nearly any news or text website, and there will likely be a small XML XML or RSS link or the RSS icon.

This is data sharing in action. While there might be copyright issues on repurposing this information, it is made available to be shared. We can save this RSS file, which often has the .xml file ending, or grab the data directly off the Internet. Either way, we now need to parse the data in order to extract the header information such as the article title, date, author, and the actual content.

Most RSS data is news stories, effectively text, sometimes accompanied by images. This does not lend itself to being displayed in 3D. Yet, some of this data represents statistics, stock prices, company portfolios, and comparative analysis—the elements of data mining. The next step is to parse this data and build 3D graphics representations.

Prepare for lift off

Our first project will be to represent the prices of various stocks. To do this, we need two items: the stock data feed coming in the form of an RSS/XML file and software to parse this file.

Real-time stock data feeds are expensive; however, NASDAQ, typically the stock exchange of the high-technology industry, makes a limited amount of data available, and while it is not live, it is delayed by just a half hour. This will be fine for our purpose. You can find the NASDAQ RSS feed web link at `http://www.nasdaq.com/services/rss.aspx`; select the **Stock Quote Feed** tab. Type in the stock market abbreviation; for example, *AAPL* for Apple or *YHOO* for Yahoo!, and this will produce a link, such as `http://www.nasdaq.com/aspxcontent/NasdaqRSS.aspx?data=quotes&symbol=AAPL`. Using the link as a web browser address will return the RSS/XML page with code listed as follows:

```
<rss xmlns:nasdaq="http://nasdaq.com" version="2.0">
  <channel>
    <title>NASDAQ.com Stock Tracker</title>
    <link>http://www.nasdaq.com</link>
    <description>
      Track your favorite stock and link to NASDAQ.com for the full
details.
    </description>
    <copyright>
      Copyright 2013 Nasdaq.com. All rights reserved.
    </copyright>
    <item>
      <pubDate>16 Oct 2013 16:00:00 EDT</pubDate>
      <title>
        16 Oct 2013 16:00:00 EDT - The latest stock information is now
available for your stocks
      </title>
      <author>isfeedback@nasdaq.com</author>
      <description>
```

```
          <![CDATA[
          <table border=0 cellspacing=0 cellpadding=0 width="200"> <TR
     bgcolor="#DDDDDD"> <TD ALIGN="LEFT" COLSPAN=2 nowrap>

     More data here -

               </TD> </TR> </TABLE>
          ]]>
        </description>
      </item>
    </channel>
  </rss>
```

Some of the repeated file data was removed. The raw stock information is saved inside the `item -> description` XML tags and within the `CDATA` brackets. Before we get to that, we need software to read and parse this data file.

Years ago, XML file parsing was left to the developer to create their own server software. Fortunately, today, Google supports a number of Internet applications. A good starting point is `https://code.google.com/` for many community resources. In addition, Google developed programs to assist in reading XML with server support, available free with examples and an API at `https://developers.google.com/feed/v1/`. We will integrate this code with 3D graphics and WebGL in a simple example beginning with a single stock.

Engage thrusters

To parse the XML file with JavaScript, we use Google's freely available *Feed* program. Google hosts the programs and provides a nice interface for us. We just need to include a link to Google's code at the start of our program:

```
<script src="//www.google.com/
    jsapi?key=AIzaSyA5m1Nc8ws2BbmPRwKu5gFradvD_hgq6G0"
    type="text/javascript">
</script>
```

Now, let's start with the first command upon loading the web page. The first line loads Version 1 of the `feeds` API. Google supports many APIs, including familiar ones such as Google Docs and Google Maps. The second line runs upon loading our web page and initiates the access to read and parse the XML file:

```
google.load("feeds", "1");

google.setOnLoadCallback(OnLoad);
```

This line calls the following code that retrieves our XML data:

```
function OnLoad() {
    //Create a feed instance that will grab the Apple data.
    var feed = new google.feeds.Feed
    ("http://www.nasdaq.com/aspxcontent/
    NasdaqRSS.aspx?data=quotes&symbol=AAPL");

    //Request the results in XML
    feed.setResultFormat(google.feeds.Feed.XML_FORMAT);
    //Calling 'load' sends a request to fetch the Apple data off
    //the NASDAQ server.  When done, the server informs us
    feed.load(feedLoaded);
}
```

We do not need to know all the functionality here, but a few items need to be identified. The `var feed` variable is simply the XML stock report; in this case, *Apple*, as noted by its symbol, *AAPL*. The next line containing `google.feeds.Feed.XML_FORMAT` specifies that this data will be in XML format. Once the XML file is loaded, we call the `feedLoaded()` function with the XML data in the `result` variable.

Inside the `feedLoaded()` function, we get references to three <DIV> tags. None of this is required to display the stock information in 3D, but these are shown in order to provide us with a learning opportunity and to better understand the data in XML format:

```
var table = document.getElementById('tablePrintOut');
var price = document.getElementById('price');
var changeAmt = document.getElementById('change');
```

The `table` tag will be the complete stock information already formatted nicely in an HTML table. The `price` tag and `changeAmt` <DIV> tags will display the results in text below our WebGL display to assist us in understanding the parsing process.

Next, we parse the XML file. A condensed version of this actual stock data was shown earlier within the <item> tags containing a <description> tag that contains **CDATA**. To get to CDATA, we must parse our way through the <item> tag to the <description> tag. If we start instead by requesting the <description> tag first, we will get the <description> tag located inside the <channel> tag. So, we must start with the <item> tag and parse our way to the <description> tag:

```
var items = result.xmlDocument.getElementsByTagName('item');
```

In this example, we only have one item—the single *AAPL* stock—but we still use the items array inside a `for` loop as if we are going to parse multiple stocks, which we will perform later:

```
for (var i = 0; i < items.length; i++) {
    var item = items[i];

    // Get the description from the element.
    // firstChild is the text node containing the first data set
    var description =
        item.getElementsByTagName('description')
    [0].firstChild.nodeValue;
        table.innerHTML = description;
```

The `description` variable is all the data parsed inside the `<description>` tags of the XML file. There is a single `<description>` tag within the `<item>` tag, so the array index value equals zero. The `firstChild` function represents the block of CDATA, and `nodeValue` is all the data within (and including) the `<table>` and `</table>` tags. The final line places the raw, unedited HTML `<table>` `</table>` data inside the table `<DIV>` tags. This HTML table will be overlaid onto our 3D scene.

Our final step is to parse the CDATA `<table>` information, which is saved in the `description` variable, to extract the current stock price of `501.114` and the price change for the day as `+2.434` contained in an HTML table. A partial listing of the data shows the current stock price after the word `Last` with the change in price for the day following it:

```
<table border=0 cellspacing=0 cellpadding=0 width="200"> <TR
bgcolor="#DDDDDD"> <TD ALIGN="LEFT" COLSPAN=2 nowrap><a href="http://
www.nasdaq.com/symbol/aapl">AAPL</a>   </TD> </TR> <TR
bgcolor="#EEEEEE"> <TD nowrap width="50%"> Last </TD> <TD nowrap
align=right width="50%">501.114 </TD> </TR> <TR bgcolor="#DDDDDD">
<TD nowrap width="50%"> Change </TD> <TD nowrap align=right
width="50%"><font color="green">+<img src=http://www.nasdaq.com/
images/greenarrowsmall.gif >2.434</font>
```

We know that the stock price follows the word `Last`, so locate `Last` and then parse data using the `>` and `<` HTML characters to isolate the data we want. The following is the substring command that excludes the text after the word `Last`:

```
priceDescriptn =
    description.substring( description.indexOf("Last"),
    description.length );
```

Getting the preceding substring leaves us with the following remaining text:

```
Last </TD> <TD nowrap align=right width="50%">501.114 < . . .
```

The next substring command searches for `<TD`:

```
priceDescriptn =
    priceDescriptn.substring(priceDescriptn.indexOf("<TD"),
    priceDescriptn.length );
```

This code leaves us with the following string:

```
<TD nowrap align=right width="50%">501.114 < . . .
```

Now, we find the next `>` character and increment one space over the `>` character:

```
priceDescriptn =
    priceDescriptn.substring(priceDescriptn.indexOf(">")+1,
    priceDescriptn.length );
```

The code leaves us with the following string:

```
501.114 < . . .
```

Finally, grab the data before `<`, leaving us with just the stock price (501.114):

```
priceDescriptn = priceDescriptn.substring
    (0, priceDescriptn.indexOf("<") );
```

Parsing for the price change activity uses a similar technique, although we also have to get the plus or minus sign, which is then followed by the actual price change. The +/- sign and stock price change are contained within separate HTML tags. It is tedious, but once done, you get into the habit of parsing XML and HTML.

We end by setting two global variables used by the 3D program, `stockPrice` and `changePrice`.

Finally, we get to some familiar WebGL. In the `drawScene()` function called for every frame, we calculate the percent of price change for the day and set the scale for the box. Have a look at the screenshot that follows the code:

```
pctChange = 100*(changePrice / stockPrice);
meshObjectArray[i].scale = [1, pctChange, 1 ];
```

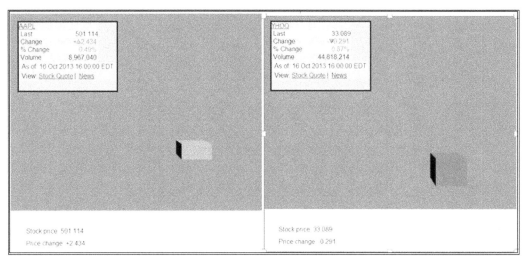

Apple's stock price gained 0.49 percent and Yahoo! lost 0.87 percent today, and thus the box is lower

The original box is 2 x 2 x 2, but we alter the scale matrix based on the percent gain or loss. The box dimensions are from -1 to 1 in both the *x* and *z* dimensions, but from 0 to 2 in the *y* dimension. Thus, if the stock loses money that day, the *y* axis scaling will be negative, which effectively flips the box over vertically.

Next, we set the color of the box. If the gain was 1 percent or higher, it is a solid green. Between 0 and 1 percent, we color the box light green; we color the box light red for losses less than 1 percent, and solid red for losses over 1 percent. There is an exception case if there was a 0 percent change in the stock price: the color will be light blue and at a height of 0.01 units:

```
if (pctChange > 1.0)
    color = [0.0, 1.0, 0.0 ]; // dark green
else if (pctChange > 0.0)
    color = [0.5, 1.0, 0.5 ]; // light green
else if (pctChange == 0.0) {
    meshObjectArray[i].scale = [1, 0.01, 1 ];
    color = [0.5, 0.5, 0.6 ]; // gray
}
else if (pctChange > -1.0)
    color = [1.0, 0.5, 0.5 ]; // light red
else color = [1.0, 0.0, 0.0 ]; // dark red
```

We finish by sending the color to the shader. Note that we did not use a texture map, although that leads us to an opportunity to use a stock logo, for example:

```
gl.uniform3f(shaderProgram.colorUniform,
    color[0], color[1], color[2] );
```

On a final note, the table `<DIV>` tags are listed after the `<Canvas>` tag inside the `<BODY>` tag, and thus print the 3D scene first. These `<DIV>` tags overlay the HTML table data over the 3D scene and then the stock price and price change below the 3D scene.

Objective complete – mini debriefing

The interesting challenge in this example involved getting access to and parsing the stock data. In contrast, the 3D component was relatively simple. With confidence, we'll be able to create more elaborate examples.

Comparing multiple stocks in 3D

After parsing and displaying the data from a single stock, we will now display the data from multiple stocks in a single scene. The level of programming jumps significantly when we grow from showing just a single stock value to showing two or more. We shall do this now by showing data from five stocks.

Engage thrusters

Not surprisingly, growing from displaying one stock to five stocks means that we have to deploy an array constructed with the global variable `var stockBoxObject = [];`. We will build the boxes that will represent our stock data inside `webGLStart()`:

```
stockBoxObject[0] = AddMeshObject
    ("texturedBox0", "texturedBox.obj",
    [-5.5, -3.0, -16.0], [1, 1, 1], [0, 0, 0], false );
  ......
stockBoxObject[4] = AddMeshObject
    ("texturedBox4", "texturedBox.obj",
    [5.5, -3.0, -16.0], [1, 1, 1], [0, 0, 0], false );
```

The boxes are numbered 0 to 4, but only the first box (number 0) and the last box (number 4) are shown in the code, with boxes 1, 2, and 3 having similar code. There are additional arrays where the stock price and price change are initialized with basically the flat boxes' values, `var stockPrice = [100, 100, 100, 100, 100];`, and some default initial values that will be overwritten quickly once the program runs `var changePrice = [-1.5, -.5, 0, .5, 1.5];`. We do not want to leave these values uninitialized. Their actual values will be set once the data is downloaded. If, for example, the stock data did not transmit immediately due to Internet traffic or general latency—a common problem with network software—the code could crash before it starts due to undefined values. Therefore, we just eliminate the issue, which is not visible to the user anyway, but we don't want to take any chances, so we always initialize the values.

NASDAQ has made getting the real-time data for multiple stocks fairly simple for us by generating the following link:

```
http://www.nasdaq.com/aspxcontent/NasdaqRSS.aspx?data=quotes&symbol=A
MAT&symbol=AAPL&symbol=FB&symbol=EBAY&symbol=INTC
```

We randomly selected Applied Materials, Apple, Facebook, eBay, and Intel as identified by their NASDAQ abbreviation stock symbols. As before, Google's code handles the tedious requests from NASDAQ to return these stock values in an XML document. We previously covered the parsing of this XML file. The `<item>` data now contains ten HTML tables, two per stock. We are really only interested in the data from the first pair of these tables. The second set of the `<table>` tags has a link to NASDAQ's website. It is useful information; it is very nicely done, and perhaps might be valuable in order to extend this demo, but we are going to step over that table here. In the previous example, we were only interested in data from the first table and ignored the rest, but now we have to skip over the second set of the `<table>` tags for each stock to get to the next set of stock data.

Tables are bound by the `<TABLE>` and `</TABLE>` HTML tags, so we figure it to be an easy search to skip over the unnecessary tags. Starting from inside the `feedLoaded()` function, as before, we get the data from the `description` node and save the text data in `tableData`:

```
    var description =
        item.getElementsByTagName
        ('description')[0].firstChild.nodeValue;
    var tableData = description;
```

We could have the code read for an almost infinite number of stocks, but we have simplified the example by displaying just five stocks and left the rest as an exercise for the reader. Thus, `stocksTracked` was set to 5.

We progressively parse through the data inside a `for` loop from 0 to 4. We first save the raw HTML table data in the `stockTableData` array. This makes for a nice display when we roll over each 3D rectangle in the scene:

```
YHOO
Last                    33.089
Change                ▼0.291
% Change              0.87%
Volume           44,818,214
As of: 16 Oct 2013 16:00:00 EDT
View: Stock Quote | News
```

Stock data from Yahoo! – already placed inside an HTML table
ready for display. No edits required.

```
for (var stockNum = 0; stockNum < stocksTracked; stockNum++ ) {
    stockTableData[stockNum] =
    tableData.substring( tableData.indexOf("<table>"),
    tableData.indexOf("</TABLE>") );
    tableData = tableData.substring
    (tableData.indexOf("</TABLE>")+1, tableData.length );
    tableData = tableData.substring
    (tableData.indexOf("</TABLE>")+8, tableData.length );
```

The final two lines skip over the second set of the `<table>` tags.

Next, we have the meticulous duty of parsing the actual table data so that we get just the stock price and the price change. The previous example where we displayed a single stock demonstrated this code. We also added just a few new lines of code to handle the rare case that the stock price is unch, or unchanged. We catch the unch value and set it to 0, so we can later perform the math and set the colors of the boxes:

```
        if ( stockPriceChange == "unch" ) {
            stockPriceChange = 0;
        }
        changePrice[stockNum] = parseFloat(stockPriceChange);
    } // end for-loop stock num
```

Finally, we go through the `drawScene()` function that displays the five boxes. Their height is set by the percent of the stock's price change.

```
    pctChange = 100*(changePrice[i] / stockPrice[i]);
    meshObjectArray[i].scale = [1, pctChange, 1 ];
```

Note that the boxes' locations were previously set in `webGLStart()`.

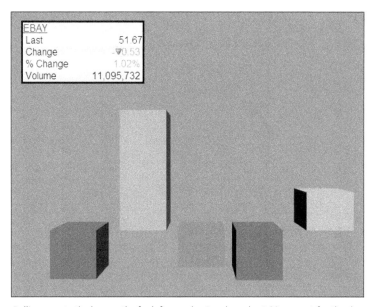

Rolling over to the box on the far left reveals eBay down by 1.02 percent for the day

This is a small example, but we can clearly see which stock is having the best day without having to look at any numbers. With multiple stocks represented by boxes, an ideal scenario is to role the mouse over any box and display the data using HTML5's `hidden` and `visibility` CSS properties.

Much of the `drawScene()` code is left intact from the previous example. The only new functionality added was detection when the mouse rolls over a box. For this, we use code from the previous projects that detects the mouse's *x* and *y* positions and then converts this from 2D screen coordinates into 3D world coordinates. We then test if the *ray*, which is just a line from the camera position of (0, 0, 0) to the 3D world coordinates, intersects any object's bounding box. Note that we have to position and scale the stock's bounding box with the same matrix in which we position and scale the box representing the stock's daily performance, with one additional line of code in `drawScene()`:

```
mat4.set(mvMatrix, meshObjectArray[i].boundingBoxMatrix);
```

The bounding box is later used in the `mouseMoveEvent()` function. The mouse is rolled over the second box from the left. Apple, with a 2.56 percent gain, can be seen in the following screenshot:

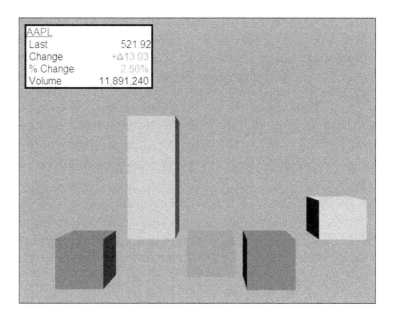

In order to detect any mouse movements, remember to set this up in `webGLStart()` with the following line of code:

```
document.onmousemove = mouseMoveEvent;
```

Inside the `mouseMoveEvent()` function, the mouse's *x* and *y* coordinates are passed in the `event` object. Previous examples used variations of this function to convert the mouse's *x* and *y* position into 3D world coordinates, so we will only review the unique code of detecting a roll-over of a box to display the data here. Of course, if no box is rolled over, then hide the `table` `<DIV>` tag:

```
var overObject = false;
var table = document.getElementById('table');
for (var i = 0; i < stocksTracked; i++ ) {
    if ( RayBoundingBoxIntersection(
        stockBoxObject[i], xWorld, yWorld ) ) {
            table.innerHTML = stockTableData[i];
            overObject = true;
            table.style.visibility = 'visible';
        }
}
if ( !overObject ) {
    table.style.visibility = 'hidden';
}
```

Here, `table` is the ID for the HTML `DIV` tags inside the `<body>` tags of this HTML document. We check if the mouse rolled over any `stockBoxObject`. We are free from checking if one box is closer to the camera than another since there are no overlapping boxes. However, this is good to note if the example is more extensive with hundreds of stocks to check. Once we detect a ray-box intersection, we take the accompanying table data previously parsed, drop it inside the table's `<DIV>` tags, and set the table to be visible. The final three lines just set the table's visibility to hidden if no boxes were rolled over by the mouse.

Objective complete – mini debriefing

One could declare that this chart need not be in 3D. The comparison of just five stocks is well suited for a traditional 2D non-interactive display. However, that misses the big picture. The goal is to bring all the pieces together in a small example. From here, we can list hundreds of stock and walkthrough these charts to identify the best performers or top 10 percent of best or worst all at a glance, and much more quickly than in 2D. This presentation is simply a starting point into a vast universe of data.

Displaying historical stock data

Presenting current real-time data is just one analysis used by investors, but to identify trends and insights, we often use historical data. Since the data is historical, we do not capture it in real time. Historical data is more readily available. NASDAQ, for example, enables one to download a company's stock price closing by days, the past few months, years, or even since the beginning of that stock's history. These are downloaded as `.csv` files, which are comma-separated text data exported and read by Microsoft Excel. Our job is to read these files, parse the data, and display it in 3D.

Engage thrusters

For past demonstrations, we have used the `meshObject.js` JavaScript file to support our work. Since the 3D mesh will be generated based on the data read from a `.csv` file and not from data built from an `.obj` file, it made sense to create a new `csvFile.js` file set of JavaScript functions that replace `meshObject.js` for this example.

The `.csv` files exported by NASDAQ are in rows and columns of data:

```
"date",           "close",        "volume",                "open",
"high",        "low"
"16:00",          "51.95",       "44,956,761",             "53.24",
"53.24",       "51.88"
"2013/10/24",  "52.4450",   "46436620.0000",     "52.3800",
"52.8400",    "51.5928"
"2013/10/23",  "51.9000",   "57037800.0000",     "51.7500",   "52.2500",
"51.1300"
```

Only the second column from the left (the stock's closing price) is of importance to us, although we could present some very interesting 3D scenes using the volume in addition to high and low price data. As we read in these closing prices, we will build our 3D mesh that will appear like a flat ribbon. The data will be saved in our new `cvsFileObject`. All of these objects—one for each stock read—will be saved in `stockArray` constructed by a call to `CreateStockObject()` in `cvsFile.js`. After declaring two global variables, `totalCSVfiles = 0;` and `var stockArray = [];`, we make our function calls to begin parsing these data files:

```
stockArray[totalCSVfiles] = CreateStockObject
    ("Nvidia", "NVidiaHistoricalQuotes.csv", [0, -20.0, -28.0],
    [ .2, .8, .2 ]  );
totalCSVfiles++;
```

This sets up the reading of the file of stock data of nVidia, the graphics chip producer, for the past three months. The call to `CreateStockObject()` sets the translation (location) and color of the 3D mesh, but its major responsibility is to use AJAX technology to read the CSV data file and inform us when the `.csv` file has been downloaded:

```
function CreateStockObject
    (stockName, csvFile, stockTranslation, stockColor ) {
    // Adds a new .csv file
    stockObject = new csvFileObject();
    stockObject.name = stockName;

    if (csvFile != null) loadAJAXcsvFile( csvFile, stockObject );
    stockObject.translation = stockTranslation;
    stockObject.color = stockColor;
    return stockObject;
} // end CreateStockObject
```

The call to `loadAJAXcvsFile()` uses AJAX technology to download the `.cvs` file in the background and inform us when that task is complete. We set `fileLoaded` to `true` in order to inform the main program that the file is in our possession, and we can now parse the complete file. The file's text data is saved in `csvFileObject.string`. Since we don't need the first line, which is just header data, we make our first call to `ParseCVSfile()`, which in turn calls `GetLine()`. This reads the first line that consists of six pieces of data, all contained inside double quotes.

In this example, we read in the stock data from four different companies: nVidia, Intel, AMD, and Yahoo!. The `tick()` program is called per frame to enable animation. We are also using `tick()` to check when the `.cvs` files have arrived and can then proceed to build our mesh:

```
for ( var csvFile = 0; csvFile < totalCSVfiles; csvFile++ ) {
    if ( stockArray[ csvFile ].fileLoaded &&
    !stockArray[ csvFile ].meshCreated) {
        initBuffers( stockArray[ csvFile ] );
        stockArray[ csvFile ].meshCreated = true;
    }
}
```

Once we receive the signal display that `stockArray[ csvFile ].fileLoaded` is true, we will call `initBuffers()` to create our 3D mesh representing the stock's daily closing price.

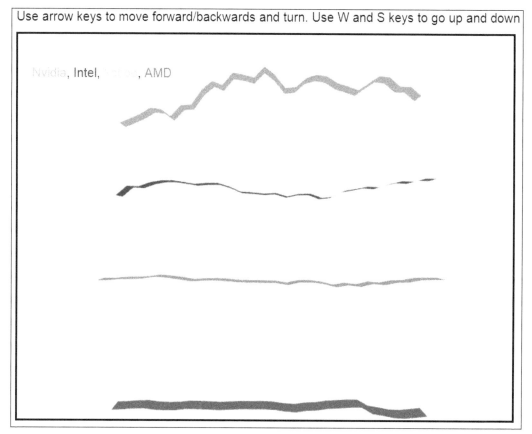

A display of the closing prices of various stocks for the past 30 business days

The `initBuffers()` function parses the data, although there is only one (the closing price) of the six pieces of important data, which becomes the *y* value to show the stock moving up and down.

Two arrays that will become the buffers loaded in the graphics card are `stockVertices = [];` and `stockVertexNormals = [];`. For this demonstration, we are limiting this application to closing stock prices of the past 30 business days, where each day will be one unit in the positive *x* direction. Since the data begins with the most recent day first, we start on the right side and work our way backwards along the negative *x* axis. Thus, to center the data, we begin at 15 units in the *x* direction and subtract 1 unit per day.

An interesting implementation of this code is the application of the **triangle strip array**. Unlike most 3D meshes with an index buffer that specifies which vertices are connected to form each polygon, a triangle strip array is more efficient. A triangle strip array connects the first three vertices, and then each new vertex connects to the previous two. For example, vertices 1, 2, and 3 connect to form our first polygon. When we add the fourth vertex, it connects with the two previous vertices, vertex 2 and 3, to construct the second polygon from vertices 2, 3, and 4. Vertex 5 connects with vertexes 3 and 4 to form the third polygon, and so on.

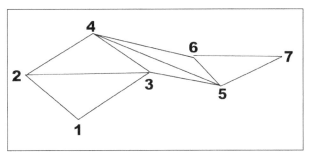

Triangle strip array

In the previous figure, vertices 1, 2, and 3 connect to form our first polygon. Vertex 4 is added to the previous two vertices to form a polygon (2, 3, 4). Vertex 5 connects to vertices 3 and 4 to form another polygon.

The width of the stock ribbon was chosen to be 2 units, so the *z* values are +1 and -1. We could have calculated the normals of each polygon so that the ribbon would shade slightly as the stock goes up and down. However, this shading was very subtle, so we decided to keep it simple and use a flat color per stock.

Each closing price added to the stock ribbon consists of two vertices. Each vertex consists of three values (*x*, *y*, *z*). Thus, each stock data point consists of six values; two vertices multiplied by three values (*x*, *y*, *z*) for each vertex.

```
for (var dataPoints = 0; dataPoints <
    stockDataPoints; dataPoints++ ) {
        var str = GetLine( csvFileObj );

    // Include the first vertex with x, y, z values
    stockVertices[ dataPoints*6 ] = stockLineX;
    stockVertices[ dataPoints*6+1 ] =
        parseFloat(str[1].replace(/,/g,''));
    stockVertices[ dataPoints*6+2 ] = 1.0;

    // Include the second vertex with the same x and
    // y values, and z values 1 and -1
    stockVertices[ dataPoints*6+3 ] = stockLineX;
    stockVertices[ dataPoints*6+4 ] =
        parseFloat(str[1].replace(/,/g,''));
    stockVertices[ dataPoints*6+5 ] = -1.0;

    // Each vertex normal points straight up
    stockVertexNormals[ dataPoints*6    ] = 0.0;
    stockVertexNormals[ dataPoints*6+1 ] = 1.0;
    stockVertexNormals[ dataPoints*6+2 ] = 0.0;

    stockVertexNormals[ dataPoints*6+3 ] = 0.0;
    stockVertexNormals[ dataPoints*6+4 ] = 1.0;
    stockVertexNormals[ dataPoints*6+5 ] = 0.0;

    stockLineX--;
}
```

One interesting line of code is `parseFloat(str[1].replace(/,/g,''))`. The closing stock price is obtained as text. The JavaScript `parseFloat()` command converts text to a floating point number. The `replace()` function parses out the commas found with stock values above 1000. Without this `replace()` function, the `parseFloat()` function will only parse until the first comma and thus not work correctly.

The rest of the `initBuffers()` code loads the buffers, which are part of each stock's `cvsFileObject`. When we return from `initBuffers()`, everything is set to render the stock ribbon, so we set `stockArray[ csvFile ].meshCreated = true;`.

Much of the code inside `drawScene()` reflects previous examples. Before rendering any individual stock ribbons, we check if the mesh has been created.

```
if ( stockArray[ csvFile ].meshCreated ) {
```

Since this is a triangle strip array, there is no index buffer to load. Also, the `drawArray()` function no longer specifies the `TRIANGLE` data, but instead a `TRIANGLE_STRIP` data.

```
gl.drawArrays(gl.TRIANGLE_STRIP, 0, stockArray
    [ csvFile ].stockVertexPositionBuffer.numItems);
```

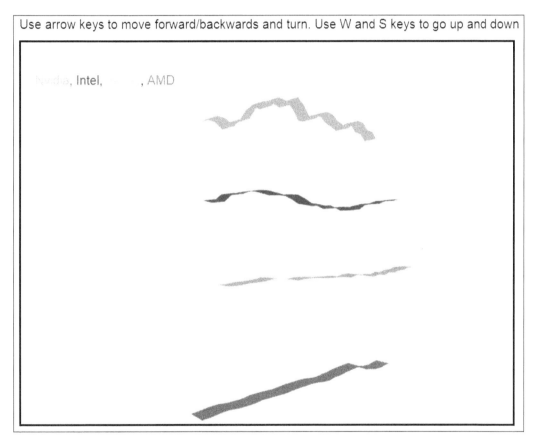

Use arrow keys to move forward/backwards and turn. Use W and S keys to go up and down

, Intel,   , AMD

The camera moved up and rotated around for a better view

Objective complete – mini debriefing

We successfully displayed the performance of multiple stocks over 30 business days. However, a few new problems may have become obvious, while other issues may not be so obvious. First, our stocks do not have the same starting price, so how can we tell if one stock is performing better than the other? Yahoo! certainly jumped up and down the most, but that does not indicate which stock has performed the best or worst. In addition, all the stocks that are shown have prices between $3 and $50. What happens if we try to display a stock such as Apple that most recently was selling for $500, or Google that hovers around $1000 per share? Neither would be visible unless we pulled the camera way out or moved our camera pretty high. Clearly, there is a better way to do this.

Presenting comparative data

To compare the performance of various stocks, we need an equal starting point. However, each stock has its own starting price. Thus, we need to adjust the data so that each begins at the same point.

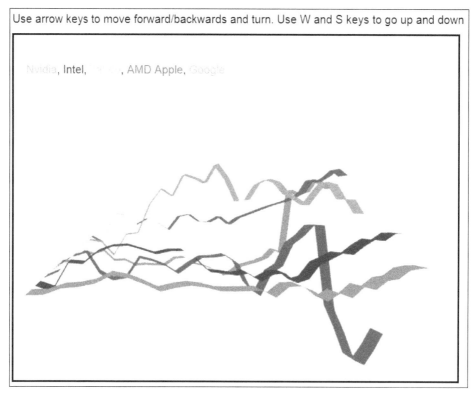

Comparing the performance of six stocks from September to mid-October, 2013

Engage thrusters

We will not know the starting point until we read in the entire file, which in our case is the past 30 days. Once we read in all 30 closing prices for each of our stocks, we will divide all 30 daily closing prices by the first day's closing price. That sets our first day's closing price equal to 1. This means that all the stocks we compare will have the same starting point. Every closing price thereafter will be a percent change. However, stock prices vary daily by about 1 percent or less. Such a chart will look almost flat. Therefore, we multiply each value by a multiplier that will accentuate the daily closing stock price. In this example, we multiply each value by 50 so that a 10 percent gain will appear as an increase of 50 units.

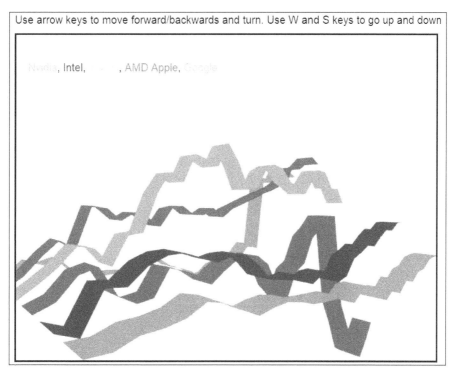

We can move the camera forward and upward for a detailed comparison

Inside `InitBuffer()`, we determine the `multiplyFactor` value by obtaining the *y* value of the last data point (we read in closing stock prices from most recent to 30 days back—that is how NASDAQ exports these `.csv` files). Then, we multiply all the *y* values and get a very interesting chart that is valuable for comparisons:

```
// determine the multiply factor using the last y-value
// while the value 50.0 was selected to what looked best
var multiplyFactor = 50.0 / stockVertices [ (stockDataPoints-1)*6+4 ];
// now multiply every y-value
```

```
for (var dataPoints = 0; dataPoints < stockDataPoints;
    dataPoints++ ) {
        stockVertices[ dataPoints*6+1 ] =
            stockVertices[ dataPoints*6+1 ] * multiplyFactor;
        stockVertices[ dataPoints*6+4 ] =
            stockVertices[ dataPoints*6+4 ] * multiplyFactor;
}
```

Objective complete – mini debriefing

We now have some interesting comparative data, virtually unlimited in 3D space as we can have hundreds of stocks to travel through—clearly, something not possible in traditional 2D charts, but walking through data presents new opportunities.

Zooming into the data – level of detail

One area where 3D shows off its capability is in the **level of detail**. This is a technique where as we get closer to an object, we see more details. As we pull away from the object, we simplify the scene by substituting the 3D mesh with one with fewer polygons. This is akin to the zoom in and zoom out feature of Google Maps when looking from entire continents down to a street map view. In 3D, level of detail ensures that we are not rendering excess polygons that are not more than a few pixels on the screen.

Level of detail can also be effective in presenting data. In the upcoming example, we are showing a year's worth of closing stock price. In a typical year, the stock market operates for 250 days. However, at a distance, we only need to see month-end data points (13 total data points for the starting month plus data points at the end of the 12 months). As we drill into the data, we display 50 weekly data points, and finally, as we navigate further, we display each day's market activity for the year.

There is one other feature in this example besides level of detail, and that is the lighting of the polygons so that large stock gains are lit differently due to slight changes in the stock price.

The shading of the stock ribbon is determined by the **normal** of the polygon. The normal can be thought of as a perpendicular or a line at a right angle to the polygon. For example, using a flat table, the normal of the tabletop would point straight up toward the ceiling. In the past projects, we used normals generated by the 3D modeling tools included inside the .obj file. Now, we are creating our own polygons representing stock price activity. Since we are creating our own polygons, we also need to create the polygon normals.

Prepare for lift off

There are a few steps to calculate a polygon's normal:

- Find the edges of the polygon in the (x, y, z) format
- Calculate the cross-product of any two of the three edges
- Make the normal a unit vector (of length one)

First, calculate the edges of the polygon by subtracting the x, y, z values from one vertex to the next in a counter-clockwise manner. Begin by labeling the vertices "0", "1", and "2" in a counter-clockwise order (it does not matter which vertex is designated vertex 0).

Edge a = *Vertex 1 (x, y, z) - Vertex 0 (x, y, z)*. Using the following diagram, edge a = *(1, 3, 1) - (3, 0, 2) = (1-3, 3-0, 1-2) = (-2, 3, -1)*.

Edge b = *(-2, -1, -1) - (1, 3, 1) = (-3, -4, -2)* and edge c = *(5, 1, -3)*. Note that by adding the three edges, we get (0, 0, 0):

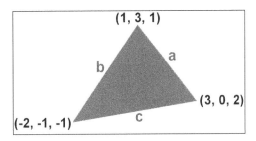

Sample polygon used to demonstrate how to calculate normals

Next, we use the cross-product formula, $a \times b$ (read as *a cross b*, not multiply):

$$a \times b = (a_y b_z - a_z b_y, a_z b_x - a_x b_z, a_x b_y - a_y b_x)$$
$$a \times b = (-2, 3, -1) \times (-3, -4, -2) = (3(-2) - (-1)(-4), (-1)(-3) - (-2)(-2), (-2)(-4) - 3(-3))$$
$$= (-6 - 4, 3 - 4, 8 - (-9)) = (-10, -1, 17)$$

Note that regardless of which two edges are used, $a \times b$, $b \times c$, or $c \times a$, we would come up with the same value (-10, -1, 17).

Shaders have a `normalize` command that converts the normal to a unit value, but let's complete the exercise by showing how we convert a vector to a unit value. Incidentally, it is proper to say that we normalize the normal:

Normalize(x, y, z) = (x, y, z) / sqrt(x² + y² + z²)
Normalize(-10, -1, 17) = (-10, -1, 17) / sqrt((-10)² + (-1)² + 17²)
= (-10, -1, 17) / sqrt((-10)² + (-1)² + 17²)
= (-10, -1, 17) / sqrt(390)
= (-10, -1, 17) / 19.75
= (-0.506, -0.051, 0.861)

Knowing how normals are generated allows us to also manipulate them. Perturbing normals can give the appearance of waves or bumpy surfaces without changing the shape of an object. Now, let us use normals to shade our stock market ribbons.

Engage thrusters

Our `cvsFileObject` already contained `stockVertexPositionBuffer` and `stockVertexNormalBuffer`. To enable level of detail, we create two additional buffers, one for the weekly data that is every fifth day of activity, and another for every twentieth day of activity representing a month. Therefore, our four new buffers are:

- `stockVertex5PositionBuffer`
- `stockVertex5NormalBuffer`
- `stockVertex20PositionBuffer`
- `stockVertex20NormalBuffer`

Beyond these four new variables, this file is identical to `cvsFile.js`.

We defined a new function, `GenerateNormals(stockVertices, stockVertexNormals);`, which calculates all the normals. We covered the algorithm previously, and thus we will not detail the code here.

Using all the available data points with the newly calculated normals, we get the following image that shows the four stocks fluctuating daily:

View of stock performance for a year for four high-tech companies

Now, we calculate the other levels of detail as we pull the camera away. To get the weekly stock data, we just grab every fifth data point. Note how the code divides the number of data points by 5, `stockDataPoints/5`:

```
// weekly data
for (var dataPoints = 0; dataPoints <= stockDataPoints/5;
    dataPoints++ ) {
    stockVertices5[dataPoints*6] = stockVertices[dataPoints*30];
    stockVertices5[dataPoints*6+1]=stockVertices[dataPoints*30+1];
    stockVertices5[dataPoints*6+2]=stockVertices[dataPoints*30+2];
    stockVertices5[dataPoints*6+3]=stockVertices[dataPoints*30+3];
    stockVertices5[dataPoints*6+4]=stockVertices[dataPoints*30+4];
    stockVertices5[dataPoints*6+5]=stockVertices[dataPoints*30+5];
}
GenerateNormals(stockVertices5, stockVertexNormals5);

// Note the buffers and arrays are for every 5th data point
csvFileObj.stockVertex5PositionBuffer = gl.createBuffer();
gl.bindBuffer(gl.ARRAY_BUFFER,
    csvFileObj.stockVertex5PositionBuffer);
```

```
gl.bufferData(gl.ARRAY_BUFFER, new Float32Array(stockVertices5),
    gl.STATIC_DRAW);
csvFileObj.stockVertex5PositionBuffer.itemSize = 3;
csvFileObj.stockVertex5PositionBuffer.numItems =
    stockDataPoints * 2/5;

csvFileObj.stockVertex5NormalBuffer = gl.createBuffer();
gl.bindBuffer(gl.ARRAY_BUFFER,
    csvFileObj.stockVertex5NormalBuffer);

gl.bufferData(gl.ARRAY_BUFFER,
    new Float32Array(stockVertexNormals5), gl.STATIC_DRAW);
csvFileObj.stockVertex5NormalBuffer.itemSize = 3;
csvFileObj.stockVertex5NormalBuffer.numItems =
    stockDataPoints * 2/5;
```

The setup of buffers for the monthly data at every twentieth data point will be virtually the same as the weekly data, except with divisions and multiplications by 20 instead of 5.

In `drawScene()`, we choose which set of vertices to render—the daily, weekly, or monthly stock prices—based on the distance between the camera's *z* value and the stock ribbon's *z* value. If the camera's *z* value is less than 16 units from the location of the stock ribbon, then the graph displays the detailed daily stock values. Between 16 and 32 units, the graph display uses the weekly data, and beyond 32 units, it uses the monthly data.

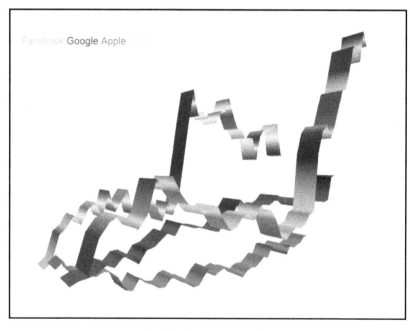

Stock performance by week

```
//since the color will be the same regardless of level-of-detail,
//setting the color for the shader was moved above.
gl.uniform3f(shaderProgram.colorUniform,
    stockArray[ csvFile ].color[0],
    stockArray[ csvFile ].color[1],
    stockArray[ csvFile ].color[2] );

if (Math.abs(eye[2]-stockArray[ csvFile ].translation[2]) < 16 ) {
// Level-of-Detail: closest
    gl.bindBuffer(gl.ARRAY_BUFFER,
        stockArray[ csvFile ].stockVertexPositionBuffer);
    gl.vertexAttribPointer(shaderProgram.vertexPositionAttribute,
        stockArray[ csvFile ].stockVertexPositionBuffer.itemSize,
    gl.FLOAT, false, 0, 0);
    gl.bindBuffer(gl.ARRAY_BUFFER,
        stockArray[ csvFile ].stockVertexNormalBuffer);

    gl.vertexAttribPointer(shaderProgram.vertexNormalAttribute,
        stockArray[ csvFile ].stockVertexNormalBuffer.itemSize,
    gl.FLOAT, false, 0, 0);
    gl.drawArrays(gl.TRIANGLE_STRIP, 0,
        stockArray[ csvFile ].stockVertexPositionBuffer.numItems);
}
else if ( Math.abs(eye[2] - stockArray[ csvFile ].translation[2])
    < 32 ){
    // Level-of-Detail: middle
    // use stockVertex5PositionBuffer and stockVertex5NormalBuffer
....
}
else {
    // Level-of-Detail: furthest
    // use stockVertex20PositionBuffer
    // and stockVertex20NormalBuffer
....
}
```

There is one additional change in the vertex shader. In the previous examples, the normal for each vertex was set to (0, 1, 0), which meant that the color of the stock ribbon would not vary despite the ups and downs of stock market activity. Now, we calculated the normals; thus, we have to normalize the normals. A line of code in the vertex shader has to be changed. Previously, the line was as follows:

```
vTransformedNormal = uNMatrix * vec3(aVertexNormal);
```

This line of code is now changed to the following:

```
vTransformedNormal = uNMatrix * normalize(vec3(aVertexNormal));
```

Inside the fragment shader, we had a single light pointing straight down. An artist may suggest other ways to light this scene.

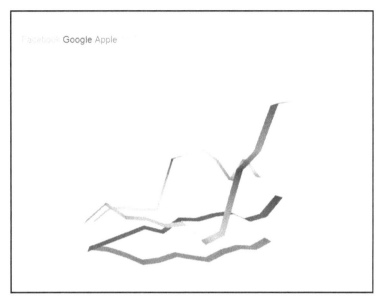

Monthly stock data from the furthest camera position. Facebook has had a good year!

Objective complete – mini debriefing

This demonstration featured two concepts unique to 3D programming: level of detail, where more details are revealed when the camera gets closer to the 3D mesh, and generating our own normals for shading. The next exercise is to include hundreds or thousands of stocks. Within these, we could add interactivity to reveal the best performers, market trends, and analytical parameters to predict stock activity. In other words, WebGL may give developers an advantage over stock analysts.

Mission accomplished

This project introduced ways to visualize *Big Data*. We used XML data from external content providers, used online tools to parse the data, and presented the information in 3D. We could easily broaden this example to include other forms of data beyond stocks, such as demographic trends, geographical mapping, or data mining. Then we will begin to see why 3D is the best way to visualize Big Data.

Project 7

Adapting Architecture, Medical, and Mechanical Engineering to Web3D

"Pay no attention to that man behind the curtain."

– Wizard of Oz

All content is now driven to the Internet. Any press release, documentation, software program, legal briefing, statistics, or transcript goes on the Web. Nearly all multimedia—video and audio—is streaming across the Web, but what about 3D designs? We see online gaming in massive multiuser environments. But much of that content came off a DVD—the character meshes, scenery, and the code itself. The online data component is quite small, usually just data packets sent among the players to specify one's position and actions.

It seems natural to take 3D models built by architects, mechanical engineers, and animators to the Web. WebGL is an obvious choice—the right technology to display this 3D content. But herein lies the problem of taking content designed for one medium and repurposing it for another. Generally, those 3D models are built for preciseness and precision. File size is hardly a factor for an architect or mechanical engineer. Mechanical drawings often go from the designer straight to the manufacturing and production process. Manufacturing tolerances are measured to 10 decimal points—thousandths of millimeters—less than the width of human hair. The result can be file sizes from megabytes to several gigabytes—hardly anything that can be downloaded in a few seconds. And even if the Internet connection speed were increased by many factors, we would run into the next bottleneck of rendering such a massive file in real time.

Repurposing content from one medium to another is not new. Live theater was the guide for motion pictures. But one could not just place a camera on a stage, film it, and call it a movie. The content had to be changed to fit the medium. The work of architects and mechanical engineers will also require them to contour their content to the medium of WebGL. Fortunately, many **Computer-aided Design (CAD)** tools include options to reduce the precision of their content from 10 decimal points down to three, and export very low polygon versions of their content. And just as movies grew from live theater enabling new content, so too may architectural drawings contoured for the Web create new opportunities such as dynamic lighting, walkthrough architectural designs, and interactivity.

Architecture is not buildings

When we think of architecture, naturally we think of buildings. And indeed, due to the proliferation of CAD, that is what we see as its output – the blueprint of a building. And much can similarly be said for the design work of mechanical engineers – the detailed design and assembly of parts to make up some final components, from the layout of an assembly line down to the individual bolts. The medical field has also made effective use of 3D graphic design tools to simulate heartbeats or design the crown on a tooth. Some of this output goes directly to the production process known as **Computer-aided Modeling (CAM)**. In the past, these were milling operations designing molds for mass production. Now, 3D printers can take this output to build the parts. The output designed by architects and mechanical engineers are 3D models. And to WebGL, 3D models are the canvas for us to paint on through textures and lighting. We will investigate the techniques for controlling the appearance of architecture using shader languages.

Mission briefing

Look around your environment – your house, workplace, or neighborhood. Everything was designed by an architect, engineer, designer, or artist. Nearly all of that was first drawn on a blueprint, sketched onto paper, or most likely, designed by a computer. We are not going to replace these designers, nor do we want to. Instead, we want to take the output of these craftsmen and enhance it for interactive 3D for the Web.

Why is it awesome?

Reflections add a sense of realism to what is essentially an Internet browser on a 2D computer screen. While specular highlights provide visual cues of the Sun and bright lights in a scene, reflection between 3D meshes creates a sense of actual materials such as polished metal or glass. Refraction creates the realism of other surfaces so that water isn't just a 3D mesh with a blue tint, but instead the physics of light traveling through liquids or partially transparent materials such as stained glass.

Few surfaces in nature are smooth either. Most have bumpy exteriors, from the Moon to an orange. Tree bark, brick walls, pavement, clothing, and furniture all have irregular surfaces. Most are bumpy, indented, weathered, and worn. This also adds character, so we shall learn ways to create irregular surfaces that look correct, and even amaze users.

Finally, one of the cool implementations of 3D rendering is the ability to create a texture map in real time from a camera inside the scene. This enables special effects such as multiple views of the world rendered from different viewpoints as if we were viewing a panel of security cameras in the same environment.

Your Hotshot objectives

We will perform the following tasks:

- Demonstrating environment mapping for reflections
- Bending of light – calculating refraction for surfaces such as water
- Creating surfaces – depth, non-smooth, natural, and realistic with normal maps
- Rendering a scene as a texture to view multiple cameras simultaneously

Mission checklist

Before starting, you will need a six-sided image in a cube format, as if the world were textured 360 degrees inside a cube. An Internet search on environment or cube maps will provide a lot of nice resources. There is a specific file naming format that must be followed, which is described later. You will also need a nice object to reflect, preferably with a lot of curves, such as the default teapot that comes with all 3D modeling programs. A 3D model of a car also makes for a nice demo since it reflects objects well.

Demonstrating environment mapping for reflections

One of the great techniques of computer graphics is reflections. The truest reflection is looking through a mirror. Since mirrors generally have no distortion, this can be achieved by rendering from a second camera. Most reflections are of other surfaces such as metal, a pane of glass, or water (such as a still lake). If the scene contains multiple reflective surfaces, it grows in complexity. Such photorealism is beyond the capabilities of WebGL, for now. But like so much in computer graphics, we deploy techniques to accomplish a close representation of reflections – environment maps. Essentially, an environment map is created by placing 3D object(s), such as the car, inside a cube where each of the six sides of the cube is texture mapped with the surrounding environment. The top of the cube may be the sky, the bottom of the cube the ground, and the four sides would be images looking north, east, west, and south.

Prepare for lift off

Light is created by photons traveling in all directions. Eventually, a few of these photons enter our eye pupils and interact with the receptors in our eyeballs, which in turn generate an image interpreted by our brains. Computers will never be able to simulate this, simply because computers cannot run at the speed of light, nor can they perform all the calculations for these bouncing photons, nor can computers manage the billions of photons traveling in space.

Since only a fraction of photons do reach our eyes, the technique for creating photorealism was solved by reversing the direction of the photons. Starting from our eyes, we work backwards, sending rays in all directions that represent photons. Most rays will hit an object where we can test which light(s) are shining at that particular point. If the ray hits a nonreflective surface such as wood or concrete, we can stop there. If the object is transparent, such as a window, then the ray will pass through until it hits a nontransparent object. And if the object is reflective, such as the surface of a car, some of the car's color will make up the pixel, but the ray will bounce off the car until it hits another object such as a tree or building, which will then be reflected in the car. These rays make up the technique known as **ray tracing**.

Rays can split if the surface is partially transparent and curved, such as an empty glass. Ray tracing can indeed become quite complex. There is a technique beyond ray tracing, radiosity, which takes into account the heat generated by a surface. For example, a white surface in a red room will have some of that red bleed into the white surface. The root word in radiosity is radiate (as in radiating heat). Some of the more advanced game engines, such as Frostbite (http://www.frostbite.com/), have techniques to simulate radiosity. Ray splitting and radiosity are the next frontier, but expect innovations sooner than you think to conquer those.

Here, we will implement environment mapping, a technique that places objects inside a textured box—each side of the box having its own texture map—and reflects those images onto the 3D mesh, giving the appearance of a reflective, silver, or metal object.

Engage thrusters

Once again, we deploy the teapot with its nice varied curves, and thus a favorite among the computer graphics community. The images are from `http://www.humus.name`, which has a wonderful variety of cube maps. The following screenshot is a cube map stitched together from six individual images. On the far right of the following screenshot is `Fatbursparken_Stockholm-negz.jpg`, the image in front of our camera; and the center image, `Fatbursparken_Stockholm-posz.jpg`, is behind our camera and will be reflected in the teapot:

Image from Fatbursparken, Stockholm; courtesy http://www.humus.name

We load the objects as we have traditionally done so far. Have a look at the following line of code:

```
cubeMapObject = AddMeshObject("cubeMapObject", "cubemap.obj",
    [0, 0, -distanceToViewPlane], [1, 1, 1], [0, 0, 0], true );
```

However, there is one exception to our usual method – note the `true` value set as the last argument. Inside `mesh3dObject.js`, this indicates the object contains a textured cube consisting of six images instead of a single texture map, and so it calls the `initCubeMapTextures()` function instead. Two important changes from a regular texture map are that instead of `gl.TEXTURE_2D` as a parameter for many of the initialization functions, we use `gl.TEXTURE_CUBE_MAP`. Also, `cubemap.obj` references `cubemap.mtl`, which lists one of the texture maps for this code: `Fatbursparken_Stockholm-negz.jpg`. The `initCubeMapTextures()` function parses this filename to get the first part, `Fatbursparken_Stockholm`, and appends the file endings, `pos` or `neg` plus *x*, *y*, or *z* to get all six texture map filenames. Have a look at the following screenshot:

Teapot with texture map reflection

Inside `drawScene()`, the following is just one line of code to bind the texture to the texture sampler, so it can be referenced in the shader, which is shown as follows:

```
gl.bindTexture(gl.TEXTURE_CUBE_MAP, cubeMapObject.textureMap);
```

This looks similar to other bind texture commands, except `TEXTURE_CUBE_MAP` is specified. The rest of the work takes place inside the shader language.

In the vertex shader, we calculate the reflection using the `reflect(vec3, vec3)` method defined by the OpenGL ES implementation. The reflection calculation can be found at `http://www.khronos.org/opengles/sdk/docs/manglsl/xhtml/reflect.xml`. And the entire documentation can be found at `http://www.khronos.org/opengles/sdk/docs/manglsl/`.

The normal vector is calculated in a similar manner to how we have calculated it in previous examples of vertex shaders: we multiply the vertex normal by the Normal matrix. The Normal matrix is a subset of the object's Transformation matrix. A Transformation matrix rotates, moves (translates), and scales each vertex so the entire 3D mesh rotates and moves. Normals are vectors and are not affected by the 3D object's movement (translation). But if the 3D mesh is rotated, the Normal vectors must be similarly rotated. The Normal matrix is just a copy of the 3D object's rotation matrix. For example, if a vertex normal were pointing straight up and the object moved a few units to the left, the vertex normal would still point straight up. But if the object rotated 90 degrees clockwise (to the right), then the vertex normal, multiplied by the Normal matrix, would also point 90 degrees to the right.

Inside the vertex shader, the `worldview` value, also known as the Incident vector, is a vector from the camera to each vertex. The `reflect(vec3, vec3)` method calculates `ReflectDir`, the ray that would bounce off the surface of the 3D mesh—in this case, the teapot—to the cube texture map, as shown in the following code:

```
vec3 worldNorm = vec3( uNMatrix * aVertexNormal );
vec3 worldView = normalize( uCameraEye - vPosition.xyz );
ReflectDir = reflect( -worldView, worldNorm );
```

The following figure shows an incident vector (`worldView`) from the camera to each pixel and the normal:

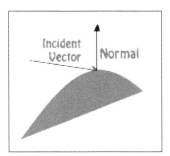

Finally, inside the fragment shader, we use another built-in OpenGL ES function, shown in the following line of code, to get the pixel from `ReflectDir` (reflection direction) against the cube map:

```
vec4 reflectColor = textureCube( uCubemap, ReflectDir );
```

Classified intel

One of the nice additions to reflections is the inclusion of specular highlights. These are the shiny spots that we often see on the hood of a car on a sunny day. Specular highlights previously required a complex equation and even then were an imprecise estimate interpolated between vertices. Instead of calculating on a pixel-by-pixel basis, we could only calculate specular highlights at each vertex, and the brightness of the pixels between vertices were an approximation. But with shader languages, we can create an accurate specular highlight with a bright center circle, plus the fall off of light at the edges. Specular highlights can now be calculated on a per-pixel basis. The following screenshot shows how the scene is reflected in the surface of our metal teapot:

A spotlight aimed directly at the teapot provides the bright specular highlight just to the right of the tower

There is no one best way to calculate specular highlights. As with so much of computer graphics, we have to balance between the physical world and what can be calculated reasonably well while maintaining frame rates of at least 30 fps (frames per second) and hopefully around 60 fps. The issue is compounded for web development because we do not know the performance of the user's computer, unlike game programming, where we are developing for a target hardware such as an Xbox or PlayStation.

Specular highlights move with the viewer's point of view. This is different than other lighting algorithms, which are the same regardless of where one is standing. Have a look at the following figure:

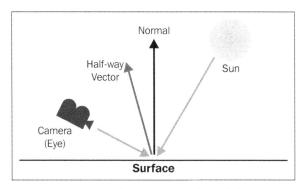

Components of calculating specular highlights

The quick implementation prior to the introduction of shader languages was to calculate a halfway vector between `eyeDirection`—the vector from the camera to the surface—and the light source to the surface, depicted as the Sun. The cosine of the angle between the halfway vector and the surface's normal would be taken to the power of the `shininess` value. For example, if the angle between the halfway vector and the surface normal were 0 degrees, then the cosine(0) would be 1. The shininess value varies from 0 to 127; the lower the number, the shinier the surface. For example, polished metal would have a small value while tree bark is not shiny at all and thus would have a high number. In our example, we used `32` for the shininess value, so 1 to the thirty-second power is 1. For white light, this would be a white spot.

Using another example, if the difference between the halfway vector and the surface normal were 10 degrees (similar to the preceding figure), we would get *cosine(10°) = 0.9848*, which taken to the thirty-second power is 0.6127, adding about 60 percent (*cosine(0.9848)^{32}*100%=61.27%*) of the color of the light to that pixel. A 20 degree angle would add just 13.7 percent of the light's color to the pixel (*cosine(20)^{32}*100%=13.7%*). At 30 degrees, it would add just 0.01 of the light's color to the overall pixel color, and beyond 30 degrees, it would be negligible.

Prior to shader languages, we could only calculate specular highlights at each vertex and interpolate between the vertices for each pixel. But with fragment shaders, we can calculate on a per-pixel basis. First, we use both `eyeDirection` and `lightDirection` to the surface, as shown in the following code:

```
vec3 eyeDirection = - normalize ( vPosition.xyz );
vec3 lightDirection =
    normalize(spotLightLocation - vPosition.xyz);
```

We now use the `reflect` function in OpenGL, calculated by the angle between the normal and the direction of the light. Have a look at the following lines of code:

```
vec3 reflectionDirection = reflect(-lightDirection, normal);
float uMaterialShininess = 32.0;
specularLightWeighting = pow(max(dot(reflectionDirection,
    eyeDirection), 0.0), uMaterialShininess);
```

Within the final line of the preceding code, the dot product, given by `dot (reflectionDi rection,eyeDirection)`, is equal to the cosine of the angle between the reflection and eye-to-surface vectors. If the angle is greater than 90 degrees (positive or negative), then the cosine of that angle is less than zero and we can ignore the reflection. That is the purpose of the inner code that begins with `max(…, 0.0)` —we will either get a positive number or zero as a minimum.

We finally take this dot product to the power of our material shininess, given by `pow(max(dot(…, 0.0), uMaterialShininess)`, and that gives us the amount of additional color at this specific pixel.

Objective complete – mini debriefing

To demonstrate the principles of reflection, a menu was added to the example to turn off the ambient lighting, pause the teapot's rotation, and set the colors of the spotlight and ambient light. In addition, the arrow keys move the camera forward, back, left, and right, though the impression is that the teapot, not the camera, is moving, as shown in the following screenshot:

Using the spotlight with ambient light almost completely off

Reflection is a great application for realism. We see this used effectively in video games such as the reflections on car windows or buildings, particularly glass or metal. And while there was some complexity in this demonstration, it is not all that bad considering the actual coding part was pretty small.

Bending of light – calculating refraction for surfaces such as water

A variation on reflection is refraction, the bending of light as it passes through a surface, or more accurately, light passing through air into another surface. We see refraction when we observe a straw in a glass of water or view the bottom of a pool. Have a look at the following screenshot:

Refraction as the image of the pen is bent and broken

Prepare for lift off

This won't become a class in physics, I promise. But we cannot ignore it either, and besides, a little physics never hurt anyone (just continue to stay out of the way of falling objects). We need to take a moment and introduce **refractive index**, which describes how light moves through a surface. Refractive index is the ratio of light moving in a vacuum (which, for our purposes, is air) versus light moving through a substance such as glass or water. In water, the refractive index is 1.33, whereas the refractive index for diamond is 2.42. Types of glass and liquids can vary. For our purposes, we shall stick with water. The Greek symbol used for refractive index is *eta*, which is derived from the wavelengths of the light passing through the surfaces. For more information on the physics of refraction, visit http://www.physicsclassroom.com/class/refrn/Lesson-1/Refraction-and-Sight.

Engage thrusters

The code in the fragment shader is just a slight variation of the reflection code. Have a look at the following screenshot:

Refraction; note that the tree appears upside down on the teapot, just like a water droplet inverts the scene

Inside the fragment shader, along with the calculations for the spotlight previously described as the lightWeighting value, the refraction code consists of just four lines, as follows:

```
float eta = 1.33;
vec3 RefractDir =
    refract( -vPosition.xyz, vTransformedNormal, eta );
vec4 fragmentColor = textureCube( uCubemap, RefractDir );
gl_FragColor = vec4(fragmentColor.rgb * lightWeighting, 1.0);
```

We are using the *eta* value to simulate the transition between air and a teapot of water. The OpenGL ES refract(vec3, vec3, float) method and other functions can be found at http://www.khronos.org/opengles/sdk/docs/manglsl/.

Finally, we use the `textureCube` command as before, with the same six-sided box to see where the rays intersect after bouncing through the teapot. Have a look at the following screenshot:

Using just the spotlight looking from the bottom of the teapot

Objective complete – mini debriefing

Refraction is a cool and simple implementation. It can be a very eye-catching effect. It will not only look great for end users, but may also demonstrate to architects and designers some of the great capabilities of WebGL as they walk through their own designs online.

Creating surfaces – depth, non-smooth, natural, and realistic with normal maps

Few things in life are smooth and reflect light predictably, such as plastic—a modern invention—and a glass-smooth lake. We know how to render such smooth meshes based on the angle between the light source at that pixel and the normal using the dot product. The dot product is calculated by multiplying the two normalized vectors (each having a length of 1 unit), $N_x * L_x + N_y * L_y + N_z * L_z$, where N is the vertex normal (N_x, N_y, N_z) and L is the light direction (L_x, L_y, L_z).

However, most objects in nature have a bumpy, irregular surface, for example, oranges, tree bark, or a choppy lake. Man-made objects also have rough surfaces, for example, fabric or brick walls. Early in computer graphics, when computation was at such a premium, we simplified the calculations as very few video games had shading. The first computer-generated movies, such as *Toy Story*, had a number of surfaces that were smooth plastic, such as toys. But those are the exceptions, and now we want reality; if for no other reason, it lends character to the 3D scene. With a few exceptions, such as the ice in a hockey game, 3D in video games is not sanitary but worn-down, pock-marked, showing its age. Its surfaces are not polished marble, but brick, and require techniques to distinguish brick-looking wallpaper from actual bricks.

To create the surfaces of a brick wall, or an orange, we could ask our over-worked 3D artists to model those. But that's cumbersome and time consuming to construct, and requires an excessive number of polygons to render. We could also texture map the object with the indentations painted on. Sometimes, this does the job on small obscure items, but not on larger, more obvious objects.

Instead, we emulate the variations of depth on an object's surface by modifying the surface normals. The 3D mesh of an orange would still be smooth, but would render with the appearance of a rough surface. And unlike using just a texture map, modifying the normals would render correctly as the object was moved or rotated. A great example of this would be a golf ball with dimples in a pattern. Those dimples assist the flight of a golf ball by creating low pressure areas, giving the ball lift. But in computer graphics, we don't need low pressure areas, yet we still want a golf ball to look like a golf ball. Instead, we use a sphere and change the surface normals to create those dimples, slightly modifying where the normals point, as shown in the following screenshot:

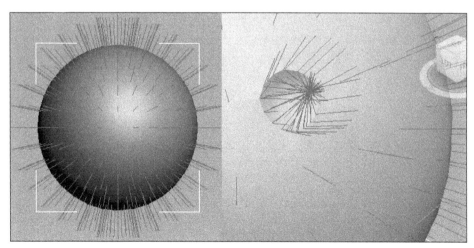

Sphere showing vertex normals (left) and normal changes for a golf ball dimple

Prepare for lift off

Normal maps are simply texture maps with the same dimensions as the original texture map, used to modify the normals during the rendering process. Some of the algorithms for normal maps compare adjacent pixels to determine the direction of that pixel's normal. For example, on a normal map, if the pixel's normal in the *y* direction (above) is lighter, then deduct from the normal's *y* value. If the pixel's normal *y* value above it is darker, then add to the normal *y* value. Adjacent pixels are rather complex, so we go with a much simpler normal map for our example of a brick pattern. Our normal texture map will use red-green-blue to set the normal's *x*, *y*, and *z* values. We use a simple formula that multiplies the RGB values by two and subtracts one. For example, let's use (0, 0.5, 1) on our normal map, which is blue plus half green. We would multiply by two and subtract one, so we have *(0, 0.5, 1)*2-1=(-1, 0, 1)* for the pixel's normal. That value would then be normalized (converted to a unit value) to be (-0.707, 0, 0.707).

Engage thrusters

This normal map matches our brick texture map and is read in as a second texture map. The predominance of blue is because the *z* value is always positive, as shown in the following screenshot:

Brick pattern normal texture map

Looking at the fragment shader, a point light is set at (0, 0, 1), just in front of the brick wall. We now calculate the `LightDirection` unit vector from that light to each pixel, as follows:

```
void main(void) {
    vec3 pointLightLoc = vec3(0.0, 0.0, 1.0 );
    vec3 lightDirection =
        normalize(pointLightLoc - vVertexPosition.xyz);
```

Next, calculate the normal at each pixel by multiplying the RGB value by two and subtracting one, and then convert it to a unit value, as presented in the following code:

```
vec4 pixelNormal =
    vec4( (texture2D(uSamplerAlt,
    vec2(vTextureCoord.s, vTextureCoord.t))
     * 2.0) - 1.0 );
vec3 normal = normalize(pixelNormal.rgb);
```

We conclude with the usual calculation of the light's angle to each pixel's normal for the light contribution to this scene, as presented in the following code:

```
float lightAngleToPixel = dot(lightDirection, normal );
if (lightAngleToPixel < 0.0) lightAngleToPixel = 0.0;
vec4 fragmentColor =
    texture2D(uSampler,
        vec2(vTextureCoord.s, vTextureCoord.t));
gl_FragColor =
    vec4(fragmentColor.rgb * lightAngleToPixel, 1.0);
}
```

Another important addition of code here is that the demonstration looks much better tiled. Fortunately, in the vertex shader, the following line of code handles the tiling for both the texture map and the normal map:

```
vTextureCoord = aTextureCoord * vec2(4.0, 4.0);
```

Have a look at the following screenshot:

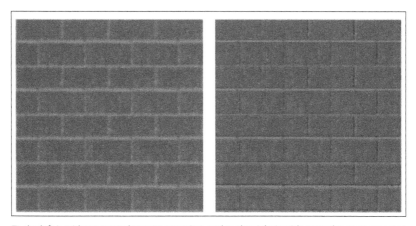

To the left is without normal texture mapping, and to the right is with normal texture mapping

Objective complete – mini debriefing

Each image in the preceding screenshot has a point light at the center and at the top. Thus, the effect of the normal texture map, while subtle, is more detectible towards the bottom where the indentation from the mortar looks a bit darker, which even adds to the sense of 3D instead of what could be mistaken for wallpaper.

As in the previous example, the use of normal maps to give surfaces a more realistic, rougher appearance in an online demonstration may truly impress architects and mechanical engineers. The technique was fairly simple, but it really shows off the power of shader languages.

Rendering a scene as a texture to view multiple cameras simultaneously

One of the more fascinating aspects of working in 3D computer graphics is not that we can recreate a photorealistic world, but that we can create worlds that cannot exist in the real world. We are unbound by physics, and can create one-way walls or walk through portals to get from one location to another in an instant. Clearly, it is not traditional architecture as we know it, nor should it be.

Until now, every 3D mesh we have sent to the `drawScene()` function has been drawn onto a canvas embedded inside a web page. But now, we are going to render the scene as a texture map, then apply that texture map onto a 3D mesh in our scene. Think of this as if we had a room with security cameras, and we wanted to show the scene from the security camera on a 3D mesh that was a television monitor.

Prepare for lift off

In rendering the scene to be later used as a texture map, we are essentially taking over part of the rendering process that had been done entirely by the graphics card. By rendering our own textures, we now have to draw the pixels saved in a memory area, plus save the depth of each pixel in a **depth buffer**, also known as a *z* buffer.

As pixels are drawn by the fragment shader, the GPU saves the pixel plus its depth. If an object is drawn at the same location, the GPU checks if the new pixel is in front of or behind the pixel already drawn there. If the new pixel has a larger depth value than the existing pixel—meaning the new pixel is further away—then the GPU ignores the new pixel. However, if the new pixel is closer than the existing pixel in the depth buffer, draw the new pixel in the raster buffer that contains the final image and save its distance in the depth buffer. Once all the 3D meshes are drawn for the current scene, we **blt** (bit block transfer) the pixels from the buffer memory to the screen, clear the depth buffer, and then get ready to render the next frame. Incidentally, the `gl.enable(gl.DEPTH_TEST);` command enables the depth test.

The depth buffer serves other purposes in a special post-rendering process. **Screen Space Ambient Occlusion (SSAO)** compares the depth of neighboring pixels in the depth buffer. If there is a great difference in the depth of these neighboring pixels, it indicates that we are at the edge of one object with another object behind it. We then use this information to darken areas around the foreground object. This appears to pull the foreground object away from the background and provides a greater illusion of depth by shadowing objects behind the foreground.

Engage thrusters

There are two parts to rendering an image onto another 3D mesh: rendering the image into a buffer or memory area, and using that image as a texture map onto a polygon. In this exercise, we shall display the scene from a default camera at (0, 0, 0) looking down the negative *z* axis, and use that image as a texture map for the objects.

Upon start-up, we create the frame buffers, which is just a technical way of saying a memory area, and generate a texture map and depth buffer of the same size, which will be filled in later. In `webGLStart()`, we call our initial program, `initTextureFramebuffer();`. There are also two global variables for the frame buffer and texture: `rttFramebuffer` and `rttTexture`, where `rtt` is simply an abbreviation for "render to texture". Have a look at the following code:

```
function initTextureFramebuffer() {
// create render-to-texture (rtt) frame buffer (memory area)
//    on the graphics card
   rttFramebuffer = gl.createFramebuffer();
   gl.bindFramebuffer(gl.FRAMEBUFFER, rttFramebuffer);
   rttFramebuffer.width = 512;
   rttFramebuffer.height = 512;
```

```
// sets texture map parameters, similar to any other texture
//    map when we download a texture file
    rttTexture = gl.createTexture();
    gl.bindTexture(gl.TEXTURE_2D, rttTexture);
gl.texParameteri(gl.TEXTURE_2D, gl.TEXTURE_MAG_FILTER,
gl.LINEAR);
    gl.texParameteri(gl.TEXTURE_2D, gl.TEXTURE_MIN_FILTER,
gl.LINEAR_MIPMAP_NEAREST);
    gl.generateMipmap(gl.TEXTURE_2D);

// binds the texture above to the memory area on the graphics
//    card (though the texture map image does not yet exist)
gl.texImage2D(gl.TEXTURE_2D, 0, gl.RGBA, rttFramebuffer.width,
rttFramebuffer.height, 0, gl.RGBA, gl.UNSIGNED_BYTE, null);

// Create the depth buffer with 16-bit depth
var renderbuffer = gl.createRenderbuffer();
gl.bindRenderbuffer(gl.RENDERBUFFER, renderbuffer);
gl.renderbufferStorage(gl.RENDERBUFFER, gl.DEPTH_COMPONENT16,
rttFramebuffer.width, rttFramebuffer.height);

// attach the rgb + depth buffer to the rtt frame buffer
gl.framebufferTexture2D(gl.FRAMEBUFFER, gl.COLOR_ATTACHMENT0,
gl.TEXTURE_2D, rttTexture, 0);
gl.framebufferRenderbuffer(gl.FRAMEBUFFER,
gl.DEPTH_ATTACHMENT, gl.RENDERBUFFER, renderbuffer);

// resets the binded buffers back to their defaults
gl.bindTexture(gl.TEXTURE_2D, null);
gl.bindRenderbuffer(gl.RENDERBUFFER, null);
gl.bindFramebuffer(gl.FRAMEBUFFER, null);
} // end initTextureFramebuffer
```

This was an extensive look at the setup of the render-to-texture buffer, but the setup is key! Much of the rest of the coding is pretty straightforward, with just a few variable changes. Inside drawScene(), we begin with three lines of code to redirect the rendering of the scene to the render-to-texture buffer, then render the scene by calling the drawRenderedTextureMap() function, and then reset the frame buffer back to draw to the GPU, as shown in the following code:

```
function drawScene() {
    // switch away from the default framebuffer (which renders to
    // the canvas) to the render-to-texture frame buffer
    gl.bindFramebuffer(gl.FRAMEBUFFER, rttFramebuffer);
    drawRenderedTextureMap();
    gl.bindFramebuffer(gl.FRAMEBUFFER, null);
```

To experience the demo, a radio button was set to switch between rendering to the texture map or rendering to canvas, and based on that we select the appropriate shader, as seen in the following code snippet:

```
var raster = document.getElementById("rasterRadioBttn").checked;
var renderToTextureShaderBttn =
document.getElementById("renderToTextureShaderRadioBttn").checked;

if (renderToTextureShaderBttn) {
currentProgram = textureMapShaderProgram;
gl.clearColor(0.2, 0.2, 0.25, 1.0); // dark gray background
}
else { // draw to the canvas
currentProgram = shaderProgram;
gl.clearColor(0.7, 0.7, 0.7, 1.0); // light gray background
}
```

Have a look at the following screenshot:

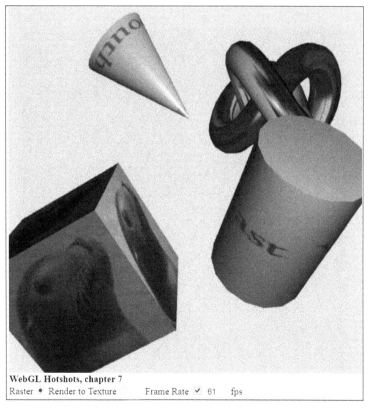

Render as a normal scene without render-to-texture

The call to `drawRenderedTextureMap()` nearly duplicates the regular rendering process of passing information to the shaders. A few changes include setting the appropriate vertex and fragment shader viewport to our frame buffers instead of the canvas, as presented in the following code:

```
gl.viewport(0, 0, rttFramebuffer.width, rttFramebuffer.height);

currentProgram = renderToTextureProgram;
gl.useProgram(currentProgram);
```

We end with the final three lines of code binding this new texture to the current 3D mesh, then generating the mipmap so the texture map can size properly on objects in the distance. After all this calculation of generating a new texture map from the 3D scene, reset the texture binding back to the default using the following code:

```
gl.bindTexture(gl.TEXTURE_2D, rttTexture);
gl.generateMipmap(gl.TEXTURE_2D);
gl.bindTexture(gl.TEXTURE_2D, null);
```

Have a look at the following screenshot:

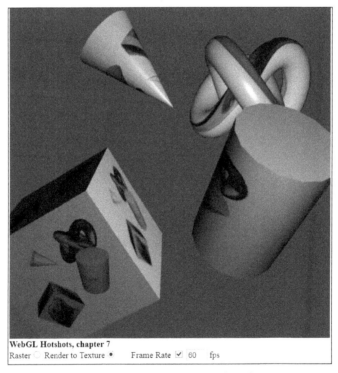

WebGL Hotshots, chapter 7
Raster ○ Render to Texture ●   Frame Rate ☑ 60   fps

First rendering the entire scene as a texture map, and then applying that texture map to each object

The shaders themselves are fairly simple. They only seem long because all the different materials were included, such as diffuse colors, emissive colors, and specular colors. Otherwise, they are standard-looking shaders with nothing particularly unique to rendering a scene to texture.

Classified intel

Prior to having programmable shaders, we had the fixed-function pipeline, part of the OpenGL ES 1.0 specification where we had no control over programming the GPU. The OpenGL ES 2.0 specification replaced the fixed-function pipeline with programmable shaders where we control lighting and texturing of each pixel inside the GPU. OpenGL ES 3.0 was announced at SIGGRAPH 2012 with greater features for drawing geometry and texture maps, and is beginning to roll out with full deployment within a few short years, all to make programming easier.

Each new advance is built upon what we have learned so far. Often, we cannot predict the next great opportunity until we solve existing problems. One of the most memorable talks from SIGGRAPH 2013 and the co-located High Performance Graphics conference discussed how vertex shaders produce the location of each polygon, and then send this directly to the fragment shader. However, if the output from vertex shaders were to be saved before calling the fragment shader, we could render the polygons from front to back, thus eliminating how we often redraw the same pixel if 3D meshes were to overlap. Much of the work of the depth buffer would be taken over by the vertex shader. It was estimated that this could conservatively give us a 30 percent performance boost. We used to talk about the performance increases in the CPU, but now, much of these geometric performance increases are occurring inside the GPU.

Objective complete – mini debriefing

An interesting addition would be to add the rendering from the point of view of a different camera. That could then be pasted onto a wall to act like a monitor or security camera looking into another room. It would be a fun addition to a video game or just for an interesting high-tech look. The key here though is that all of this can be expanded to create more complex scenes. Here, we just gave a taste as to what was possible.

Learning about rendering to a texture map and using that later is certainly something few, if any, web designers would have previously come across. Rendering to a texture map also provides insights into the process that the GPU performs and may inspire a few of you into the world of graphics chip programming.

Mission accomplished

Most of the demonstrations here have focused on simple aspects of rendering: reflection, refraction, normal mapping, and rendering to a texture map to build more complex architecture or mechanical applications. Together, these compose some of the more difficult yet impressive techniques in 3D computer graphics.

Hotshot challenges

A great challenge would be to combine all these features—reflection, refraction, normal maps, and rendering to a texture map—into a dark city scene. The normal mapping of brick patterns with spotlights can be compelling and eye catching. Add to that windows with reflections, and if you dare, water pools with refraction. This is a great time as well to engage with 3D artists to create some great architecture for you to light. Together, you can create some impressive worlds.

Project 8

3D Websites

"The World Wide Web is like the discovery of a new world, populated by the content of our own imaginations"

– Mark Pesce, Co-Inventor of VRML (Virtual Reality Modeling Language)
from "VRML: Browsing and Building Cyberspace," 1995

One of the most difficult yet fun creative aspects of 3D web design is to brainstorm for clever metaphors in order to navigate a 3D website. The phrase "think outside the box" does not come close. "Think outside the cube" is a little closer, or beyond that, think outside the fourth dimensional sphere. We are sailing into unchartered and undiscovered cyberspace.

It is a pretty safe bet that 100 percent of your audience would have never seen a 3D website. Even right now, you likely cannot envision what a 3D website would be. Perhaps an Internet site where instead of clicking on web pages, you walk through, navigating down hallways and looking for doors to open. You might also be thinking about QuickTime VR, used effectively and inexpensively by realtors to show homes. Others say that something is 3D by adding shadows to text and images, or if it was designed with the help of 3D modeling tools. In my years of evangelizing interactive Web3D, I was surprised by how varied people's perception was of what defined 3D, and all were correct. However, my stricter, technical definition involves rendering 3D models and navigating in 3D space.

Regardless of any definition of 3D, it is safe to say that our audiences have never been to a 3D website. Even video game players may not be familiar with a Web3D environment. Therefore, we must invent the third dimension for users. So, how do we educate and engage users to *walk-through* and navigate a 3D website without relying on text for instructions? After all, no one wants to come to a website that needs instructions. Going from the 2D web to a 3D web presents a challenge that may be the same leap taken when going from command-line prompts such as DOS to Apple's graphical user interface.

Mission briefing

Since we are talking about 3D and the Web, why not talk about Web3D sites? We will look at some original Web3D designs, the lessons learned, and the challenges ahead, such as navigating and prompting users to engage in an interactive 3D environment.

Traditional 2D web coalesced around standard designs, which were often three columns of text with interspersed images and perhaps advertisements overlaid on top. It took a quarter century from the beginning of the Internet in the 1960s to the first commercial applications using web browsers in the early 1990s. Therefore, perhaps the 3D web is just a matter of time. We will look again at X3D as we did in *Project 1*, *Building Great Web3D*, and some techniques only available in 3D to create engaging websites, and maybe, make interactive 3D the media standard of this century.

Why is it awesome?

The Web has been a catalyst for a lot of great creative content and has connected society through channels such as Facebook and distribution sites such as YouTube. In many ways though, the Web has been a technology that, while making content more personal, has also replaced one technology with another. Twitter is the modern day Morse code, limited to 140 characters or less. Online shopping is the modern day version of the Sears catalog from yesteryear; it is multi-user and more rapid, but websites still comprise of text and images.

However, Web3D is a new medium similar to video games that have changed the way we engage with entertainment. Web3D will create websites that are more than just ways to get information—it will engage users and make their experience naturally interactive. Users will not just view a website; they will be inside a website. Moreover, for the web designer, you are about to create the new frontier for the next century.

Your Hotshot objectives

The major tasks required to complete our project are as follows:

- Building a 3D website
- Creating engaging scenes
- Portals to navigate virtual spaces

Building a 3D website

When I began 3D-Online, or more specifically, `www.3d-online.com`, I was determined to have interactive Web3D on the home page, as shown in the following screenshot. After all, if Web3D was going to prove itself, then interactive 3D graphics had to be in front of people right on the home page. Web3D companies at that time, such as PULSE 3D, attracted a lot of attention at SIGGRAPH 2000 in New Orleans with their Web3D examples on distant pages of their website. You had to go through a few links from the home page just to see interactive Web3D. Of course, you had to download and install their plugin first. While it was a great technology and PULSE 3D's efforts were noble, this seemed a timid presentation of one's own product and industry.

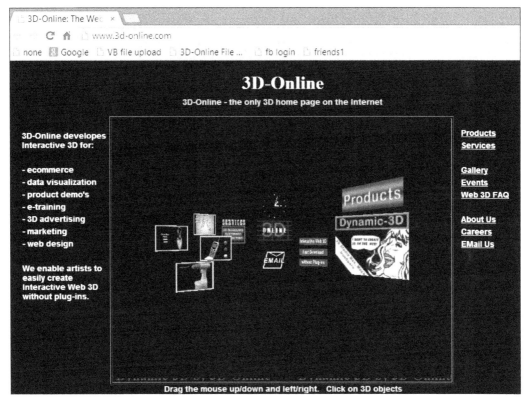

The original 3D-Online website

To create awareness for Web3D, it had to be on the home page. This meant that plugins such as PULSE 3D could not be used. No one is going to download a plugin just to see your home page. The only reliable solution prior to WebGL was Java, which was often preinstalled on many computers to run applets. However, Java runs slowly for 3D, and thus Web3D could not be too complex. In addition, search engines cataloged websites based on the amount of text on the home page—something Web3D was also not well suited for. When 3D-Online was launched as one of the first Web3D home pages, I went to public locations such as Apple stores to display the 3D-Online website on Apple's store computers to see the reaction from customers. Clearly, no one was familiar with Web3D. Rarely did anyone navigate forward through the website. If they did drag the mouse, the user would often drag the mouse to the left and right and the scene would disappear.

A quick fix was to add text at the bottom instructing users to drag the mouse forward and backward in order to navigate through the website and to click on the objects. Still, users needed something more; so, the scene opened with the camera moving forward, giving users the sense of walking through the website. Moreover, to prevent users from going too far, the camera pulled back until some objects were visible. I saw that for 3D websites, we had to give visual cues to users.

Eventually, all the text was removed so that the home page would be a pure 3D website. The 3D web was on its way. However, technologies do perish, and the Java-based software was replaced by WebGL. So, let us take a look at 3D-Online using X3D and the techniques used to engage users by controlling the camera and ongoing animations.

Engage thrusters

This demonstration uses X3D first discussed in *Project 1, Building Great Web3D*. For review, X3D is a file format used to specify a 3D scene. There are several solutions that can parse the X3D file. I prefer X3DOM (http://www.x3dom.org/) and thus included it in the header of the **XHTML** file: `<script type="text/javascript" src="x3dom.js"></script>`. This is an XHTML file since it uses a strict XHTML tag structure. The `<body>` tag contains the X3D scene data, and JavaScript controls the clicks on the 3D objects as well as the hands on the clock.

Immediately after the XHTML file is read, we set up the callback to the `myTimer` time inside the `<script>` tag called every 15 milliseconds, plus links to the clock hands' `<Transform>` tag, plus `currentVP` (our camera's current viewpoint), each updated in the 3D scene through JavaScript:

```
var myVar=setInterval(function(){myTimer()},15);
var secondHandTransform = document.getElementById("secondHand");
var minuteHandTransform = document.getElementById("minuteHand");
var hourHandTransform   = document.getElementById("hourHand");
var currentViewpoint = document.getElementById("currentVP");
```

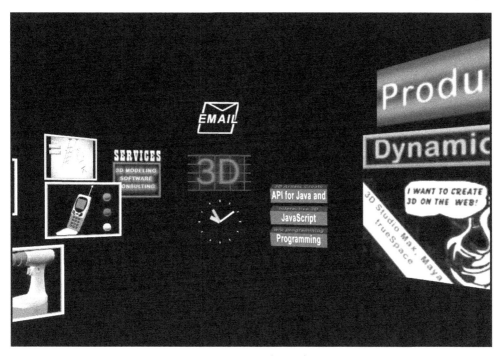

The 3D-Online website designed in X3D

The `<Transform>` tag for the second hand (in yellow) also follows the HTML5 standard of the tag being identified by an ID:

```
<Transform id="secondHand" translation="0 0 15"
    rotation="0 0 1 0">
```

All the 3D meshes in the scene are contained inside the `<Transform><Shape>` and `</Shape></Transform>` tags.

The `myTimer()` function is called every 15 milliseconds. We have chosen 15 milliseconds because it gives us about 60 frames per second—the refresh time that is often used in video games. JavaScript's `Date` object methods get the seconds, minutes, and hours:

```
function myTimer() {
    var d=new Date();
    var seconds = d.getSeconds();
    var minutes = d.getMinutes();
    var hours = d.getHours();
    var zSecondsRotation = -seconds * Math.PI / 30.0;
    var zMinutesRotation = -minutes * Math.PI / 30.0;
    var zHourRotation = -(hours % 12) * Math.PI / 6.0 +
        (zMinutesRotation / 12.0);
```

```
        secondHandTransform.setAttribute('rotation', '0 0 1 ' +
            zSecondsRotation );
        minuteHandTransform.setAttribute('rotation', '0 0 1 ' +
            zMinutesRotation );
        hourHandTransform.setAttribute('rotation', '0 0 1 ' +
            zHourRotation );
    }
```

Calculations for minutes and seconds are pretty simple. Here, we're given a value from 0 to 59, and the value is multiplied with *(2π/60)* to convert seconds and minutes to radians. The value of *(2π/60)* is reduced to *(π/30)*, and the value is negated because rotations in computer graphics are generally counterclockwise.

Hours are given in military time, between 0 and 23, so we use the modulo function (`%`), which gives the remainder of a division by 12 to produce values between 0 and 11. Multiply hours with *(2π/12)* and reduce to *(π/6)*. So that the hour hand does not *jump* every hour, we add in the minutes so that the hour hand increments smoothly each minute.

The final step is to use the `setAttribute()` function to set the rotation parameter inside the `<Transform>` tag for the second, minute, and hour hands. These are important animations so that customers do not think that the website is frozen. In gaming, these are known as fidget animations. Just to the right-hand side of the clock are three rotating marquees. Since the marquees are not time-dependent like the clock, we can use X3D's animation functions that begin with the `<TimeSensor>` tag sending a signal to an interpolator that computes the amount of rotation based on the time. Back in *Project 1*, *Building Great Web3D*, we used similar interpolators for the rotations of the planets. The interpolator outputs a rotation to each of the marquee's three `<Transform>` tags, identified by the names `marquee1`, `marquee2`, and `marquee3`:

```
<TimeSensor DEF="marqueeTIMER" cycleInterval="16.7" loop="true"/>
<OrientationInterpolator DEF="marqueeInterpolator"
    key="0 .2 .25 .45 .5 .7 .75 .95 1"
    keyValue="1 0 0 0   1 0 0 0   1 0 0 1.57   1 0 0 1.57
    1 0 0 3.14   1 0 0 3.14   1 0 0 4.71   1 0 0 4.71
    1 0 0 6.28" />
<ROUTE fromField="fraction_changed" fromNode="marqueeTIMER"
    toField="set_fraction" toNode="marqueeInterpolator"/>
<ROUTE fromField="value_changed" fromNode="marqueeInterpolator"
    toField="rotation" toNode="marquee1"/>
<ROUTE fromField="value_changed" fromNode="marqueeInterpolator"
    toField="rotation" toNode="marquee2"/>
<ROUTE fromField="value_changed" fromNode="marqueeInterpolator"
    toField="rotation" toNode="marquee3"/>
```

Another fidget animation, more subtle, is **ONLINE** that appears every few seconds in front of **3D** and perhaps encourages the user to walk forward to get a closer look.

To give users the perception that they are in 3D space and are not just watching a video or a QuickTime VR animation, the camera moves forward when the user enters the space. In addition, if the camera is outside bounds in either the positive or negative *z* direction, the camera is animated back into the scene. Earlier upon startup, we obtained a reference to the `<Viewpoint id="currentVP">` tag. We get the *x*, *y*, and *z* values for the camera position as a string—one of the annoying issues with programming X3D with JavaScript—and thus the value must be parsed by separating the string between each space character:

```
var vpPos = currentViewpoint.getAttribute('position');
var vpPosX = vpPos.substring( 0, vpPos.indexOf(" ") );
var vpPosY = vpPos.substring(
    vpPos.indexOf(" "),vpPos.lastIndexOf(" ") );
var vpPosZ = vpPos.substring(
    vpPos.lastIndexOf(" "), vpPos.length );
```

Then, we either increment or decrement the *z* value depending on whether *z* is out of the predetermined boundaries, and use HTML5's `setAttribute()` command to set the viewpoint's position value. The values to constrain the viewpoint between 1100 and -1550 were simply selected on what works best. The goal is to not let the user stray too far:

```
if (vpPosZ > 1100) {
    if (drag == false) {
        vpPosZ -= .4 * vpPosZ / 900.0;
        currentViewpoint.setAttribute('position',
            vpPosX + ' ' + vpPosY + ' ' + vpPosZ  );
    }
}
if (-vpPosZ > 1550) {
    vpPosZ = -1545;
    currentViewpoint.setAttribute('position',
        vpPosX + ' ' + vpPosY + ' ' + vpPosZ  );
}
```

The next issue is controlling the mouse click and drag. Once the page loads, `document.onload = function()` is called to set up the event listeners in order to call the `mouseDown()`, `mouseMove()`, and `mouseUp()` functions:

```
x3dScene.addEventListener('mousedown', mouseDown, true);
x3dScene.addEventListener('mouseup', mouseUp, false);
x3dScene.addEventListener('mousemove', mouseMove, true);
```

Event listeners inform us when an event occurs. When we are driving a car and see a stop light turn red, it's an example of a *red light* event that we need to react to and use the brakes. When the mouse is clicked or moved, this generates a *mouse down* event that informs the `mouseDown` function. The `mouseDown` function saves the location of where the mouse was clicked as well as the position and rotation (orientation) of the camera. In this demonstration, the camera only rotates around the *y* axis:

```
function mouseDown(event) {
    bgnMousePos = runtime.mousePosition(event);
    drag = true;
    // parse the viewpoint position provided in a string format
    viewpointPosMouseDown =
        currentViewpoint.getAttribute('position');
    viewpointPosXMouseDown = viewpointPosMouseDown.substring( 0,
        viewpointPosMouseDown.indexOf(" ") );
    viewpointPosYMouseDown = viewpointPosMouseDown.substring(
        viewpointPosMouseDown.indexOf(" "),
        viewpointPosMouseDown.lastIndexOf(" ") );
    viewpointPosZMouseDown = viewpointPosMouseDown.substring(
        viewpointPosMouseDown.lastIndexOf(" "),
        viewpointPosMouseDown.length );
    // Get the rotation angle, which is the last of 4 values
    viewpointOrientationMouseDown =
        currentViewpoint.getAttribute('orientation');
    viewpointOrientationAngleMouseDown =
        viewpointOrientationMouseDown.substring(
    viewpointOrientationMouseDown.lastIndexOf(" "),
        viewpointOrientationMouseDown.length );
}
```

With the initial mouse data saved, the back and forth dragging of the mouse is an event to call our `mouseMove` function. Dragging the mouse up and down changes the mouse's *y* value. The mouse dragged horizontally from the left-hand side to the right rotates the camera around the *y* axis. The `drag` value was set to true in the `mouseDown()` function. Without this true/false drag value, the camera would move whenever the mouse rolled over the 3D scene, regardless of whether a mouse was clicked or not. Therefore, drag controls our camera movements only when the mouse button is pressed down:

```
function mouseMove(event) {
    if (drag) {
        currentMousePosition = runtime.mousePosition(event);
        var zVp = viewpointPosZMouseDown -
            6*(bgnMousePos[1] - currentMousePosition[1]);
        currentViewpoint.setAttribute('position',
            viewpointPosXMouseDown + ' ' +
            viewpointPosYMouseDown + ' ' + zVp );
```

```
            var angleVp = viewpointOrientationAngleMouseDown -
                .001*(currentMousePosition[0] - bgnMousePos[0]);
            currentViewpoint.setAttribute('orientation',
                '0 1 0 ' + angleVp );
        }
    }
```

Here, the constant values, such as multiplying the change in the mouse's *y* position by 6 or multiplying the change in the mouse's *z* position by 0.001, were simply chosen as what looked best.

The final block of code turns `drag` to `false` when the mouse is no longer clicked:

```
function mouseUp() {  drag = false;  }
```

The final feature is to program what happens when the textured panels in the scene are clicked, which either hyperlinks to a new web page or sends an e-mail:

```
document.onload = function()  {
    var x3dScene = document.getElementById("x3dObj");
    runtime = x3dScene.runtime;

    var aboutUs = document.getElementById("AboutUs");
    aboutUs.addEventListener('mousedown',
        mouseDownAboutUs, false);
    aboutUs.addEventListener('mouseover', mouseOverEvent, false);
    aboutUs.addEventListener('mouseout', mouseOutEvent, false);
    . . .
}
```

The `x3dObj` ID specifies the `<X3D>` `</X3D>` tags containing the entire 3D scene:

```
<X3D id="x3dObj"
xmlns=http://www.web3d.org/specifications/x3d-namespace
width="1024px" height="768px">
```

The first `<Transform . . . id="AboutUs">` identifies the `AboutUs` object. The next three lines set up the listeners for the events: `mouseover`, `mouseout` (moving off the 3D mesh), and clicking on the **3D** and **Online** textured panels.

All 3D meshes that can be clicked on provide a visual cue by changing the mouse icon:

```
function mouseOverEvent() {
    runtime.getCanvas().style.cursor = "pointer";
}
function mouseOutEvent() {
    runtime.getCanvas().style.cursor = "auto";
}
```

Finally, the code that specifies what to do when the mouse clicks on the **About Us** panel is as follows:

```
function mouseDownAboutUs() {
    window.open("./Web3DSuppPages/AboutUs.htm", "_self");
}
```

This code is replicated for all the other panels in the 3D scene that link to other web pages with the one minor exception of the e-mail panel that naturally launches an e-mail:

```
function mouseDownEmailItem() {
    window.open(
        "mailto:info@3D-Online.com?SUBJECT=email from 3D-Online",
        "_self");
}
```

Objective complete – mini debriefing

While it seemed like a lot of code, in reality, it would be rather simple to take some existing images from your current website, replace them here, change the web pages that would be clicked on in the scene, and navigate through your own 3D website in a matter of an hour or less. The X3D code, which is XML-based and specifies a 3D space and JavaScript, is nothing new to even a novice HTML5 developer.

I have had the good fortune to be at the onset of Web3D and have seen many failures, but each of these small steps pointed us into new directions to conquer the next hurdle. Never before have we had such a simple technology like X3D, a ready and waiting audience, and a wide, open field for new designers.

Creating engaging scenes

There is no adopted style for a 3D website. No metaphor can best describe the process of designing the 3D web. Perhaps what we know the most is what does not work. Often, our initial concept is to model the real world. An early design that was used years ago involved a university that wanted to use its campus map to navigate through its website. One found oneself dragging the mouse repeatedly, as fast as one could, just to get to the other side of campus. A better design would've been a book shelf where everything was in front of you. To view the chemistry department, just grab the chemistry book, and click on the virtual pages to view the faculty, curriculum, and other department information. Also, if you needed to cross-reference this with the math department's upcoming schedule, you could just grab the math book.

Each attempt adds to our knowledge and gets us closer to something better. What we know is what most other applications of computer graphics learned—that reality might be a starting point, but we should not let it interfere with creativity. 3D for the sake of recreating the real world limits our innovative potential.

When a project begins, it is natural to model the exact scene. Following this starting point, strip out the parts bound by physics, such as support beams or poles that serve no purpose in a virtual world. Such items make the rendering slower by just existing. Once we break these bounds, the creative process takes over—perhaps a whimsical version, a parody, something dark and scary, or a world-emphasizing story. Characters in video games and animated movies take on stylized features. The characters are purposely unrealistic or exaggerated. One of the best animations to exhibit this is Chris Landreth's *The Spine*, *Ryan* (Academy Award for best-animated short film in 2004), and his earlier work in *Psychological Driven Animation*, where the characters break apart by the ravages of personal failure (`https://www.nfb.ca/film/ryan`).

This demonstration will describe some of the more difficult technical issues involved with lighting, normal maps, and the efficient sharing of 3D models. The following scene uses 3D models and textures maps from previous demonstrations but with techniques that are more complex.

Engage thrusters

This scene has two lampposts and three brick walls, yet we only read in the texture map and 3D mesh for one of each and then reuse the same models several times. This has the obvious advantage that we do not need to read in the same 3D models several times, thus saving download time and using less memory. A new function, `copyObject()`, was created that currently sits inside the main WebGL file, although it can be moved to `mesh3dObject.js`. In `webGLStart()`, after the original objects were created, we call `copyObject()`, passing along the original object with the unique name, location, rotation, and scale. In the following code, we copy the original `streetLight0Object` into a new `streetLight1Object`:

```
streetLight1Object = copyObject( streetLight0Object,
    "streetLight1", streetLight1Location, [1, 1, 1], [0, 0, 0] );
```

Inside `copyObject()`, we first create the new mesh and then set the unique name, location (translation), rotation, and scale:

```
function copyObject(original, name, translation, scale, rotation)
{
    meshObjectArray[ totalMeshObjects ] = new meshObject();
    newObject = meshObjectArray[ totalMeshObjects ];
    newObject.name = name;
    newObject.translation = translation;
    newObject.scale = scale;
    newObject.rotation = rotation;
```

The object to be copied is named `original`. We will not need to set up new buffers since the new 3D mesh can point to the same buffers as the original object:

```
newObject.vertexBuffer = original.vertexBuffer;
newObject.indexedFaceSetBuffer =
    original.indexedFaceSetBuffer;
newObject.normalsBuffer = original.normalsBuffer;
newObject.textureCoordBuffer = original.textureCoordBuffer;
newObject.boundingBoxBuffer = original.boundingBoxBuffer;
newObject.boundingBoxIndexBuffer =
    original.boundingBoxIndexBuffer;
newObject.vertices = original.vertices;
newObject.textureMap = original.textureMap;
```

We do need to create a new bounding box matrix since it is based on the new object's unique location, rotation, and scale. In addition, `meshLoaded` is set to `false`. At this stage, we cannot determine if the original mesh and texture map have been loaded since that is done in the background:

```
newObject.boundingBoxMatrix = mat4.create();
newObject.meshLoaded = false;
totalMeshObjects++;
return newObject;
}
```

There is just one more inclusion to inform us that the original 3D mesh and texture map(s) have been loaded inside `drawScene()`:

```
streetLightCover1Object.meshLoaded =
    streetLightCover0Object.meshLoaded;
streetLightCover1Object.textureMap =
    streetLightCover0Object.textureMap;
```

This is set each time a frame is drawn, and thus, is redundant once the mesh and texture map have been loaded, but the additional code is a very small hit in performance. Similar steps are performed for the original brick wall and its two copies.

Most of the scene is programmed using fragment shaders. There are four lights: the two streetlights, the neon **Products** sign, and the moon, which sets and rises. The brick wall uses normal maps that have been described in the previous project. However, it is more complex here; the use of spotlights and light attenuation, where the light fades over a distance. The faint moon light, however, does not fade over a distance.

Opening scene with four light sources: two streetlights, the **Products** neon sign, and the moon

This program has only three shaders: LightsTextureMap, used by the brick wall with a texture normal map; Lights, used for any object that is illuminated by one or more lights; and Illuminated, used by the light sources such as the moon, neon sign, and streetlight covers.

The simplest out of these fragment shaders is Illuminated. It consists of a texture map and the illuminated color, uLightColor. For many objects, the texture map would simply be a white placeholder. However, the moon uses a texture map, available for free from NASA that must be merged with its color:

```
vec4 fragmentColor =
    texture2D(uSampler, vec2(vTextureCoord.s, vTextureCoord.t));
gl_FragColor = vec4(fragmentColor.rgb * uLightColor, 1.0);
```

The light color also serves another purpose, as it will be passed on to the other two fragment shaders since each adds its own individual color: off-white for the streetlights, gray for the moon, and pink for the neon sign.

Since the streetlight covers' location is 3 units left and 10 units above the base of each streetlight, an offset of (-3, 10, 0) was built into the model. If you examine the streetLightCover.obj file, the center of the thin cylinder is (-3, 10, 0), so we can use the same location for both the streetlight and the cover.

The next step is to use the `shaderLights` fragment shader. We begin by setting the ambient light, which is a dim light added to every pixel, usually about 0.1, so nothing is pitch black. Then, we make a call for each of our four light sources (two streetlights, the moon, and the neon sign) to the `calculateLightContribution()` function:

```
void main(void) {
    vec3 lightWeighting =
        vec3(uAmbientLight, uAmbientLight, uAmbientLight);
    lightWeighting += uStreetLightColor *
        calculateLightContribution(uSpotLight0Loc,
        uSpotLightDir, false);
    lightWeighting += uStreetLightColor *
        calculateLightContribution(uSpotLight1Loc,
        uSpotLightDir, false);
    lightWeighting += uMoonLightColor *
        calculateLightContribution(uMoonLightPos,
    vec3(0.0, 0.0, 0.0), true);
    lightWeighting += uProductTextColor *
        calculateLightContribution(uProductTextLoc,
        vec3(0.0, 0.0, 0.0), true);
```

All four calls to `calculateLightContribution()` are multiplied by the light's color (white for the streetlights, gray for the moon, and pink for the neon sign). The parameters in the call to `calculateLightContribution(vec3, vec3, vec3, bool)` are: location of the light, its direction, the pixel's normal, and the point light. This parameter is `true` for a point light that illuminates in all directions, or `false` if it is a spotlight that points in a specific direction. Since point lights such as the moon or neon sign have no direction, their direction parameter is not used. Therefore, their direction parameter is set to a default, `vec3(0.0, 0.0, 0.0)`.

The `vec3 lightWeighting` value accumulates the red, green, and blue light colors at each pixel. However, these values cannot exceed the maximum of 1.0 for red, green, and blue. Colors greater than 1.0 are unpredictable based on the graphics card. So, the red, green, and blue light colors must be capped at 1.0:

```
if ( lightWeighting.r > 1.0 )  lightWeighting.r = 1.0;
if ( lightWeighting.g > 1.0 )  lightWeighting.g = 1.0;
if ( lightWeighting.b > 1.0 )  lightWeighting.b = 1.0;
```

Finally, we calculate the pixels based on the texture map. Only the street and streetlight posts use this shader, and neither have any tiling, but the multiplication by uTextureMapTiling was included in case there was tiling. The `fragmentColor` based on the texture map is multiplied by `lightWeighting`—the accumulation of our four light sources for the final color of each pixel:

```
vec4 fragmentColor = texture2D(uSampler,
    vec2(vTextureCoord.s*uTextureMapTiling.s,
    vTextureCoord.t*uTextureMapTiling.t));
```

```
gl_FragColor =
    vec4(fragmentColor.rgb * lightWeighting.rgb, 1.0);
}
```

In the `calculateLightContribution()` function, we begin by determining the angle between the light's direction and point's normal. The dot product is the cosine between the light's direction to the pixel and the pixel's normal, which is also known as Lambert's cosine law (http://en.wikipedia.org/wiki/Lambertian_reflectance):

```
vec3 distanceLightToPixel = vec3(vPosition.xyz - lightLoc);
vec3 vectorLightPosToPixel = normalize(distanceLightToPixel);
vec3 lightDirNormalized = normalize(lightDir);
float angleBetweenLightNormal =
    dot( -vectorLightPosToPixel, vTransformedNormal );
```

A point light shines in all directions, but a spotlight has a direction and an expanding cone of light surrounding this direction. For a pixel to be lit by a spotlight, that pixel must be in this cone of light. This is the *beam width* area where the pixel receives the full amount of light, which fades out towards the *cut-off angle* that is the angle where there is no more light coming from this spotlight:

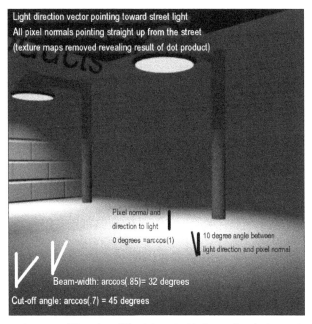

With texture maps removed, we reveal the value of the dot product between the pixel normal and direction of the light

```
if ( pointLight) {
    lightAmt = 1.0;
}
else { // spotlight
```

```
        float angleLightToPixel =
            dot ( vectorLightPosToPixel, lightDirNormalized );

        // note, uStreetLightBeamWidth and uStreetLightCutOffAngle
        //  are the cosines of the angles, not actual angles
        if ( angleLightToPixel >= uStreetLightBeamWidth ) {
            lightAmt = 1.0;
        }
        if ( angleLightToPixel > uStreetLightCutOffAngle ) {
            lightAmt = (angleLightToPixel - uStreetLightCutOffAngle) /
            (uStreetLightBeamWidth - uStreetLightCutOffAngle);
        }
    }
}
```

After determining the amount of light at that pixel, we calculate attenuation, which is the fall-off of light over a distance. Without attenuation, the light is constant. The moon has no light attenuation since it's dim already, but the other three lights fade out at the maximum distance. The `float maxDist = 15.0;` code snippet says that after 15 units, there is no more contribution from this light. If we are less than 15 units away from the light, reduce the amount of light proportionately. For example, a pixel 10 units away from the light source receives *(15-10)/15* or *1/3* the amount of light:

```
attenuation = 1.0;
if ( uUseAttenuation ) {
    if ( length(distanceLightToPixel) < maxDist ) {
        attenuation =
            (maxDist - length(distanceLightToPixel))/maxDist;
    }
    else attenuation = 0.0;
}
```

Finally, we multiply the values that make the light contribution and we are done:

```
lightAmt *= angleBetweenLightNormal * attenuation;
return lightAmt;
```

Next, we must account for the brick wall's normal map using the `shaderLightsNormalMap-fs` fragment shader. The previous project introduced the normal texture map, but just for review; we use the red, green, and blue components of a texture to map for the *x*, *y*, and *z* coordinates of the pixel's normal. The normal is equal to **rgb * 2 − 1**. For example, rgb (1.0, 0.5, 0.0), which is orange, would become a normal (1.0, 0.0, -1.0). This normal is converted to a unit value or *normalized* to (0.707, 0, -0.707):

```
vec4 textureMapNormal = vec4( (texture2D(uSamplerNormalMap,
    vec2(vTextureCoord.s*uTextureMapTiling.s,
    vTextureCoord.t*uTextureMapTiling.t)) * 2.0) - 1.0 );
vec3 pixelNormal =
    normalize(uNMatrix * normalize(textureMapNormal.rgb) );
```

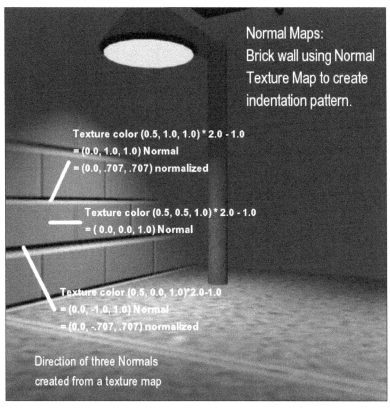

A normal mapped brick (without red brick texture image) reveals how changing the pixel normal alters the shading with various light sources

We call the same `calculateLightContribution()` function, but we now pass along `pixelNormal` calculated using the normal texture map:

```
calculateLightContribution(uSpotLight0Loc, uSpotLightDir,
pixelNormal, false);
```

From here, much of the code is the same, except we use `pixelNormal` in the dot product to determine the angle between the normal and the light sources:

```
float angleLightToTextureMap =
    dot( -vectorLightPosToPixel, pixelNormal );
```

Now, `angleLightToTextureMap` replaces `angleBetweenLightNormal` because we are no longer using the vertex normal embedded in the 3D mesh's `.obj` file, but instead we use the pixel normal derived from the normal texture map file, `brickNormalMap.png`.

A normal mapped brick wall with various light sources

Objective complete – mini debriefing

This comprehensive demonstration combined multiple spot and point lights, shared 3D meshes instead of loading the same 3D meshes, and deployed normal texture maps for a real 3D brick wall appearance. The next step is to build upon this demonstration, inserting links to web pages found on a typical website. In this example, we just identified a location for **Products** using a neon sign to catch the users' attention. As a 3D website is built, we will need better ways to navigate this virtual space and this is covered in the following section.

Portals to navigate virtual spaces

Even before the World Wide Web, linking to data non-sequentially was introduced in Apple's **Hypercard**. We know it today as hyperlinks or simply *links* in a website. Prior to this, most data was linear, such as this book or an article, where we read from the beginning to end. It took time for links to become intuitive. However, now when we see text underlined, a different color, or the mouse icon change, we know that clicking on hyperlinks takes us to another web page.

Virtual worlds have an even better navigation system—the **portal**. Perhaps our first portal could be attributed to the *Star Trek* transporter that could beam you from the *Enterprise* to another planet. So popular was the transporter that the phrase *beam me up* is part of our culture. Star Trek was hardly the first although, as other fictional works conceived vortexes to transfer from place to place. However, now 3D worlds make practical use of these portals, enabling us to navigate virtual worlds without having to drag our mouse hundreds of times to get across the virtual 3D website.

Engage thrusters

To create a portal, there is just one item required—an object representing the portal. We could just texture map that object, click on it, and go through the portal. Since no one wants to go someplace lifeless, we need animated objects inside the portal showing us that there is life on the other side. In addition, while we are at it, we will need some way to get back. Our two new portals are `portalWall1Object` and `portalWall2Object`. In the previous project, we introduced rendering the scene onto a texture map. This time we will declare two texture maps to render inside `webGLStart()` and name them `rttFramebuffer1` (render-to-texture) and `rttFramebuffer2`:

```
rttFramebuffer1 = gl.createFramebuffer(); // buffer memory area
rttTexture1 = gl.createTexture(); // render-to-texture texture
initTextureFramebuffer(rttFramebuffer1, rttTexture1);

rttFramebuffer2 = gl.createFramebuffer();
rttTexture2 = gl.createTexture();
initTextureFramebuffer(rttFramebuffer2, rttTexture2);
```

The call to `initTextureFramebuffer()` is the same as in the last project, although we now pass on the unique variables for each buffer memory area and the **rtt (render-to-texture)** map.

The `drawScene()` function is broken up so that the panels that are used for the portals use the same code to render the scene as the main camera. Thus, we now have a new function, `renderer()`, with a single parameter—the camera from where the scene should be rendered, once for each of the two portals and once for the 3D scene itself. Within `drawScene()`, we set the parameters to render the scene from the first portal camera and save it to `rttFramebuffer1`. Then, set up the parameters for the second portal camera, save its rendered image to `rttFramebuffer2`, and finally render the scene from the original camera:

```
function drawScene() {
    // switch from default to the render-to-texture frame buffer
    gl.bindFramebuffer(gl.FRAMEBUFFER, rttFramebuffer1);
    mat4.lookAt(portal1eye, portal1target, portal1up,
        portalCamera);
```

```
        drawRenderedTextureMap(rttFramebuffer1, rttTexture1,
            portalCamera );
        gl.bindFramebuffer(gl.FRAMEBUFFER, null);

        gl.bindFramebuffer(gl.FRAMEBUFFER, rttFramebuffer2);
        mat4.lookAt( portal2eye, portal2target, portal2up,
            portalCamera );
        drawRenderedTextureMap(rttFramebuffer2, rttTexture2,
            portalCamera );
        gl.bindFramebuffer(gl.FRAMEBUFFER, null);

        gl.clearColor( fogColor[0], fogColor[1], fogColor[2], 1.0);
        gl.viewport(0, 0, gl.viewportWidth, gl.viewportHeight);
        gl.clear(gl.COLOR_BUFFER_BIT | gl.DEPTH_BUFFER_BIT);
        target[0] = eye[0] + Math.sin(cameraRotation) *targetDistance;
        target[2] = eye[2] - Math.cos(cameraRotation) *targetDistance;
        mat4.lookAt( eye, target, up, camera );
        renderer(camera);
    } // end drawScene
```

The `drawRenderedTextureMap()` function sets the width and height of our memory area (preferably in dimensions of 2), and then calls the same `renderer()` function used to draw the original scene. On being returned from the `renderer()` function, we bind the `rttTexture` texture map object, which saves this image. As a texture map, we generate mipmaps, the previously discussed process that makes half-sized copies of the texture map blending neighboring pixels. Finally, we reset variables to null to build the next texture map:

```
    function drawRenderedTextureMap( rttFramebuffer, rttTexture,
        portalCamera ) {
        gl.clearColor(0.25, 0.25, 0.5, 1.0);
        gl.viewport(0,0, rttFramebuffer.width, rttFramebuffer.height);
        gl.clear(gl.COLOR_BUFFER_BIT | gl.DEPTH_BUFFER_BIT);
        renderer(portalCamera);
        gl.bindTexture(gl.TEXTURE_2D, rttTexture);
        gl.generateMipmap(gl.TEXTURE_2D);
        gl.bindTexture(gl.TEXTURE_2D, null);
    }   // end drawRenderedTextureMap
```

The textures have been created and are ready to be used inside the `renderer()` function. Within the `for` loop that draws all the 3D meshes, we check whether the current mesh is `portWall1Object` or `portalWall2Object`. The key line, `gl.bindTexture(gl.TEXTURE_2D, rttTexture1)`, assigns our generated portal texture as the texture map for our 3D mesh portal object:

```
if ( meshObjectArray[i] == portalWall1Object ) {
    gl.activeTexture(gl.TEXTURE0);
    gl.bindTexture(gl.TEXTURE_2D, rttTexture1 );
    gl.uniform1i(shaderProgram.samplerUniform, 0);
}
else if ( meshObjectArray[i] == portalWall2Object ) {
    gl.activeTexture(gl.TEXTURE0);
    gl.bindTexture(gl.TEXTURE_2D, rttTexture2 );
    gl.uniform1i(shaderProgram.samplerUniform, 0);
}
```

To see the effect of cameras in each portal, the rotating Earth and a teapot were added and can be seen in the portals on the left-hand side of the screen.

The new scene has the rotating teapot and Earth and the portals on the left

Now that the portal planes are rendering the scene live in real time, we have to detect when to go through the portal. We create a box named `portalActiviationBox` and set its coordinates to (5, 0, 2) in front of each portal. If the camera is within five units in front of the portal and two units in either direction of the center of the portal, we go through the portal. A distance of five units allows the user to see the entire portal texture map. We check the camera position for every frame inside the `tick()` function right after `handleKeys()` to see if we entered the portal area. Incidentally, this scene rotates the teapot and Earth inside the `tick()` function:

```
if ( (eye[0] > portalWall2Location[0]) &&
     (eye[0] < (portalWall2Location[0]+portalActiviationBox[0])) &&
     (eye[2] < (portalWall2Location[2]+portalActiviationBox[2])) &&
     (eye[2] > (portalWall2Location[2]-portalActiviationBox[2])) )
      {
      eye[0] = portal2target[0]-3.0;
      eye[2] = portal2target[2];
      cameraRotation = 1.57;
}
```

Once we go through the portal, the camera's view matches the portal's view. Therefore, if you walk towards the portal with the picture of the teapot, you come out on the other side looking at the teapot as shown in the following screenshot:

An up close view of the two portals where cameras are pointed in the opposite direction

The 3 percent gray borders surrounding the portal's texture maps were added to the `textureMapPortal` fragment shader to separate the portal from the background:

```
void main(void) {
    vec4 textureColor = texture2D(uSampler,
        vec2(vTextureCoord.s, vTextureCoord.t));
    if ( (vTextureCoord.s <= 0.03) || (vTextureCoord.s >= 0.97) )
        textureColor = vec4( 0.5, 0.5, 0.5, 1.0 );
    else if ((vTextureCoord.t <= 0.03)||(vTextureCoord.t >= 0.97))
        textureColor = vec4( 0.5, 0.5, 0.5, 1.0 );
    gl_FragColor = vec4(textureColor.rgb, 1.0);
}
```

Objective complete – mini debriefing

Designing portals is a cool feature in 3D web design. It made good use of code sharing between the existing scene renderer and only needed you to insert the new camera's transformation matrix.

Classified intel

The video game *Portal* and the *Unreal game engine editor* display portals as circles. Perhaps this gives a vortex effect that is a fairly simple modification in the shader. We only need to display pixels within a radius from the center of our portal, and then add a gray border as done previously.

A portal using a circle rather than a rectangle

Modify the `textureMapPortal` fragment shader by first calculating the distance from the center of the texture map to each pixel. In this example, our radius is 1, so any pixel within our radius will be displayed. Beyond a distance of 1, that pixel will be discarded as if it were transparent. Note that the texture map coordinates are from 0 to 1, so by multiplying the texture map's s and t coordinates with 2 and then subtracting one will give us coordinates from -1 to 1 in the *x* and *y* dimensions:

```
void main(void) {
    float distanceFromCenter =
        sqrt( pow((vTextureCoord.s * 2.0) - 1.0, 2.0) +
        pow((vTextureCoord.t * 2.0) - 1.0, 2.0) );
    vec4 textureColor = texture2D(uSampler,
        vec2(vTextureCoord.s, vTextureCoord.t));
    if ( distanceFromCenter > 1.0) discard;
    else if  ( distanceFromCenter > .97)
        textureColor = vec4( 0.5, 0.5, 0.5, 1.0 );
    gl_FragColor = vec4(textureColor.rgb, 1.0);
}
```

Another interesting illusion is having the portal camera look at the portal. Much like when a video camera is aimed at a television, the television displays smaller versions of itself as shown in the following screenshot. This is known as recursion and can be a cool effect in virtual spaces.

The camera is aimed at the portal and thus recursively displays the image. Note the rising moon in each image.

Another neat trick is to see ourselves in the portal. If we step in front of the portal's camera, we see ourselves—the current camera, which is our current position. The *Mario* video games were among the first to do this, as Mario looked into a mirror and saw a camera floating behind him. It captures the user's attention and reinforces the portal concept. The video game *Portal* used a generic female character instead of the movie camera when its two portals looked across from each other and you as the game player were in the middle.

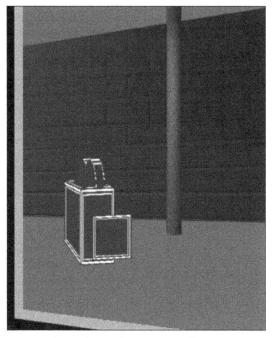

Seeing ourselves in the portal, as represented by a camera object

The 3D model movie camera is encasing the scene's camera. Since the actual camera is now inside our 3D modeled movie camera, it is important to include `gl.enable(gl.CULL_FACE)` to `webGLStart()`. This *culls* or removes the backsides of objects so that we can see through them from the inside. Incidentally, backface culling also speeds up performance since we don't render the backsides of objects.

In `drawScene()`, we moved up the camera transformation code to the beginning and set the translation of our new `cameraObject` to the same location as the camera. The camera rotates only around the *y* axis, but we have to negate this *y* value since the rendering of a camera rotates opposite the calculation of the actual camera. It's like looking into a mirror. If you step twice to the left, the mirror image looks as if you stepped twice to the right:

```
function drawScene() {
    target[0] = eye[0] + Math.sin( cameraRotation ) *
        targetDistance;
```

```
target[2] = eye[2] - Math.cos( cameraRotation ) *
    targetDistance;
mat4.lookAt( eye, target, up, camera );
cameraObject.translation = [eye[0], eye[1], eye[2]];
cameraObject.rotation = [0, -cameraRotation, 0];
. . .
```

Mission accomplished

We are at a point where it is time for our imagination to run wild. The missing elements are fun and creativity. We have looked at interesting lighting examples, converting textures that looked like wallpaper into textures with depth and an organic look, and virtual spaces with portals. Like most work in the field of computer graphics, we demonstrated the technical issues first and then allowed the designers to create the engaging scenery that connects us emotionally with their story.

Perhaps this final image poses the questions, "What do we see when we see ourselves designing WebGL websites? What do we see when we look deeper and deeper into virtual space?"

Portal camera looking into a portal; we can see ourselves over and over again

Project 9

Education in the Third Dimension

"If I were again beginning my studies, I would follow the advice of Plato and start with mathematics."

— Galileo Galilei

3D graphics for education just seems natural. What better way to learn than through experiential knowledge. And what better way to experience, aside from actually being on-location, than in a 3D environment. In fact, a 3D environment might be better than reality because virtual worlds can perform worst-case scenarios and test the extremes without any actual damage. We can simulate weak building structures, the effects of fire spreading, or navigation errors without a physical collapse, real destruction, or loss of life, such as training to avoid a plane crash.

Imagine not only learning a foreign language or reading a novel, but actually walking through a 3D virtual town in another country or a Shakespeare setting. We could also walk into microscopic spaces such as the heart or brain, or macroscopic spaces such as experiencing the conditions on another planet. From history to languages, from science to math, for creating art or for commerce, 3D is as natural a learning environment as any school or classroom.

Mission briefing

My introduction into 3D graphics came from developing educational video games. Upon learning the math algorithms used in moving objects and calculating lights, I knew 3D graphics would be a great educational tool. Few things engage students more and can be fun, whimsical, creative, and educational. The demonstrations focus on selecting atomic elements from the periodic chart where each item is a square, followed by countries from a map where the borders are irregular. The final example involves a mathematical demonstration of different algorithms for rotations. Thus, we shall use 3D graphics to learn math used in 3D graphics.

Why is it awesome?

Interactive 3D graphics offers such great opportunities to broaden education. It can be used to immerse oneself into environments to learn foreign languages, or go back into history to learn about cultures and world events. We can demonstrate physics, chemical experiments, or test math algorithms. Some of the first video games were *edutainment*—a term used to describe learning while playing—including *Oregon Trail*, *Reader Rabbit*, and *Math Blaster*, where I was Manager of Software. Education also includes job training. Reading a user manual would likely lead to much lower retention than an interactive 3D presentation. One of my first Web3D projects trained submarine commanders the control panel for the U.S. Department of Defense. Educators today are competing for attention with more stimulating media such as video games. Interactive 3D has the potential to be more engaging and fun to learn.

Your Hotshot objectives

The major tasks required to complete our project are as follows:

▶ Selecting locations on a texture map

▶ Selecting locations from a rotated texture map and perspective correction

▶ Selecting irregular shapes from a textured 3D mesh

▶ Using WebGL to teach math

Mission checklist

It seems logical that a project on applying 3D graphics to education should itself involve some background depth into the math behind 3D graphics. We shall learn how the graphics card actually draws texture maps upon objects that are often rotated and in perspective view. You may find yourself recalling old math algorithms from algebra, such as the equations of a line. This may reinforce the concept that 3D graphics is a terrific tool for education.

Selecting locations on a texture map

This first demonstration will show how we select specific points on a texture map facing the camera, without rotation. We shall use the periodic table from chemistry to select specific atomic elements. While we have performed ray-bounding box intersections in previous examples, this is quite different in that we want to select a specific location within the texture map. Such an application is well suited to select an item from a textured wall, such as an image of a doorknob, a light switch, or in education, pointing to specific organs of a human being.

Prepare for lift off

Our first example is applied to chemistry but the actual demonstration is picking an exact point in a polygon. We are using the mouse to select one of the over one hundred elements from the periodic table. We need to click on that table to select a specific element. Because we need a specific point on the 3D mesh, we cannot simply use bounding boxes to determine if we clicked on an entire 3D mesh. We have to use math that can detect the intersection of a ray (line) with a polygon. And we have to calculate this for every polygon in the 3D mesh until we find an intersection or until we exhaust the list of polygons in the 3D mesh. This may sound mathematically intensive, time consuming, and prohibitive in real time, but if we can limit the 3D mesh to just a few polygons, then we can get precise ray-polygon intersection in real time.

If you are video game player, perhaps you have noticed the inaccuracies of hitting a target, such as a pass thrown in Madden NFL that was caught yet nowhere near the receiver. Or you have played Call of Duty and knew you hit a target but it never registered. In video games, characters and objects are often made up of thousands of polygons, so we are limited to bounding-box collision detection. Ray-polygon detection would be too time-consuming for video games. We should also note that ray-tracing, which reflects surfaces of other surfaces, such as polished metal and glass, also uses ray-polygon intersection.

Ray-polygon intersection uses **Barycentric coordinates** – a series of matrices and determinates to detect the 3D point of intersection. We begin by labeling the vertices of a 3-vertex polygon as *a*, *b*, and *c*. We wish to find a point in the polygon intersected by the ray, labeled *(α, β, γ)*, the Greek lowercase letters alpha, beta, and gamma, as shown in the following figure:

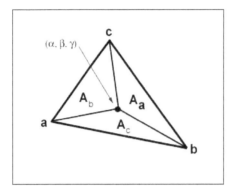

Triangle (*a*, *b*, *c*) searching for the ray intersection at (*α*, *β*, *γ*)

In this figure, the areas A_a, A_b, and A_c, all labeled opposite their vertices, add up to the total area of the triangle: $A_a + A_b + A_c$ = *area of the triangle*.

To calculate the point of intersection, we use a series of **determinants** based on 3 x 3 matrices, but before we do that, we need to know how we calculate determinants. We've been given a 3 x 3 matrix, with the nine values labeled from **a** to **i**. Since a 3 x 3 determinant is a series of 2 x 2 matrices, the calculation of that 2 x 2 determinant is shown first, as follows:

2 x 2 matrix

$$\begin{bmatrix} a & b \\ c & d \end{bmatrix}$$

determinant: ab - bc

3 x 3 matrix

$$\begin{bmatrix} a & b & c \\ d & e & f \\ g & h & i \end{bmatrix} = a \begin{bmatrix} e & f \\ h & i \end{bmatrix} - d \begin{bmatrix} b & c \\ h & i \end{bmatrix} + g \begin{bmatrix} b & c \\ e & f \end{bmatrix}$$

determinant:

a(ei - hf) - d(bi - ch) + g(bf - ce) =
aei - ahf - bdi + bfg + cdh - ceg

Determinant of a 2 x 2 matrix, and a 3 x 3 matrix, which is a series of 2 x 2 matrices

Now that we know how to calculate determinants from 3 x 3 matrices, let's utilize the equations of the various matrices. We are looking for the point *(α, β, γ)* if and where our ray goes through the polygon. This point also fits the equation using the earlier figure. We will apply determinants to calculate the areas of triangles A_a, A_b, A_c, and *A* as follows:

$$\alpha = A_a/A$$
$$\beta = A_b/A$$
$$\gamma = A_c/A$$

Another way to write this is *point(α, β, γ) = α a+β b+γ c*, where *a*, *b*, and *c* are the *x*, *y*, and *z* vertices of the triangle. We can also write this in the following expanded form:

$$point(\alpha, \beta, \gamma) = \alpha(a_x, a_y, a_z)+\beta(b_x, b_y, b_z)+\gamma(c_x, c_y, c_z)$$

We know the *x*, *y*, and *z* coordinates of the points of the three vertices, so we now need to find: *α*, *β*, and *γ*.

Let's start with *A*:

$$A = \begin{bmatrix} a_x - b_x & a_x - c_x & d_x \\ a_y - b_y & a_y - c_y & d_y \\ a_z - b_z & a_z - c_z & d_z \end{bmatrix}$$

Triangle area matrix using the three triangle vertices and the mouse-click point converted to 3D

We know *a*, *b*, and *c* refer to the *x*, *y*, and *z* values for each vertex. The *d* value refers to the distance plane. This is the location where the mouse clicks on (on our 2D screen), which gets converted to 3D space (the equation was covered in detail in *Project 6, 3D Reveals More Information*), and creates the ray from the camera into the 3D scene. In the program, this value is rayMouseDown = [xWorld, yWorld, -distanceToViewPlane, 1];, where xWorld and yWorld are 3D coordinates after the conversion from 2D screen coordinates and distanceToViewPlane = 1 / Math.tan((fieldOfView * Math.PI/180.0) / 2); is where fieldOfView is set to 45 degrees.

Once we find A, the determinant of the matrix, the determinants for β and γ are just variations. We need not calculate α since these three values must add up to A. If β or γ are less than 0 or greater than 1, the ray passes the polygon without intersection. If α, β, or γ equals 0 or 1, then the ray hits an edge. If two of the values are 0, then the ray hits a vertex. If after these calculations, $0 <= \beta <= 1$, $0 <= \gamma <= 1$, and $(\beta+\gamma) <= 1$, then we have met the requirements and confirmed the ray intersects the polygon and we can now calculate the exact point of intersection, as follows:

$$\beta = \frac{\begin{bmatrix} a_x & a_x - c_x & d_x \\ a_y & a_y - c_y & d_y \\ a_z & a_z - c_z & d_z \end{bmatrix}}{A}$$

$$\gamma = \frac{\begin{bmatrix} a_x - b_x & a_x & d_x \\ a_y - b_y & a_y & d_y \\ a_z - b_z & a_z & d_z \end{bmatrix}}{A}$$

β and γ matrices, divided by the determinant of the area matrix

Before the final ray-polygon intersection calculation, let's pause and have a look at a right triangle, vertices at (1, 8, 0), (1, 2, 0), and (9, 2, 0) and ray going through at (5, 4, 0) that illustrates the point:

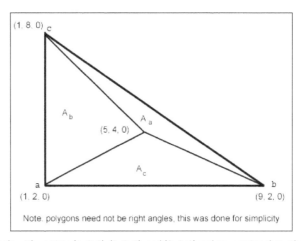

Right triangle with vertices (1, 8, 0), (1, 2, 0), and (9, 2, 0) and ray passing through at (5, 4, 0)

The area of a right triangle is 1/2 base times height. The base is *9-1 = 8*, and the height is *8-2 = 6*. Therefore, the area is *1/2 x 8 x 6 = 24*.

A_b (area of triangle b) is calculated by dividing the triangle into two right triangles from (5, 4, 0) to (1, 4, 0), shown as follows:

▶ The area of the upper triangle is *1/2 x (8-4) x (5-1) = 8*

▶ The area of the lower triangle is *1/2 x (4-2) x (5-1) = 4*

▶ Add both *8* and *4*, which gives us *12*, the area of A_b

A_c (area of triangle c) is also subdivided into two right triangles, each with a height of *(4-2)=2*. The left portion has a base of *(5-1)=4*, and the right portion a base of *(9-5)=4*. Thus, the total area is *(1/2×2×4)+(1/2×2×4)=8*.

Finally, triangle A_a is the remainder *24-(12+8)=4*. Let's go back to Barycentric coordinates:

$$\alpha = A_a/A = 4/24 = 1/6$$
$$\beta = A_b/A = 12/24 = 1/2$$
$$\gamma = A_c/A = 8/24 = 1/3$$
$$point(\alpha, \beta, \gamma) = \alpha\ a+\beta\ b+\gamma\ c = 1/6*(1, 2, 0)+1/2(9, 2, 0)+1/3(1, 8, 0)$$
$$(1/6+9/2+1/3, 2/6+2/2+8/3, 0+0+0) = (5, 4, 0)$$

A lot of work indeed, but hopefully this example provided some insights to Barycenteric coordinates. The last step is that once we determine that α, β, and γ are each greater than 0 and less than 1, and thus determine that the ray intersects the polygon, we can then calculate the exact point of intersection in the polygon by calculating the determinant of the *t* matrix, and multiplying our ray by *t* for the exact coordinate on the polygon. Based on this point on the polygon, we can find the point on the texture map. Readers may wish to review the *Using the mouse for interactivity* section in *Project 2, WebGL for E-Commerce*, for more details on the point of intersection. Have a look at the following figure:

$$t = \frac{\begin{bmatrix} a_x - b_x & a_x - c_x & a_x \\ a_y - b_y & a_y - c_y & a_y \\ a_z - b_z & a_z - c_z & a_z \end{bmatrix}}{A}$$

t is derived from calculating the determinant. Multiply t by the (x, y, z) rayMouseDown value for the exact point of ray-polygon intersection

Engage thrusters

For this demonstration, the user will click on the periodic table used for the atomic elements, and display an enlarged version of that element in the panel to the left. If the user clicks on a place other than an atomic element or outside the 3D mesh, then we revert to the original scene, as shown in the following screenshot:

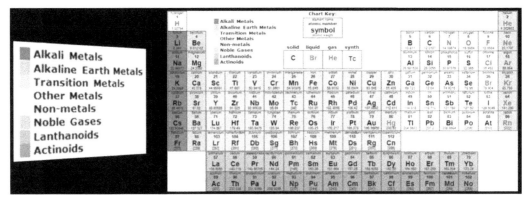

Opening scene – periodic chart on the right with a textured plane on the left displaying the chart's legend

As we have done before with intersections, when there is a `mouseDownEvent()`, we check if the ray intersected the bounding box. This is for efficiency so we only check for ray-polygon intersections once we first determined that the mouse intersects the object's bounding box. Once we determine the mouse click was within the periodic table mesh's bounding box, we perform our refined ray-polygon intersection. We multiply the periodic table's original coordinates by its transformation matrix, previously saved in the `boundingBoxMatrix` to give us a set of transformed vertices. Recall that inside the shaders, we multiply the vertices by the transformation matrix, but now we perform this multiplication so we can check for ray-polygon intersection. We have to perform this check for each polygon in the 3D mesh and that is why this is inside a `for` loop. We copy the vertices from the `periodicTableObject` in the `vertex` array, transform the vertices by the bounding box matrix, and save the result in `transformedVertexArray`, as shown in the following code:

```
if ( RayBoundingBoxIntersection( periodicTableObject, xWorld,
    yWorld ) ) {
    for (i = 0; i < periodicTableObject.vertices.length/3; i++ ) {
        var vertex = [ periodicTableObject.vertices[i*3],
            periodicTableObject.vertices[i*3+1],
        periodicTableObject.vertices[i*3+2], 1 ];
    var transformedVertex = [];
    mat4.multiplyVec4( periodicTableObject.boundingBoxMatrix,
      vertex, transformedVertex);
```

```
      transformedVertexArray[i*3] = transformedVertex[0];
      transformedVertexArray[i*3+1] = transformedVertex[1];
      transformedVertexArray[i*3+2] = transformedVertex[2];
   }
```

The next step involves setting up the three matrices—*area*, *β*, and *γ*—followed by calculating the determinants for each. Following the algorithm, both the *β* and *γ* determinants are divided by the area determinant. It should be noted that these three determinants can be negative values depending on which vertex we start with, but dividing two negatives will result in a positive, as shown in the following code:

```
set3x3Matrices(0);
var detA = get3x3MatrixDerminent(area);
var detBeta = get3x3MatrixDerminent(beta);
var detGamma = get3x3MatrixDerminent(gamma);
var detBetaDivArea = detBeta / detA;
var detGammaDivArea = detGamma / detA;

if ( ((detBetaDivArea + detGammaDivArea) < 1) &&
     (detBetaDivArea > 0) && (detGammaDivArea > 0) ) {
        var element = getIntersectionPt(detA);
        if (element != 0) clickedOnChart = true;
        else clickedOnChart = false;
}
```

Though we covered the math for setting the 3 x 3 matrices, the following code is a portion of set3x3Matrices() to create the *β* matrix. The offset value is either 0 for the first triangle using the *x*, *y*, and *z* values for the first three vertices (a total of nine numbers) in transformedVertexArray, or it is 1 for the second triangle, which is the next nine values in transformedVertexarray, as shown in the following code:

```
beta[0] = transformedVertexArray[offset*9];// ax
beta[1] = transformedVertexArray[offset*9] -
     transformedVertexArray[offset*9+6];// ax - cx
beta[2] = rayMouseDown[0]; // dx
beta[3] = transformedVertexArray[offset*9+1];// ay
beta[4] = transformedVertexArray[offset*9+1] -
     transformedVertexArray[offset*9+7];// ay - cy
beta[5] = rayMouseDown[1];// dy
beta[6] = transformedVertexArray[offset*9+2];// az
beta[7] = transformedVertexArray[offset*9+2] -
     transformedVertexArray[offset*9+8]; // az - cz
beta[8] = rayMouseDown[2];// dz
```

The `get3x3MatrixDeterminent()` function is the code for calculating the matrix, as presented in the following code:

```
function get3x3MatrixDeterminant(matrix3x3) {
    var det = matrix3x3[0] *
    ((matrix3x3[4]*matrix3x3[8]) - (matrix3x3[7]*matrix3x3[5]));
    det -= matrix3x3[3] *
    ((matrix3x3[8]*matrix3x3[1]) - (matrix3x3[7]*matrix3x3[2]));
    det += matrix3x3[6] *
    ((matrix3x3[1]*matrix3x3[5]) - (matrix3x3[2]*matrix3x3[4]));
    return det;
}   // end get3x3MatrixDeterminent
```

After calculating the determinants and area percentages, we apply the test that β and γ are both greater than 0, but summed to be less than 1. If this test passes, we find the intersection point of the ray with the triangle by calling `getIntersectionPt(detA);`.

The `getIntersectionPt()` function creates the matrix for finding the *(x, y, z)* intersection point between the ray and the polygon. The first task is to create the *t* matrix and then its determinant. Multiplying this `detTpt` value by the ray will give us the actual intersection point on the polygon, as shown in the following code:

```
function getIntersectionPt(detA) {
    . . .
    var detTpt = get3x3MatrixDeterminant(tPt);
    intersectionPt[0] = rayMouseDown[0] * detTpt/detA;
    intersectionPt[1] = rayMouseDown[1] * detTpt/detA;
    intersectionPt[2] = rayMouseDown[2] * detTpt/detA;
```

This is the intersection of the ray and polygon. We now have to convert this to the location on a texture map by offsetting this point by the lower-left corner of the 3D mesh using the following `for` loop:

```
for (i=0; i < 3; i++) {
    intersectionPt[i] -= transformedVertexArray[i+3];
}
```

The final step is to determine which atomic element was clicked on. The periodic chart is textured on a 8 x 4 polygon. We have to convert this into a polygon that is 1 x 1 so we divide the *(x, y)* values of the intersection point by 1/8 for the *x* value, and 1/4 for the *y* value. The atomic chart is divided into a grid of 18 columns by 9 rows. To get the specific atomic element, the *x* and *y* values are divided by 18 and 9. Since the 2D screen's *y* value increments vertically, that is, 0 is the top of the 2D screen and the values increase as we go down, but the *y* value in 3D increases as we go up, the values get inverted by subtracting from 8, as shown in the following code:

```
            periodTableElementTextureCoord =
                [ intersectionPt[0]/8.0, intersectionPt[1]/4.0 ];
            var xPos = parseInt(periodTableElementTextureCoord[0] * 18);
            var yPos = 8 - parseInt(periodTableElementTextureCoord[1]* 9);
            periodTableElementTextureCoord = [xPos/18.0, (8.0-yPos)/9.0 ];
            return periodicChart[xPos + yPos * 18];
    }
```

The final step seen in the preceding code snippet is to get the specific atomic element (Hydrogen is 1, Helium is 2, and so on) using a look-up table that is an array of 18 by 9, representing the squares on a periodic table. If an element is clicked on, such as Helium, then 2 is returned from the array; otherwise, 0 is returned, meaning we clicked on a whitespace in the periodic chart and we revert to the original image.

If the ray did not intersect the first polygon, we test the second polygon using the same steps except we change the parameter in `set3x3Matrices()` from 0 to 1.

In the `renderer()` function, called each time we redraw the image, we send `periodTableElementTextureCoord`, the lower-left texture coordinates of the element we clicked on, to the shader. The shader will then know which portion of the periodic chart element to display on the left panel using the following line of code:

```
    gl.uniform2f(shaderProgram.periodTableElementTextureCoordUniform,
        periodTableElementTextureCoord[0],
        periodTableElementTextureCoord[1] );
```

It also tests which texture map to use for `atomicElementObject` if the chart were clicked. If we clicked on an element in the periodic table, then we use the coordinates for that element off the chart. For example, **Oxygen**, the eighth element in row 2, column 16 has its lower left texture coordinates as (0.83, 0.78), using the equation *((column-1)/18, (9-row)/9) = (15/18, (9-2)/9)*. If we clicked elsewhere, then we display the default legend as seen in the previous screenshot using the following code:

```
    if (clickedOnChart)
        gl.bindTexture(gl.TEXTURE_2D, periodicTableObject.textureMap);
    else
        gl.bindTexture(gl.TEXTURE_2D, atomicElementObject.textureMap);
```

In the following screenshot, the example displays after clicking on element 8, Oxygen:

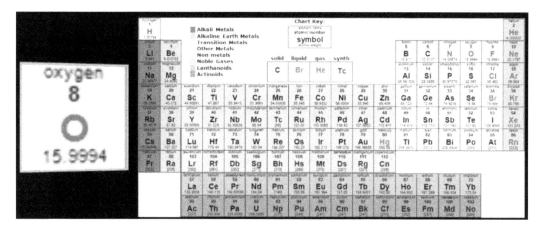

The atomic element has its own fragment shader that receives `uPeriodTableElementTextureCoord`, the coordinates of the lower left corner of the element just clicked on. The texture coordinate's width equals *1/18=0.055*, since there are 18 columns, and height equals *1/9=0.11*, since there are 9 rows. The portion of the periodic table texture maps that has Oxygen is (0.83, 0.78) in the lower left to (0.886, 0.889) in the upper right. Finally, a gold border is drawn around the box, as presented in the following code:

```
void main(void) {
    vec2 dimen = vec2( 1.0/18.0, 1.0/9.0 );
    vec4 textureColor = texture2D(uSampler, vec2(
        uPeriodTableElementTextureCoord.s +
        (vTextureCoord.s * dimen.s),
        uPeriodTableElementTextureCoord.t +
        (vTextureCoord.t * dimen.t) ) );
    if ( (vTextureCoord.s <= 0.02) || (vTextureCoord.s >= 0.98) )
        textureColor = vec4( 0.8, 0.7, 0.0, 1.0 );
    else if ((vTextureCoord.t <= 0.02)||(vTextureCoord.t >= 0.98))
    textureColor = vec4( 0.8, 0.7, 0.0, 1.0 );
    gl_FragColor = vec4(textureColor.rgb, 1.0);
}
```

Objective complete – mini debriefing

This was a good exercise on getting precise coordinates on a texture map. Yet this example was simplified to a grid on a flat plane. The camera did not rotate, and we could only move forward and back. Next, we will look at selecting texture map coordinates when the 3D meshes and/or camera are rotated.

Selecting locations from a rotated texture map and perspective correction

The next challenge is clicking on a specific region of a texture map when the camera or mesh is rotated. The number of vertical and horizontal pixels will not be the same and nor will they be located in the same place. The texture coordinates will need to be precise and rotated. Using the California flag, shown in the following screenshot, the distance of the star from the left edge is smaller once the flag is rotated. In addition, the letters are equally spaced above but not when the flag is rotated.

The California state flag rotated to show how clicking on individual regions needs to adjusted for rotations

Engage thrusters

As before, we generate a ray into the 3D scene based on the mouse click with one of the ray's endpoints beginning at the camera that sits at the origin at (0, 0, 0). If the ray intersects the mesh's bounding box, we then call getElementIntersection(), which is a revision from the previous example's getIntersectionPt() function.

We know the periodic table is a grid of 18 columns by 9 rows, so we need to generate texture map coordinates for each position on this 18 x 9 grid. We will use this information for detecting ray-polygon intersections. In the previous example, we only checked two polygons, now there will be a grid of 18 x 9, and each cell will consist of two polygons for each chemical element on the periodic chart. Then we check if the ray intersects any one of these nearly 400 polygons (18 x 9 x 2). First, we create the texture coordinates. The width and height values are taken from the x and y vertices of the 3D mesh we just clicked. We are still using the periodic table that is 18 x 9 in size, as shown in the following code:

```
function getElementIntersection() {
    var width = (clickedOnObject.vertices[6] -
        clickedOnObject.vertices[0])/18;
    var height = -(clickedOnObject.vertices[1] -
        clickedOnObject.vertices[4])/9;
    var elementBoxArray = [];
    for (row = 0; row <= 9; row++ ) {
        for (col = 0; col <= 18; col++) {
            elementBoxArray[(col + row*19)*3] =
                clickedOnObject.vertices[0] + width * col;
            elementBoxArray[(col + row*19)*3+1] =
                clickedOnObject.vertices[1] + height * row;
            elementBoxArray[(col + row*19)*3+2] = 0;//z value
        }
    }
}
```

Following this, we rotate the texture coordinates the same as the 3D mesh, again using the boundingBoxMatrix, which has the meshes rotation. We take each texture map coordinate saved in the elementBoxArray, following the matrix multiplication one coordinate at a time. We save the new transformed array, transformedTextureMapVertexArray, as presented in the following code:

```
var textureMapVertex = [];
var transformedTextureMapVertex = [];
var transformedTextureMapVertexArray = [];
```

```
for (var i = 0; i < elementBoxArray.length/3; i++ ) {
    textureMapVertex = [ elementBoxArray[i*3],
        elementBoxArray[i*3+1], elementBoxArray[i*3+2], 1 ];
        mat4.multiplyVec4( clickedOnObject.boundingBoxMatrix,
    textureMapVertex, transformedTextureMapVertex);
    transformedTextureMapVertexArray[i*3] =
    transformedTextureMapVertex[0];
    transformedTextureMapVertexArray[i*3+1] =
    transformedTextureMapVertex[1];
    transformedTextureMapVertexArray[i*3+2] =
    transformedTextureMapVertex[2];
}
```

Now we go through each pair of polygons formed by the transformed texture coordinates to determine if the ray intersects a cell on the atomic periodic table. This code is similar to the previous example—it just has many more polygons. Of course, for all those polygons, we use `for` loops to check each cell on the periodic chart, a series of 9 rows by 18 columns x 2 polygons, as presented in the following code:

```
for (row = 0; row < 9; row++) {
    for (col = 0; col < 18; col++) {
        // set-up the next polygon
        polygon = [
            transformedTextureMapVertexArray[(row*19+col)*3+3],
            transformedTextureMapVertexArray[(row*19+col)*3+4],
            transformedTextureMapVertexArray[(row*19+col)*3+5],
            transformedTextureMapVertexArray[(row*19+col)*3+0],
            transformedTextureMapVertexArray[(row*19+col)*3+1],
            transformedTextureMapVertexArray[(row*19+col)*3+2],
            transformedTextureMapVertexArray[((row+1)*19+col)*3+0],
            transformedTextureMapVertexArray[((row+1)*19+col)*3+1],
            transformedTextureMapVertexArray[((row+1)*19+col)*3+2]
        ]
    set3x3Matrices(polygon);
. . .
```

The following screenshot displays rotating meshes and camera demonstrating clicking on a mesh:

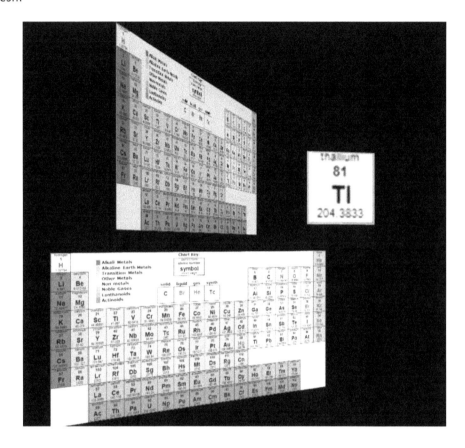

The function assembles three vertices to create the polygon that gets passed to the set3x3Matrices() function, modified slightly to handle an unlimited number of polygons. The previous code assumed only two polygons made up the mesh. Since each cell is made up of two polygons, the preceding code is repeated to check for the second polygon.

Objective complete – mini debriefing

We can click on individual items now in a periodic chart or any other image assembled in nice neat boxes or triangles. It was a lot of work too, first checking if we clicked on the object contained inside the bounding box and then searching each pair of triangles that made up a cell on the chart to identify the actual cell that was clicked on. Finally, we looked up if this cell was part of the periodic chart.

We took advantage of an image laid out in a pattern of squares and were able to rotate around the object from any angle. But, what happens when the items on a texture map are not in boxes, but random dimensions, such as countries with jagged borders and coastlines? That is what awaits us next.

Selecting irregular shapes from a textured 3D mesh

3D for education has unlimited possibilities because it adapts so well to demonstrations and presentations. For instance, we can click on organs of the body to teach Biology. But, as we have seen previously, this can be tedious to model. We may be better off applying a texture map and then clicking on individual components. Unfortunately, none of these components, such as the organs of the body fit into nice easy boxes like our periodic table of elements. Instead, we need to select individual pixels on the texture map, and have a system that identifies a particular pixel with the component. Clicking on a pixel within the image of the heart identifies the object that was clicked on as the heart. That alone requires some special programming. But, there is another issue, **texture map perspective correction**, that up until now was handled by the graphics card when we send the vertices and texture map to the fragment shader. However, we must now program this ourselves.

Prepare for lift off

Perspective projection is one of the issues that gives 3D its 3D look. Perspective projection means when objects in the distance look smaller than in the foreground. Nearly all our programs have passed a perspective matrix, pMatrix, to the shaders. The math for perspective projection is an additional matrix multiplication. However, laying down the texture map is a bit more of a complex task. If a polygon is at an angle to the camera, the more distant portions of that polygon use fewer and fewer pixels from the texture map. We end up skipping over every few pixels. Fortunately, the graphics card handles this for us. However, if we need to select a specific pixel, we will need to perform this operation too.

To understand perspective correction, it helps to see what happens without perspective correction. Since 3D meshes are made up of 3-vertex polygons, without perspective correction, they would render as if the mesh were a flat plane—the texture map has no concept of the depth of the vertices. Separately, these polygons look just fine, as shown in the following screenshot:

Two polygons that make up the California flag

However, when they are combined, as shown in the following screenshot, the problem is apparent because perspective correction has not been implemented:

Combining the two polygons reveals this bent rather than perspective look

The following figure represents an overhead view of a 3D plane angled to the camera on the left. The line on the far right, labeled **(x, z, u)**, is the original textured polygon at an angle to the camera. The rendering process places all 3D objects into perspective view and draws the entire scene onto a flat plane, represented by the line **z' = d**. Objects further back will appear smaller on the perspective view plane.

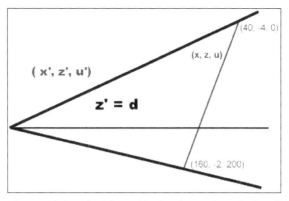

The polygon angled on the right, and final rendering where z' = d on the left

The process of taking pixels from the original object onto the flat plane while skipping pixels to preserve the perspective view begins with the equation of a line, as follows:

$$y=mx+b$$

Here (x, y) are points on a line, m is the slope, and b is the y intercept. This may be recalling your days in algebra. Modifying the equation for our perspective changes in the x and z horizontal direction, our new equation becomes $x = mz+b$. The slope m is calculated by the following equation:

$$m=(x_1-x_0)/(z_1-z_0)$$

Applying sample values, let's assume that the polygon's x value (width) goes from 40 to 160 units, and the depth from -4 to -2 units. By putting these values in the equation, we get the following:

$$m=(160-40)/(-2-(-4))=120/2=60$$

Coming back to our original equation, $x = mz+b$, and inserting (40, -4), we get the following:

$$b=x-mz=40-60*(-4)=280$$

Now, just like the right line uses (x, z), the line in perspective-view uses (x', z'), pronounced x prime and z prime. And the ratio is related as $x'/z' = x/z$. Recall that z' equals d, the distance from the camera to the perspective view plane and is calculated from the equation $d=1/Math.tan(fieldOfView/2)$. With a 45 degree field-of-view, $d = 2.41$. However, to keep this example simple, let's use the field-of-view of 90 degrees, which will make $d = 1$. Back to our equation and with a little rearranging, we get the following:

$$x'=x*z'/z=x*d/z$$

Plugging in some known values like (40, -4) and (160, -2), we get the following:

$$x'_0=40*(-1/-4)=10 \text{ and } x'_1=160*(-1/-2)=80$$

Therefore, the width of our polygon is from 40 to 160 units, but the perspective view polygon is from 10 to 80 units. To see how perspective view works, let's see what happens to the mid-point of our original line, (100, -3): $x'_m = 100*(-1/-3) = 33$. The mid-point in our original polygon is now just 23 pixels from the left edge and 47 pixels from the right edge in perspective view. The pixel in the center of our texture map would now be closer to the left side than the right side in perspective view.

There is one last step in this process that the graphics card is required to perform and that is texture—not just the pixels on the edges and at the mid-point—but pixels in between, which in our case is $x'0=10$ on the left edge to $x'1=80$ on the right edge, one pixel at a time.

Let's rearrange a previous equation, $x=zx'/d$, and then replace x into our original equation, $x=mz+b$, so the new equation is $zx'/d=mz+b$. For the purposes of demonstration, we set $d=-1$, so we get $-zx'=mz+b$. After a little rearranging, $z(x'+m)=b$ and then $z=b/(x'+m)$.

With the equation $z=b/(x'+m)$, we have everything we need. We know x' steps for each pixel 10 through 80, and we previously calculated b, the line-intercept, and m, the slope. There is still one efficiency problem—we would like to step through this formula linearly. The final value for z at pixel 10, 11, 12, through 80 is not a simple addition. For example, the values for z at pixel 10, 11, 12, 13, and 14 will be the following:

$$z_{10} = 280/(10+60) = 4$$
$$z_{11} = 280/(11+60) = 3.94$$
$$z_{12} = 280/(12+60) = 3.89$$
$$z_{13} = 280/(13+60) = 3.84$$
$$z_{14} = 280/(14+60) = 3.78$$

The values were rounded off, but the differences between z_{10} and z_{11} are 0.06, between z_{11} and z_{12} are 0.05, and continuing on 0.05 and 0.06. At the end of the line, the difference between the final points, z_{79} and z_{80} are $z_{79} = 280/(79+60) = 2.014$ and $z_{80} = 280/(80+60) = 2$.

The problem is we cannot perform a simple addition to step through from the beginning of the line at pixel 10 to pixel 80. Moreover, in real-time computer graphics, we need fast calculations. However, if we flip the equation, $1/z = (x'+m)/b$, the equation becomes linear. Now, x' is simply incremented by 1 each time, as follows:

$$1/z_{10} = (10+60)/280 = 0.25$$
$$1/z_{11} = (11+60)/280 = 0.2536$$
$$1/z_{12} = (12+60)/280 = 0.2571$$
$$1/z_{13} = (13+60)/280 = 0.2607$$
$$1/z_{14} = (14+60)/280 = 0.2643$$

The difference between each pixel is 0.25357. To get each progressive _1/z_ value, just add 0.25357 (rounded off), which is much simpler.

Let's relate this to grabbing a texture map pixel for each _x'_ location based on the _1/z_ value. We return to a modified equation of a line, $u = m_t * z + b_t$, using the _t_ subscript (for the texture map) to distinguish from the previous line equation, and _u_ is the texture map coordinate.

In our example, _u_, the texture map's horizontal dimension is from 0 to 200. The _z_ depth values remain from -4 to -2. We will calculate the slope for the texture map, m_t as follows:

$$m_t = (u_1 - u_0)/(z_1 - z_0) = (200-0)/(-2-(-4)) = 200/2 = 100$$

Next, calculate the intercept b_t as follows:

$$b_t = u - m_t * z = 200 - 100*(-2) = 200+200 = 400$$

We can now combine the equations _z=b/(x'+m)_ and $u=m_t*z+b_t$ to input the _x'_ values and get a _u_ value. Fortunately, the graphics card and **OpenGL ES** does all this work for us. Moreover, the equations for getting the texture map pixel vertically is a similar equation, just replace _x_ and _u_ with _y_ and _v_. Now let's program the picking up of a pixel on a texture map.

Engage thrusters

Our example will allow us to click on a world map and tell us the country. The example begins with the map rotated but we can also move the camera. We limited the example to clicking on Canada, Great Britain, and the United States (including Alaska and Hawaii), but there is no limit to the entire world's map. The following screenshot shows a world map, where we can click on any country:

This example builds on the first example, where we check if we clicked within the bounding box that encompasses the world map mesh and then check if we clicked inside one of the two polygons. If the mouse did click inside either polygon, we call a modified version of `getIntersectionPt()` from the first example. Midway through the code, after we establish the intersection point of the ray with the world map mesh, we get the *x-z-u* perspective correction.

We begin by calculating the slopes *m* and m_t and intercepts *b* and b_t for both the original mesh and the texture map, as presented in the following code:

```
// x-z-u perspective correction
// slope for the 3D mesh
var xzSlope =
    (transformedVertexArray[6] - transformedVertexArray[0]) /
    (transformedVertexArray[8] - transformedVertexArray[2]);
// slope for the texture map
var uzSlope =
    (EarthWallMapObject.textureMap.image.width - 0) /
    (transformedVertexArray[8] - transformedVertexArray[2]);

// b intercept for 3D mesh and texture map
var xzIntercept = transformedVertexArray[0] -
    xzSlope * transformedVertexArray[2];
var uzIntercept = - uzSlope * transformedVertexArray[2];
```

Next, we determine the *x'* (`xPrime`) value, which produces *1/z* (`OneOverZ`), giving us our final u value for the horizontal pixel location, as shown in the following code:

```
// x' = x*z'/z where z' = d
var xPrime = intersectionPt[0] * -distanceToViewPlane /
    intersectionPt[2];
var uIntersectionPt = (EarthWallMapObject.textureMap.image.width *
    intersectionPt[0]) /
(transformedVertexArray[6] - transformedVertexArray[0]);
OneOverZ = (xPrime - xzSlope * -distanceToViewPlane) /
    (xzIntercept * -distanceToViewPlane);
var u = uzSlope * (1/OneOverZ) + uzIntercept;
```

The vertical v value is calculated in a similar way, except instead of x and u, we use the v and y values. Since the texture map is only rotated around the *y* axis, there is no perspective distortion in the vertical direction and thus the `vIntersectionPt` is all we need to calculate.

We have found the texture points, but those are floating point numbers so we need to round off to get the nearest pixel by adding 0.5 and converting it to an integer value, using the following line of code:

```
texturePt = [ parseInt(u + .5), parseInt(vIntersectionPt + .5) ]
```

We now have to relate this texture map point to an actual country. For that, we have an additional texture map color-coded to indicate which country is clicked on. The portion of the texture map shown has Canada as red (dark gray), Great Britain in gold (light gray), and the United States in blue (black in the figure). This texture map, `earthMapTexture`, has the same dimensions as the original world map. Have a look at the following screenshot:

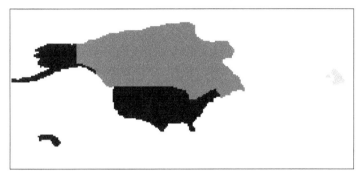

The Earth map texture showing pixels that are dark gray (red) for Canada, light gray (gold) for Great Britain, and black (blue) for the United States

Reading in `earthMapTexture` in the `alternateTextureMap` function saves the image in the graphics card buffer. We call our newly added function, `initTextureMapFrameBuffer()`, to retrieve the copy of `earthMapTexture` so we can read the individual pixels. Normally, reading individual pixels has been the job of the shader languages.

First, we save an array of bytes the size of the texture map, multiplied by 4 for the red, green, blue, and alpha byte that makes up each pixel. A frame buffer is then created, which allows us to read and write into and then proceed to copy the texture map into the frame buffer. After validating that the frame buffer was created correctly, the `gl.readPixels` command copies the pixels into the `earthMapPixels` array, as shown in the following code:

```
function initTextureMapFramebuffer( altTextureMap ) {
    earthMapPixels = new Uint8Array(altTextureMap.image.height *
        altTextureMap.image.width * 4);
    var fb = gl.createFramebuffer();
    gl.bindFramebuffer(gl.FRAMEBUFFER, fb);
    gl.framebufferTexture2D(gl.FRAMEBUFFER, gl.COLOR_ATTACHMENT0,
        gl.TEXTURE_2D, altTextureMap, 0);
```

```
        if (gl.checkFramebufferStatus(gl.FRAMEBUFFER) ==
            gl.FRAMEBUFFER_COMPLETE) {
            gl.readPixels(0, 0, altTextureMap.image.width,
            altTextureMap.image.height, gl.RGBA,
                gl.UNSIGNED_BYTE, earthMapPixels);
            gl.bindFramebuffer(gl.FRAMEBUFFER, null);
        }
    }
```

Back in the `getIntersectionPt()` function, we previously found the *x* and *y* pixel coordinates by clicking on the map. Pixels in this array begin in the upper-left corner of the texture map, across 512 pixels, and then begin with the next row. Once we find which pixel number (`pixelNum`) was clicked on, we match the pixel's colors: red for Canada (gray), blue for the United States (black in the physical book), and Gold (light gray), using the RGB values of 230, 205, and 0 respectively for Great Britain, as shown in the following code:

```
var pixelNum = (( texturePt[1] *
    EarthWallMapObject.textureMap.image.width) + texturePt[0])*4;
if ( (earthMapPixels[pixelNum] == 230) &&
    (earthMapPixels[pixelNum+1] == 205) &&
    (earthMapPixels[pixelNum+2] == 0) ) {
    countryDivTag.innerHTML = "GREAT BRITAIN";
}
else if ( (earthMapPixels[pixelNum] == 255) &&
    (earthMapPixels[pixelNum+1] == 0) &&
    (earthMapPixels[pixelNum+2] == 0) ) {
    countryDivTag.innerHTML = "CANADA";
}
else if ( (earthMapPixels[pixelNum] == 0) &&
    (earthMapPixels[pixelNum+1] == 0) &&
    (earthMapPixels[pixelNum+2] == 255) ) {
    countryDivTag.innerHTML = "UNITED STATES";
}
else { countryDivTag.innerHTML = ""; }
```

The variable `countryDivTag` refers to an HTML `<DIV>` tag saved in the initial `webGLStart()` function as shown in the following line of code:

```
countryDivTag = document.getElementById('idCountry');
```

Our options are virtually unlimited with this method as there are 256 red, green, and blue colors, providing over 16.7 million color combinations, so identifying all the world's countries would be no problem.

Objective complete – mini debriefing

Once again, a lot of code built upon math formulas to demonstrate how to pick a specific point on a texture map. This also introduced us to what happens behind the scenes deep inside the graphics chip that executes the rendering of texture maps. Perspective texture map correction is a tricky concept but is quite valuable for identifying specific regions of a texture map, which in turn has unlimited applications. Up until now, we have pushed math that enables 3D graphics. Next, we will use 3D graphics to teach math.

Using WebGL to teach math

The number one selling educational game, or edutainment, back in 1995 was *Math Blaster*. Children were playing the hero's role, defeating evil, being challenged, having fun, all while they were learning. That game was 2D. It was an obvious match then to use 3D graphics technology to teach math concepts. One advantage of teaching with real-time 3D graphics is that you can experiment with the formulas by changing variables. This next demonstration is not only a practical example of rotations in 3D graphics, but we will also learn how animating rotations of 3D objects works using **quaternions**.

Prepare for lift off

Before we walk through the code, we need to cover two concepts: animation and rotations with quaternions. Animations can be an object moving, rotating, or scaling in one or more dimensions. Animation has three variables: the beginning transformation, the ending transformation, and a timer. This is also known as **key-frame animation** where the beginning and ending points are the key frames, and the computer generates the frames in between. Often, animations have multiple key frames; for example, a door opening may begin with an animation of the doorknob turning, followed by the door opening, then closing. For our purposes, however, we will limit ourselves to just the beginning and ending key frames.

The animation will occur over a designated amount of time, such as 4 seconds. At one second, the timer will equal 0.25 (1/4), at two seconds it will be 0.5, at three seconds the timer will be 0.75 (3/4), and when it is complete, the timer will equal 1. The calculation of an animation is as follows:

$$Animation_t = animation_{start}*(1-t)+animation_{end}*t$$

Here, *t* is the percent of time, $animation_{start}$ is the starting point, and $animation_{end}$ is the ending point. For example, if an object were to move from (-2, 1, 0) to (6, -3, 8) over 4 seconds, then at 1 second, *t = 1/4* and we would be at the following location:

$$(-2, 1, 0)*(1-0.25)+(6, -3, 8)*0.25 = (-1.5, 0.75, 0)+(1.5, -0.75, 2) = (0, 0, 2)$$

At the half-way point, we would be at the following location:

$$(-2, 1, 0)*(1-0.5)+(6,-3,8)*0.5 = (-1, 0.5, 0)+(3,-1.5,4) = (2,-1,4)$$

If we limit animation to a rotation around just one axis, calculations would be simple. However, rotations in 3D require multiplying three 4 x 4 matrices. Each 4 x 4 matrix multiplication would require *((4 multiplications plus 3 additions)*16 values)* for 64 multiplications + 48 additions for the rotation around the *x* axis and *y* axis: *Rx(φ)*Ry(ϑ)*. This result is then multiplied by the rotation *Rz(Φ)* around the *z* axis for another 64 multiplications and 48 additions. Quite time consuming for a real-time animation. Have a look at the following equations:

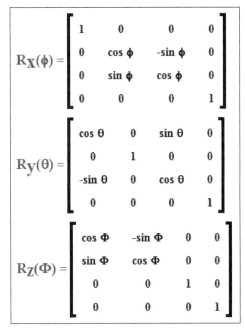

Matrices for rotation around the *x*, *y*, and *z* axis

This three-matrix multiplication is not only time consuming when the graphics are trying to render as fast as possible, but it may not produce the smoothest, most-direct animation either. For example, consider a flight from Los Angeles to Tokyo. On a globe, this appears to be a circular route flying close to the Hawaiian Islands. However, the actual shortest distance is the polar route flying over Anchorage, Alaska. Efficient rotation animations can be deceiving.

To solve this problem, we move up one dimension. For example, when we rotate around a circle, which is two dimensions, we are in fact rotating around the z axis, which is the third dimension. For rotations in 3D, we add the fourth dimension using an area of math known as quaternions. Since the fourth dimension is theoretical, and thus hard to visualize, we express it mathematically. We know the definition of a circle with a radius of 1 is $x^2+y^2 = 1$. The equation of a sphere with a radius of 1 is $x^2+y^2+z^2 = 1$. Therefore, the definition of a fourth dimensional sphere with a radius of 1 is as follows:

$$w^2+x^2+y^2+z^2 = 1$$

Now let's go from theory to practice – rotations are often specified in axis-angle format (ϑ, x, y, z), where ϑ is the angle and x, y, and z are the axis values that must be normalized, meaning a unit length, $x^2+y^2+z^2 = 1$. You might think of (x, y, z) as a location on a unit sphere, and the angle ϑ as the object's rotation on the sphere's edge. The conversion of axis-angle to a quaternion is performed as follows:

$$q = [cos(\vartheta/2), sin(\vartheta/2)*x, sin(\vartheta/2)*y, sin(\vartheta/2)*z]$$

Let's use an example to illustrate the conversion using *axis-angle = (1.2, 0.8, -0.5, 0.33)*. Note that (x, y, z), which is (0.8, -0.5, 0.33), is a unit value.

$$0.8^2+(-0.5)^2+0.33^2 = 1$$
$$q = [cos(1.2/2), sin(1.2/2)*0.8, sin(1.2/2)*(-0.5), sin(1.2/2)*0.33]$$

Reducing the calculations, we have the following:

$$q = [cos(0.6), sin(0.6)*0.8, sin(0.6)*(-0.5), sin(0.6)*0.33]$$
$$q = [0.825, 0.452, -0.2825, 0.1865]$$

Note, a unit value is as follows:

$$0.825^2+0.452^2+(-0.2825)^2+0.1865^2 = 1$$

For an animation, we will want to convert the beginning and ending axis-angles into quaternions labeled q_0 and q_1 for the start and end of the rotations respectively. The formula to interpolate between two quaternions to generate frames in between them is called **SLERP (Spherical Linear Interpolation)**:

$$SLERP\ (t;\ q_0,\ q_1) = [q_0*sin(\phi*(1-t)) + q_1*sin(\phi*t)]/sin(\phi)$$

Here, ϕ is the dot product of the two quaternions, which is the multiplication of their values. Note that the dot product $(q_0 \cdot q_1)$ calculates the cosine of the angle between the two quaternions. The inverse cosine, $arcos(q_0 \cdot q_1)$, returns the actual angle between the two quaternions as follows:

$$\Phi = arcos(q_0 \cdot q_1) = arcos(x_0*x_1+y_0*y_1+z_0*z_1+w_0*w_1)$$

The value *t* is time, a familiar value from 0.0 to 1.0. Let us try a simple example beginning with axis-angles values from (1.57, 1, 0, 0), a rotation of 90 degrees around the *x* axis, to (1.57, 0, 1, 0), a rotation of 90 degrees around the *y* axis using the following formula:

$$q_0 = (0.707, 0.707, 0, 0) \text{ and } q_1 = (0.707, 0, 0.707, 0)$$
$$\Phi = arcos(0.707*0+0*0.707+0*0+0.707*0.707) = 1.047$$

We will use 0.4 for time, which is 40 percent through the animation in the following formulae:

$$SLERP(0.4; q_0, q_1) = [q_0*sin(1.047*(1-0.4))+q_1*sin(1.047*0.4)]/sin(1.047)$$
$$SLERP(0.4; q_0, q_1) = [q_0*sin(0.6282)+q_1*sin(0.4188)]/0.866$$
$$[q_0*0.588+q_1*0.407]/0.866 = [q_0*0.679+q_1*0.470]$$
$$SLERP(0.4; q_0, q_1) = (0.707, 0.707, 0, 0)*0.679+(0.707, 0, 0.707, 0)*0.470$$
$$SLERP(0.4; q_0, q_1) = (0.480, 0.480, 0, 0)+(0.332, 0, 0.332, 0)$$
$$SLERP(0.4; q_0, q_1) = (0.812, 0.480, 0.322, 0)$$

Note that this value is a length of 1: $0.812^2+0.480^2+0.322^2+0^2 = 1$.

The final step is to convert this into a matrix that can be used in the rotation where the quaternion $q = (w, x, y, z)$, as follows:

$$
\begin{bmatrix}
1-2y^2-2z^2 & 2xy-2wz & 2xz+2wy & 0 \\
2xy+2wz & 1-2x^2-2z^2 & 2yz-2wx & 0 \\
2xz-2wy & 2yz+2wx & 1-2x^2-2y^2 & 0 \\
0 & 0 & 0 & 1
\end{bmatrix}
$$

Equation for converting a quaternion (*w, x, y, z*) to a matrix

Quaternions identify another efficiency that axis-angle does not by correcting for the shortest rotation direction. If a rotation is greater than 180 degrees, then rotating in the opposite direction will be shorter. For example, flying from Los Angeles to London could have the plane flying west over the Pacific Ocean to Japan, Russia, and Eastern Europe till we reach our final destination. However, we know flying east over New York and across the Atlantic Ocean and finally landing in London is much shorter.

If the dot product of the two quaternions is negative, then we know that rotation is greater than 180 degrees. To correct this, just negate q_1 and rotate as before. Recall that a rotation of 220 degrees is the same as rotating -140 degrees. Thus, consider the following calculation:

$$\Phi = arcos(q_0 \cdot q_1) = arcos(x_0*x_1+y_0*y_1+z_0*z_1+w_0*w_1)$$

Here, if Φ is negative, then set $q_1 = (x_1, y_1, z_1, w_1)$ to be $-q_1 = (-x_1, -y_1, -z_1, -w_1)$.

Quaternions may seem like a lot of work, but they are highly efficient and, as you shall see in the next demonstrations, create a smooth, minimal rotation.

Engage thrusters

This example includes a user interface to demonstrate an animated rotation using axis-angle values, and quaternions based on the axis-angle values. You can also set the total time for the animation. The following screenshot is a demonstration with the user interface to set the start and end rotations, time, and quaternion versus axis-angle:

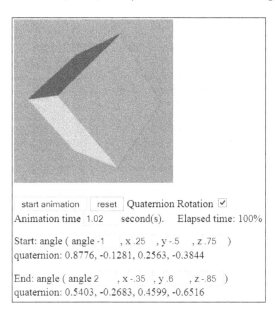

Much of the code is devoted to the user interface. When we click on the **start animation** button, we call the setRotation() function to perform the initial setup. After reading the axis-angle values set in the user interface, call another function to convert the axis-angle values into quaternions, as follows:

```
function setRotation() {
    axisAngleBgn = [parseFloat(tagStartX.value),
        parseFloat(tagStartY.value), parseFloat(tagStartZ.value),
        parseFloat(tagStartAngle.value)];
    axisAngleEnd = [parseFloat(tagEndX.value),
        parseFloat(tagEndY.value), parseFloat(tagEndZ.value),
        parseFloat(tagEndAngle.value)];
    quaternion0 = ConvertAxisAngleToQuaternion(axisAngleBgn);
    quaternion1 = ConvertAxisAngleToQuaternion(axisAngleEnd);
```

Inside the `ConvertAxisAngleToQuaternion()` function, we implement the following equation:

$$q = [cos(\vartheta/2), sin(\vartheta/2)*x, sin(\vartheta/2)*y, sin(\vartheta/2)*z]$$

Remember to normalize the values so the quaternion is of length 1, as follows:

```
function ConvertAxisAngleToQuaternion ( axisAngle ) {
    var q = [0, 0, 1, 0];
    q[0] = Math.cos( axisAngle[3]/2 );
    var qV = Math.sin( axisAngle[3]/2 );
    // normalize the axis values
    var denominator = Math.sqrt( axisAngle[0]*axisAngle[0] +
        axisAngle[1]*axisAngle[1] + axisAngle[2]*axisAngle[2] );
    for (var i = 0; i < 3; i++ ) {
        q[i+1] = qV * axisAngle[i]/denominator;
    }
    return q;
}
```

Returning to `setRotation()`, we complete the initialization by getting the angle between the two quaternions; checking if that angle is negative, in which case we negate the second quaternion; and finally setting animation constants *Φ* (theta), the angle between the quaternions, and *sin(Φ)*. Have a look at the following code snippet:

```
function setRotation() {
. . .
    angleBetweenQuaternions = 0;
    for (i = 0; i < 4; i++ ) {
        angleBetweenQuaternions +=
            (quaternion0[i] * quaternion1[i]);
    }
    if ( angleBetweenQuaternions < 0) {
        // rotation between quaternions greater than 180 degrees
        // therefore, inverse the second quaternion.
        angleBetweenQuaternions = 0;
        for (i = 0; i < 4; i++ ) {
            quaternion1[i] = -quaternion1[i];
            angleBetweenQuaternions +=
                (quaternion0[i] * quaternion1[i]);
        }
    }
    slerpTheta = Math.acos( angleBetweenQuaternions );
    sinTheta = Math.sin( slerpTheta );;
}
```

Now we begin the actual animation in the `drawScene()` function, performing the SLERP animation in a separate function. The first part of the `SLERP()` function performs the `SLERP(t; q0, q1)` calculation and the second part of the function saves the values in the Transformation matrix. The time variable t (`timePct`) is calculated in the `animate()` function based on the computer's clock and duration of time, as shown in the following code:

```
function SLERP() {
    var sinTheta0 = Math.sin(slerpTheta*(1.0 - timePct));
    var sinTheta1 = Math.sin(slerpTheta * timePct);
    for (i = 0; i < 4; i++ ) {
        qSLERP[i] = (quaternion0[i]*sinTheta0 +
            quaternion1[i]*sinTheta1)/sinTheta;
    }
}
```

After that, we convert the quaternion to a matrix shown in the following figure:

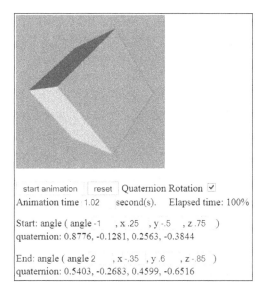

Since the calculations to set the matrix values repeat, such as x^2, we perform all the unique calculations and then combine these values to set the rotation portion of the Transformation matrix, as presented in the following code:

```
var xSqr2 = 2 * qSLERP[1] * qSLERP[1];
var ySqr2 = 2 * qSLERP[2] * qSLERP[2];
var zSqr2 = 2 * qSLERP[3] * qSLERP[3];
var wx2 = 2 * qSLERP[0] * qSLERP[1];
var wy2 = 2 * qSLERP[0] * qSLERP[2];
var wz2 = 2 * qSLERP[0] * qSLERP[3];
var xy2 = 2 * qSLERP[1] * qSLERP[2];
var xz2 = 2 * qSLERP[1] * qSLERP[3];
var yz2 = 2 * qSLERP[2] * qSLERP[3];
```

```
    // set the upper left 3x3 rotation portion of the matrix
    mvMatrix[0] = 1 - (ySqr2 + zSqr2);
    mvMatrix[4] = xy2 - wz2;
    mvMatrix[8] = xz2 + wy2;

    mvMatrix[1] = xy2 + wz2;
    mvMatrix[5] = 1 - (xSqr2 + zSqr2);
    mvMatrix[9] = yz2 - wx2;

    mvMatrix[2] = xz2 - wy2;
    mvMatrix[6] = yz2 + wx2;
    mvMatrix[10]= 1 - (xSqr2 + ySqr2);
}
```

And we are done! The alternative method using axis-angle to set the rotation of the transformation matrix is also included when the check box on the user interface is deselected. The axis-angle code looks more compact as it calculates a value between the beginning and ending axis-angle values based on the same `timePct` duration of the animation. However, the live demonstration reveals that axis-angle produces a non-optimal animation with a number of odd spins and turns, as shown in the following code:

```
mat4.rotate(mvMatrix,
    ((axisAngleEnd[3] - axisAngleBgn[3])*timePct + axisAngleBgn[3]),
    [((axisAngleEnd[0] - axisAngleBgn[0])*timePct + axisAngleBgn[0]),
    ((axisAngleEnd[1] - axisAngleBgn[1])*timePct + axisAngleBgn[1]),
    ((axisAngleEnd[2] - axisAngleBgn[2])*timePct + axisAngleBgn[2])]);
```

Objective complete – mini debriefing

This exercise was a great demonstration of both quaternions, fourth dimensional spaces, and how 3D graphics is a terrific tool for learning math principles, and used internally in graphics cards.

Mission accomplished

Each educational application of 3D graphics will be unique, but what they have in common is their ability to be engaging and interactive. It was always a great moment as a teacher when my students would perform math calculations and then validate their results in a 3D graphics environment.

Education is evolving to keep in step with our students, who engage in social media, web, and mobile applications. Students of all ages and levels of education and training are familiar with 3D graphics for entertainment both in games and movies. WebGL therefore is a natural fit as an education resource.

Project 10

The New World of 3D Art

"All the world's a stage, and all the men and women merely players: they have their exits and their entrances; and one man in his time plays many parts."

— William Shakespeare

3D graphics and art are virtually synonymous. The tools of technology find their ways into the hands of the craftspeople. Computer graphics first solved technical and military problems, enabled production and architecture, before finding its way to solving visual effects problems. Then, it took on a life of its own, moving center stage; computer graphics now creates movies and parts using 3D printers. It has come full circle—the technology that created art is now the art that creates technology.

There is no way to quantify or define art. As the saying goes, we know great art when we see it. However, we can present our own work and inspirations. We can present examples that might inspire further exploration and development. And quite possibly, WebGL may be the new art.

Mission briefing

The Web is certainly a great place to display art. Prior to the Web, there were books. While art is timeless, books are static and limited in displaying art shows. So, the Web has been a boom for artists to present works for the entire world to see. However, an art gallery is an experience where one encompasses within its surroundings. Museums stand apart and stand alone as art itself, synergized with painting and sculptures to form palaces of presentations. Two such examples are the Getty in the Santa Monica Mountains overlooking West Los Angeles and the Art Institute of Chicago. Route 66, the Main Street of America, connects these two museums, which is an inspiration for songs and movies and the destination for dreamers to create new art and new lives. This project and these tasks look at WebGL and its role in both creating the environment for presenting art and as art itself. WebGL acts as the canvas, brush, and paint in creating works of art. In this project, we will achieve the following two objectives:

▸ First, we will create our own art museum with the prestigious architecture of one of the great art museums in the world, the Art Institute of Chicago. We shall construct the beveled columns that are a key feature of the museum and use shader languages and normal bump maps.

▸ In the second part of the project, we will create an interactive 3D diorama that we can walk through, based on the style of the pop artist Roy Lichtenstein. We will then modify the scene for cel shading.

Art Institute of Chicago

Why is it awesome?

New directions in art have been preceded by technical innovation. Artists and visionaries learn to take the technology and invent new art forms and storytelling techniques. This past century has seen the advent of motion pictures and content broadcasting through the airwaves for radio and television. Amplified audio enabled rock music. Computer technology has changed the way we play games. The Internet is still evolving, yet it has already become a mainstream entertainment media. WebGL now adds the capability for interactive 3D, enabling art to be experienced by walking around and through it. Never before has the artist had such opportunities with design to engage the public.

We often look at the past for our future course and our environments for inspiration. We too shall look to our past and our surroundings to create a new art form based on WebGL.

Your Hotshot objectives

We will perform the following tasks:

- Experiencing the art museum
- Inventing interactive 3D art

Experiencing the art museum

The goal is to recreate the Art Institute of Chicago. The grounds are expansive with many rooms housing various exhibits, likely beyond what we could download over the Web for a real-time exhibit. So, we chose instead to display the main atrium highlighting its major features. What impresses people the most about the museum's architecture is the strength of the columns supporting the structure and the balanced lighting—there are no dark shadows. This is, however, not ambient lighting, which would wash out the beveling of the support columns.

For real-time 3D graphics, this presents a dilemma: pervasive ambient light often flattens out the look of 3D. What gives 3D its look is the shading or fall off of light around the edges. Yet, here we want to feature the columns, if for no other reason but to pay tribute to this sanctuary of art.

Main hall of the Art Institute of Chicago

One way to display the museum's interior would be to model the columns in 3D. This would be a tough task (although I am sure that artists would enjoy the challenge and do a great job). Instead, I took the mathematical approach and used shader languages and normal maps to perform the task. The dominant reason being that I enjoy the technical challenge and don't want artists to have all the fun. It also reveals more techniques in WebGL.

Engage thrusters

Like previous demonstrations where we tiled a single brick pattern to create an entire wall, here too we will use a single pattern and tile it around each column. This proves to be a rather complex way to create the columns, but the challenge teaches us about shader languages with complex patterns over curved surfaces.

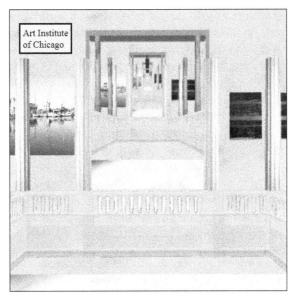

Opening scene

The scene contains only one 3D-modeled column that is copied thirteen times. Along with reading in the 3D-modeled column, which is simply a cylinder in 3D Studio Max that tapers in slightly at the top, a normal map image, `museumColumnNormalMap`, was also read and is pictured in the following figure:

Normal map for columns

The colors near the left-hand side edge are (0.9375, 0.5, 1) and on the right-hand side bluer edge are (0.0625, 0.5, 1). The red component is progressively reduced from 0.9375 to 0.0625. In the center, the color is (0.5, 0.5, 1). Inside the `shaderLightsNormalMap-fs` GPU fragment shader, this color is used per pixel to create the beveled look of each column, as presented in the following code snippet:

```
vec4 textureMapNormal = vec4( (texture2D(uSamplerNormalMap,
    vec2( vTextureCoord.s*uTextureMapTiling.s,
    vTextureCoord.t*uTextureMapTiling.t)) * 2.0) - 1.0 );
```

Inside the fragment shader, the normal map is referred to as `uSamplerNormalMap`. The fragment shader picks the pixel that corresponds to the location on the column: the upper-left corner of the column will pick the upper-left corner of the normal map. Similar to the brick walls from previous projects, the color is multiplied by two and then one is subtracted. For example, (0.0625, 0.5, 1) will become a normal of (-0.875, 0, 1). This value will then be normalized to a unit vector of (-0.6585, 0, 0.7526) with a length of 1 unit. This normal points slightly to the left in the negative *x* direction and towards us in the positive *z* direction. This scene has multiple lights, but if a light is coming straight down the *z* axis, (0, 0, -1), in the same direction as in the opening scene, then we reverse the light's direction to (0, 0, 1) and use the dot product to calculate how much light hits this pixel of the column. *(-0.6586*0+0*0+0.7526*1)=0.7526* or about 75 percent of the maximum light, basically a light gray, hits this pixel of the column. A light with direction (0.6, 0, -0.8)—after reversing the light's direction, using the dot product *(-0.6*-0.6586+0*0+0.8*0.7526)=0.99724* or about 99.72 percent, almost pure white.

Recalling the brick wall example from previous projects, the indentation of the bricks to give depth to the mortar worked very well because the wall was flat. However, the columns are curved, and in addition, the normal map is tiled 12 times to create the beveled look of the columns. Thus, the normal map vectors described in the previous paragraph have to be rotated to fit the curve of the column.

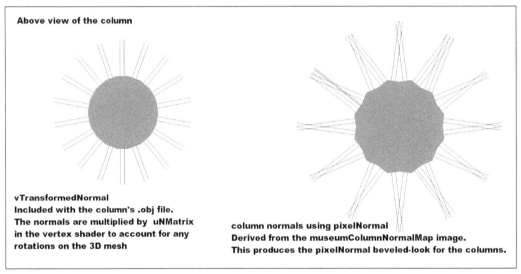

Above view of the column

vTransformedNormal
Included with the column's .obj file.
The normals are multiplied by uNMatrix
in the vertex shader to account for any
rotations on the 3D mesh

column normals using pixelNormal
Derived from the museumColumnNormalMap image.
This produces the pixelNormal beveled-look for the columns.

View above the columns: left shows the 3D meshes normals, and right shows the normals after applying the normal map

The fragment shader calculates the column's own normals on a pixel-by-pixel basis, stored in the `vTransformedVertexNormal` variable. From this, we can derive the normal map's rotation. Since normals are unit values (having a length of 1 unit) and the *y* value is always 0 for the columns as the bevel look is achieved by altering only the *x* and *z* values, we can find where a particular pixel is rotated around the column based on the normal.

For a unit circle with a radius of 1 unit, any (*x, y*) point on that circle can be found by (cos θ, sin θ). For example, at 60 degrees, the (*x, y*) point is *(cos 60, sin 60)=(0.5, 0.866)*. Except, now, we are given (0.5, 0.866) and must derive the rotation. But cos (300 degrees) is also 0.5, so the sine value will help us determine the `columnAngle` value if cos⁻¹(0.5) is 60 degrees or 300 degrees. Have a look at the following code:

```
float columnAngle = acos(vTransformedVertexNormal.x);
float columnAngleNegate = asin(vTransformedVertexNormal.z);
if ( columnAngleNegate < 0.0)
    columnAngle = PI*2.0 - columnAngle; // 2*PI - column angle
```

If the `asin(vTransformedVertexNormal.z)` value in the preceding code is negative, then the actual `columnAngle` rotation is 2π – `columnAngle`.

Now we know how much this pixel is rotated around the column, so we must create a 3 x 3 rotation matrix, `columnPixelRotationMatrix`, to rotate our normal map value. There was one final offset of -90 degrees since the normals exported by 3D Studio Max, the modeling tool, are 90 degrees off from WebGL. So, we add $3/2\pi$ (which is 270 degrees; the same as rotating the column by -90 degrees) and use a modulo function so that the final rotations over 360 degrees will be back within 360 degrees. For example, (390 % 360) produces the remainder of the division 390/360, which is 30 degrees.

```
// rotate 90 degrees but keep angle positive
columnAngle = mod((columnAngle + PI*3.0/2.0), PI*2.0);
```

Next, we create our rotation matrix, `columnPixelRotationMatrix`, as shown in the following code snippet:

```
mat3 columnPixelRotationMatrix;
columnPixelRotationMatrix[0] =
    vec3(cos(columnAngle), 0.0, sin(columnAngle));
columnPixelRotationMatrix[1] = vec3(0.0, 1.0, 0.0);
columnPixelRotationMatrix[2] =
    vec3(-sin(columnAngle), 0.0, cos(columnAngle));
```

This rotation matrix equation was shown in *Project 9*, *Education in the Third Dimension*, but has been repeated here. However, we only use the upper-left 3 x 3 region where rotations occur:

$$R_y(\theta) = \begin{bmatrix} \cos\theta & 0 & \sin\theta & 0 \\ 0 & 1 & 0 & 0 \\ -\sin\theta & 0 & \cos\theta & 0 \\ 0 & 0 & 0 & 1 \end{bmatrix}$$

4 x 4 rotation matrix around the *y* axis. For rotations, we only need the upper-left 3 x 3 matrix.

Finally, we can get the adjusted normal for each pixel by multiplying the normal map's rotation matrix, `columnPixelRotationMatrix`, with the column's rotation, `uNMatrix`, and the pixel's normal map value, `textureMapNormal`. Note that in this demonstration, there are no rotations on the columns—the columns stand straight up, so the multiplication with `uNMatrix` is unnecessary. If there were a rotation on the columns, then multiplying by `uNMatrix` would be required, as shown in the following line of code:

```
vec3 pixelNormal = normalize(columnPixelRotationMatrix * uNMatrix
    * normalize(textureMapNormal.rgb) );
```

Getting the normal of each pixel involves a lot of work, but now we can perform the calculations for the lighting. We add some ambient light to ensure that no objects are pitch black and then calculate a series of point lights that shine on the columns, as presented in the following code:

```
vec3 lighting = vec3(uAmbientLight, uAmbientLight, uAmbientLight);
float lightsContribution = 0.0;
lightsContribution += calculateLightContribution(
    vec3( 14.0,8.0,-32.0), vec3(0.0,0.0,0.0), pixelNormal, true);
. . .
lightsContribution += calculateLightContribution(
    vec3(-14.0,8.0,32.0), vec3(0.0, 0.0, 0.0), pixelNormal, true);
```

There were 12 point lights in this scene, but only the first and last are shown in the preceding code. The point lights are in two rows and 12 to 16 units apart between the columns and 14 units on both sides of the scene. A variation of the `calculateLightContribution()` function from *Project 8, 3D Websites*, is used. However, only point lights are used and no spot lights, so there is no light direction; point lights shine in all directions unlike spot lights. Point lights are preferred because ambient light alone produces a flat look that does not flatter the architecture of a museum, and direct lights either leave unlit areas associated with heavy shadows or give a washed-out look similar to ambient lights.

Inside the `calculateLightContribution()` function, called for each light in the scene, we first calculate the distance from the light to each pixel of the column (one column at a time) and then convert it to a normalized unit vector, as shown in the following code:

```
vec3 distanceLightToPixel = vec3(vPosition.xyz - lightLoc);
vec3 vectorLightPosToPixel = normalize(distanceLightToPixel);
vec3 lightDirNormalized = normalize(lightDir);
```

The next step is to calculate the angle between the light vector, `vectorLightPosToPixel`, and the pixel's normal, `pixelNormal`, previously found based on the normal map, rotated around the column, then passed in as a parameter to this function. If the dot product is less than zero, then the angle between the light and the normal is greater than 90 degrees, which means that no light is shining on this pixel, so set `angleLightToNormalMap` to 0, as follows:

```
float angleLightToNormalMap =
    dot( -vectorLightPosToPixel, pixelNormal );
if (angleLightToNormalMap < 0.0) angleLightToNormalMap = 0.0;
```

We now know how much light will shine on this pixel based on the light's angles and normal maps. We only have point lights in this museum example; however, the implementation of spot lights to highlight a painting or sculpture has been included. While spot lights have been covered in earlier projects, one must use caution when using normal maps. The normal map tells us the shading at each pixel. However, to calculate whether the pixel is within the spot light's beam, we use the normal from the column, not from the normal map.

We previously calculated a vector from the light to the pixel, `vectorLightPosToPixel`. In the next figure, the direction of the spot light is straight down (0, -1, 0). The pixels within the beam width (the inner circle) receive the full amount of light. As described before, the angle between the light-to-the-pixel and normal is found by reversing the direction of the light and then calculating the dot product as follows:

$$N \bullet L = (N_x * L_x + N_y * L_y + N_z * L_z)$$

The dot product is also the cosine of the angle between the light L and normal N vectors:

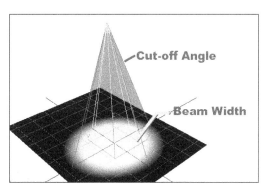

Spot light above showing the inner circle beam width and a fading cut-off angle

Pixels between the inner beam width and the outer cut-off angle receive progressively less light as they get closer to the cut-off angle until the amount of light is 0.

If we have a point light such as a light bulb, there is neither a cut-off angle nor areas outside the beam's width. Thus, the following code shows `if ( pointLight ) { lightAmount = 1.0; }`. However, if we have a spot light, we must determine the angle from the spot light to the pixel. If this angle is within the spot light's beam width, then `lightAmount = 1.0` is just like a point light. But if the angle is between the cut-off angle and the beam width, only a percentage of the light is used. Note that instead of comparing angles, we are comparing the cosines of the angles. So, as the angle between the light's direction and the pixel grows, the cosine of the angle between the light's direction and the pixel's normal gets smaller. Therefore, to determine whether the angle is within the beam width, `if ( angleLighttoPixel >= uSportLightBeamWidth)`, we use a >= sign and not <=, as shown in the following code:

```
float lightAmt = 0.0;
if ( pointLight) {
    lightAmt = 1.0;
}
else { // spot light
    vec3 lightDirNormalized = normalize(lightDir);
    // The smaller the number, the more direct the light hits the pixel
    float angleLightToPixel =
        dot( vectorLightPosToPixel, lightDirNormalized );
    //note, these are the cosines of the angles, not actual angles
    if ( angleLightToPixel >= uSpotLightBeamWidth ) {
        lightAmt = 1.0;
    }
    if ( angleLightToPixel > uSpotLightCutOffAngle ) {
        lightAmt = (angleLightToPixel - uSpotLightCutOffAngle) /
            (uSpotLightBeamWidth - uSpotLightCutOffAngle);
    }
}
```

The final calculation is attenuation—the fall off of light over a distance. In real-world physics, light falls off as the inverse of the squares of the distance—double the distance, and the light is one quarter as bright. For a distance d, the amount of light in quadratic attenuation is $1/d^2$. However, in 3D graphics, quadratic attenuation never looks quite right. Perhaps that's because we never really simulate true light with photons. Thus, we often use linear attenuation, which is a one-to-one ratio of the distance to the fall off of light. In linear attenuation, double the distance and half as much light will be received. Linear attenuation is also a little easier to calculate, as presented in the following code:

```
// calculate attenuation (fall off of light over distance)
float maxDist = 32.0;
float attenuation = 1.0;
if ( uUseAttenuation ) {
    if ( length(distanceLightToPixel) < maxDist ) {
```

```
        attenuation =
            (maxDist - length(distanceLightToPixel))/maxDist;
    }
    else attenuation = 0.0;
}
```

Three values are combined to calculate the lighting at one pixel for a single light source using `lightAmt`, which calculates the beam widths and cut-off angles for spot lights; `angleLightToNormalMap`, the angle between the light's direction and the pixel's normal based on the normal map to create the beveled look of the columns; and `attenuation`, which is the fall off of light over a distance. We multiply these three values together to get the proper lighting of the pixel on this column, as follows:

```
lightAmt *= angleLightToBumpMap * attenuation;
return lightAmt;
```

We perform this calculation for every pixel, light source, and column:

Beveled look of the columns

It is hard to imagine that these columns are perfect cylinders, yet the normal maps combined with lighting give them a beveled appearance.

There are a few additional features added to this impression of the Art Institute of Chicago. Earlier projects featured the portal look of viewing from other cameras that were textured onto a plane. This is observed in the opening, giving the appearance of additional wings of the museum and depth.

A final note on the columns and JavaScript: We read in the 3D model of the columns just once and copy the 3D mesh for the other 13 columns. This naturally saves time on download and memory space. However, every time we render a frame in the `renderer()` function, we check the state of the `meshLoaded` and `textueMap` functions for every column, as follows:

```
museumColumn1Object.meshLoaded = museumColumnObject.meshLoaded;
museumColumn1Object.textureMap = museumColumnObject.textureMap;
```

Repeat this process for all the copies of the museum columns. It is a small price to pay in comparison to downloading these columns 14 times.

Another repeated architecture is the gothic marble railings. In fact, there are two sets of railings: the railings in each corner and the railings not adjacent to any corners, which are double the length of the smaller corner railings. Each railing is a combination of two texture maps—white gothic marble and a transparency mask. The mask image uses pink—a combination of red plus blue (1, 0, 1)—for the empty space within the railings. Inside the fragment shader, we discard any pink pixels, as presented in the following code:

```
void main(void) {
    vec4 textureMaskColor = texture2D(uSamplerMask,
        vec2(vTextureCoord.s, vTextureCoord.t));
    vec4 fragmentColor = texture2D(uSampler,
        vec2(vTextureCoord.s, vTextureCoord.t));
    if ( (textureMaskColor.r > .95) && (textureMaskColor.g < .05)
        && (textureMaskColor.b > .95) )  discard;
    else gl_FragColor = vec4(fragmentColor.rgb, 1.0);
}
```

Have a look at the following screenshot:

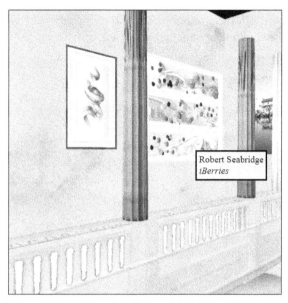

Transparencies between the railings and the labels on the paintings

This works quite well; however, remember that texturing in WebGL as well as video games use mipmaps—copies of the original texture map but half the size in both directions. So, an original texture map with the dimensions 512 by 256 pixels (width by height) will create duplicates that are half its size, 256 x 128 pixels. It performs this operation recursively, so we get texture maps that are of the dimensions 128 x 64, 64 x 32, and so on. These reduced-dimension mipmaps blend neighboring pixels. For example, if a texture map has three orange vertical stripes followed by one blue stripe, the smaller mipmaps blend these pixels together so that some of the blue color is preserved among the three orange pixels. As the camera pulls away from the textured 3D object, the smaller mipmaps look pretty good from a distance.

Mipmaps have one side effect; the pink in the transparency masks also blends with the nonpink when we generate smaller mipmaps. Since these smaller mipmaps are used at a distance, it may not be noticeable that a pixel that was previously transparent is now visible. To reduce the problem, instead of checking if the transparent pixel is (1, 0, 1), we check whether the red and blue values are 0.95 or above and the green value is 0.05 or below. We are still checking for transparent pink pixels but allowing blending issues.

One final feature of our WebGL Chicago Art Institute museum is labeling of the images as the mouse rolls over the picture. We have the artist and name of the painting, but one could add detailed background information, similar to how the museum presents its exhibits.

Much of the code uses previous examples of the ray-box intersection. Once we detect an intersection indicating that the mouse is over a painting, we display the information relative to the mouse's position, 15 pixels below and to the right of the mouse. By offsetting the label, as shown in the following code, we enable people to view the picture without obscuring the painting:

```
function mouseMoveEvent(event) {
    mouseDownX = event.clientX;
    mouseDownY = event.clientY;

    var xWorld = ( (mouseDownX - windowLeft) - gl.viewportWidth/2)
        * ( 2.0 / gl.viewportWidth);
    var yWorld = -((mouseDownY - windowTop) - gl.viewportHeight/2)
        * ( 2.0 / gl.viewportHeight);
    rayMouseDown = [ xWorld, yWorld, -distanceToViewPlane, 1 ];

    var overObject = false;
    var table = document.getElementById('table');
    for (var i = 0; i < totalMeshObjects; i++ ) {
        if ( RayBoundingBoxIntersection( paintingSeabridge1Object,
            xWorld, yWorld ) ) {
            table.innerHTML = "Robert Seabridge<BR><I>iBerries</I>";
            overObject = true;
            table.style.left = mouseDownX + 15;
            table.style.top = mouseDownY + 15;
            table.style.visibility = 'visible';
        }
    …. // continue for the other images
    }
    if ( !overObject ) {
        table.style.visibility = 'hidden';
    }
}
```

Objective complete – mini debriefing

Perhaps like no other technology, WebGL provides the sense of being at the museum. It is beyond just an Internet slideshow—a chance to walk through a building constructed as a monument to creative talents and visions. One of the more difficult issues in such a presentation is color matching and lighting. In fact, this has long been an issue of any reproduction. The first color printers stressed over this issue, and it continues today. We can come close but can never match the paint on a canvas. 3D offers additional lighting issues—we can never replicate the true physics of light to match what is observed in an art gallery. However, these problems become opportunities. Creating interactive 3D worlds enables us to go beyond the physical world. We can present images during the day or night with the flip of a switch. And like the imaginations of great artists, we can present a vision not found in the everyday world.

Inventing interactive 3D art

After looking at museums—a repository of the past—we now look at the future: new art displayed through interactive 3D. Video games and animated movies brought this art into the mainstream. In 1991, Disney's *Beauty and the Beast* received the Golden Globe Award for Best Motion Picture and was the first animated movie to be nominated for the Best Picture award at the Oscar's. There may have been some sense in the fact that the Motion Pictures Academy was about to have the Best Picture award go to a movie with no live actors. Perhaps that is why a decade later, the Motion Pictures Academy introduced a new category for animated movies.

Video games have also established themselves as works of art and music. *Video Games Live* (`http://www.videogameslive.com/`) founded by Tommy Tallarico is a world-traveling concert featuring symphonies and choirs that perform music from the most popular video games, honoring composers, musicians, and game developers with guest appearances and on-stage game challenges. Such efforts are engaging young audiences with orchestras that lost touch with classical music.

The Academy of Interactive Arts and Sciences (`http://www.interactive.org/`) honors its game of the year that includes a separate art exhibition called *Into The Pixel* (`http://www.intothepixel.com/`) presented at E3, the Electronic Entertainment Expo. *Into the Pixel* highlights great art from the video games industry. It shows another side of this industry that is often criticized for its content and confirms that video games are designed by true creative professionals.

3D modeling and 3D printers have enabled new sculptures that simply were not possible with traditional sculpting. The inner details could have never been achieved by the hands of even the finest sculptures. This is best demonstrated in the works of Kevin Mack (`http://www.kevinmackart.com/`) who uses his complex 3D models in detailed prints as well as outputs his models to the same 3D printers that produce parts for medical applications and airplane assemblies:

The sculptures by Kevin Mack made using 3D modeling and produced on 3D printers

Art has a tradition of evolving from other applications. Pop art was inspired by the byproducts of our mass production society. Andy Warhol's Campbell soup can, Coke bottles sculpture, and Brillo pad and Del Monte produce boxes represent art that are the throwaways of consumerism. Roy Lichtenstein painted using a dot-style, representing the printing process from newspapers and comic strips. Lichtenstein often used a limited color palette, simulating the production inking process of the mid-twentieth century. His art is often two dimensional—there is no shading to convey depth. Yet, Lichtenstein's 2D art style is an inspiration for a new 3D art form where the patron can walk into the scene:

Street poster from Lichtenstein's exhibit at the Art Institute of Chicago, 2012

Prepare for lift off

We always respect the copyright-protected works of content developers and artists, so the demonstrations here will not draw from Lichtenstein's work. Instead, the images used were adapted from free clip art websites such as *Public Domain Clip Art* (http://www.pdclipart.org/) and *Free Vintage Posters* (http://www.freevintageposters.com/). Our goal is to create a flat 2D Lichtenstein-style pop art, then walk into the painting and change the color palette, lighting, and other aspects of 3D interactivity, as shown in the following screenshot:

Opening scene: looking at my Lichtenstein-style painting

Imagine our opening scene. We walk towards the image and then we move through the image to arrive inside a 3D diorama. Now imagine a gallery with dozens of pictures; each takes you to a new interactive 3D art piece. The texture map is not a screenshot, but a rendering of the art piece just beyond the brick wall applied to the flat plane. This enables the art to come alive! *Project 8, 3D Websites*, described how to render to a texture map. As changes such as different lighting or animation occur in the 3D diorama, these changes are reflected in the rendered texture map.

The 3D diorama is made up of a clip art that is textured onto a flat plane. Only the *Foreign Trade* poster was rotated. What makes this diorama so effective is that the beagle and red wagon are 2D images that were drawn in a perspective view as if they were 3D images. In the following screenshot, the telephone and newspaper have a subtle perspective view too in a Liechtenstein style:

Walking through the wall into the 3D scene

The depth of the objects was determined by their relative size. The red wagon is one of the smallest clip art images in the scene, yet it was brought into the foreground so that it appears larger than the other objects. Much of Roy Lichtenstein's work was flat with objects disproportionate to their actual size. This was likely because the artist liked having some fun and because of his desire to ensure smaller objects were not diminished in the background. Lichtenstein did a series of paintings in his later life of the *Artist's Studio*, depicting his studio, living room, bedroom, and so on. Often, his earlier paintings were repainted into his artist's studio series.

To create transparencies, texture maps have a second texture known as the mask. Pixels from the mask that are pure green (0, 255, 0) will be discarded, creating the transparency, as shown in the following screenshot:

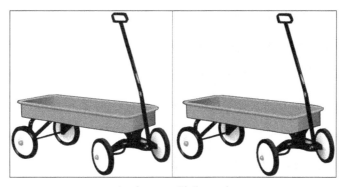

A red wagon with the mask

I preferred having the second image as the mask. If I had only one image with the wagon surrounded in green, the green would blend in with the red wagon due to the mipmap process. Unfortunately, we were still left with some dotted white areas around each image. One way to remove this is to have a white background, but a better solution would be to add additional black pixels to outline the object.

Since this scene is intended to be interactive, lighting was added that can be turned on by a checkbox. Inside the fragment shader, we first add some ambient light. If the pixel is close to pure green, we discard that pixel. If the pixel is close to black, we retain it. Otherwise, set the pixel to white and calculate its color based on the three color lights, as shown in the following code:

```
void main(void) {
    vec3 lightWeighting =
        vec3(uAmbientLight, uAmbientLight, uAmbientLight);
    vec4 fragmentColor = texture2D(uSampler,
        vec2(vTextureCoord.s, vTextureCoord.t));
    vec4 textureMaskColor = texture2D(uSamplerMask,
        vec2(vTextureCoord.s, vTextureCoord.t));
    // if mask is green, discard the pixel making it transparent
    if ( (textureMaskColor.r < .05) && (textureMaskColor.g > .95)
        && (textureMaskColor.b < .05) ) {
        discard;
    }
    else {
        // if pixel is NOT black, make it pure white
        if ( (fragmentColor.r  > .01) || (fragmentColor.g  > .01)
            || (fragmentColor.b  > .01) )
        {
            fragmentColor.r = 1.0;
```

```
                fragmentColor.g = 1.0;
                fragmentColor.b = 1.0;
            }
        }
        // A red light at (-10, 0, -50), the green light
        //  at (0, 10, -40) and the blue light at (10, 0, -30)
        lightWeighting += vec3(1.0, 0.0, 0.0) *
            calculateLightContribution( vec3(-10.0,   0.0, -50.0),
            vTransformedNormal);
        lightWeighting += vec3(0.0, 1.0, 0.0) *
            calculateLightContribution( vec3(  0.0, 10.0, -40.0),
            vTransformedNormal);
        lightWeighting += vec3(0.0, 0.0, 1.0) *
            calculateLightContribution( vec3( 10.0,   0.0, -30.0),
            vTransformedNormal);

        // any colors above 1 must be capped at 1
        if ( lightWeighting.r > 1.0 ) lightWeighting.r = 1.0;
        if ( lightWeighting.g > 1.0 ) lightWeighting.g = 1.0;
        if ( lightWeighting.b > 1.0 ) lightWeighting.b = 1.0;

        gl_FragColor = vec4(fragmentColor.rgb * lightWeighting, 1.0);
    }
```

Much of the `calculateLightContribution()` function is simplified from the previous museum example; however, we don't have to calculate bump and normal maps nor spot lights. This is shown in the following code:

```
    float calculateLightContribution(vec3 lightLoc, vec3 pixelNormal) {
        vec3 distanceLightToPixel = vec3(vPosition.xyz - lightLoc);
        vec3 vectorLightPosToPixel = normalize(distanceLightToPixel);

        float angleBetweenLightAndNormal =
            dot( -vectorLightPosToPixel, pixelNormal );
            // if the angle is > 90 degrees (where cos(angle) < 0),
            // then no light hits this pixel
        if (angleBetweenLightAndNormal < 0.0)
            angleBetweenLightAndNormal = 0.0;

        // calculate attenuation (fall off of light over distance)
        float maxDist = 40.0;
        float attenuation = 0.0;
        if ( uUseAttenuation ) {
            if ( length(distanceLightToPixel) < maxDist ) {
                attenuation =
                    (maxDist - length(distanceLightToPixel))/maxDist;
            }
        }
```

```
      float lightAmt = angleBetweenLightAndNormal * attenuation;
      return lightAmt;
}
```

In the `renderer()` function, we have to attach the correct mask with the object, so there are a series of `if` statements for each 3D mesh object. This sends the mask to the GPU that is used inside the fragment shader, as seen in the following code:

```
else if (meshObjectArray[i] == poster1Object) {
    if ( poster1Mask != null ) {
        gl.activeTexture(gl.TEXTURE1);
        gl.bindTexture(gl.TEXTURE_2D, poster1Mask);
        gl.uniform1i(shaderProgram.samplerMaskUniform, 1);
    }
}
```

The results certainly create an interesting effect. It also eliminates the white pixels that were seen to surround some of the items in the previous screenshot. Red, green, and blue colored lights were placed in the foreground. Using attenuation, objects in the distant background were slightly darker, which helped with our depth perception, as shown in the following screenshot:

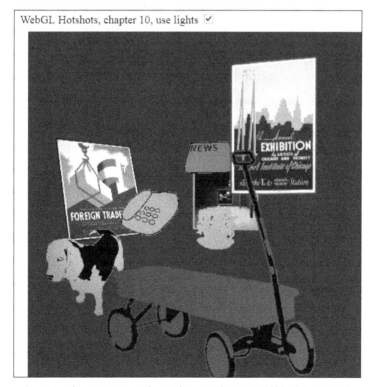

Removing the texture map colors and using red, green, and blue lights instead

Cel shading is a popular technique for games and art to show depth. Often, comic book characters have two tones—brighter colors for sunlight and slightly darker colors for shadows. However, we aren't limited to two tones. Previously, we checked to make sure no colors exceed 1.0. Now, we check if the red, green, or blue is 0.8 or greater, in which case we set these colors to 1.0. Any red, green, or blue amount from 0.6 to 0.8 will be set to 0.6, and so forth, as shown in the following code:

```
// Only the red is shown. Repeat for the green and blue
if ( lightWeighting.r >= .8 ) lightWeighting.r = 1.0;
else if ( lightWeighting.r >= 0.6 ) lightWeighting.r = 0.6;
else if ( lightWeighting.r >= 0.4 ) lightWeighting.r = 0.4;
else if ( lightWeighting.r >= 0.2 ) lightWeighting.r = 0.2;
else lightWeighting.r = 0.0;
```

This is a great place to experiment with different values. In addition, the background was changed to white to have the colors stand out better, as seen in the following screenshot:

Cel shading effect inside the fragment shader

One final addition to this 3D diorama is to get back to our original room. For this, we deploy the same portal's previous demonstrations that we have been using; however, now the portal's camera is pointing to the original opening location. Inside the `handleKeys()` function, we check if the camera's *z* value, `eye[2]`, has reached a certain depth, and if so, we reset the camera's location based on the portal's point-of-view value, `portal2eye`, as presented in the code that follows the screenshot:

A closer view of the portal that sends us back to our original location

```
function handleKeys() {
    if (currentlyPressedKeys[38]){//up arrow, camera moves forward
        eye[0] += Math.sin( cameraRotation ) * .4;
        eye[2] -= Math.cos( cameraRotation ) * .4;

        // check if we transport back to the original location
    if ( eye[2] <= (portalWall2Location[2]+5) ) {
        for (i = 0; i < 3; i++) {
            eye[i] = portal2eye[i];
        }
    }
    }
}
```

Objective complete – mini debriefing

The previous exercise did a pretty interesting job of getting us closer to the comic book, pop art style of Roy Lichtenstein. However, as it is said so often, *art is never complete, only abandoned*. To put this another way, WebGL for art is only limited by our imagination. Web3D and art is awaiting the creativity and vision of many to build something inspiring.

Mission accomplished

The course that twenty-first century art takes probably won't be known until we reach the next century, when we can look back and identify the trends. At this point, we are left with our instincts, and we can try to blend cultures and technologies to see what happens. As media becomes more interactive, more people engage in media and there is more participation, so too may art follow that course. Art could very well blend trends such as Facebook and mobile applications, sharing content, interactive yet asynchronous, group projects in cyberspace. One aspect is certain—it will be interactive and in 3D, and here, WebGL will play a major role.

Index

transparency order
about 92
restacking 93-97

U

uCamRotMatrix function 109
uMVMatrix function 109
user interfaces
creating, in 3D environment 103-109
user interfaces, in 3D environment
billboarding 103
HMD 103

V

vertexBuffer object 46
vertex shader 43
Virtual Reality Modeling Language. *See* **VRML**
virtual spaces navigation
portals, creating for 220-227
visual design
and interactivity 86-91
VRML 9
VRML 2.0 9

W

W3C 136
W3Schools
URL 42
Web3D Consortium
about 11
URL 11, 14
Web3D Gaming
about 101-103
objectives 103
WebCL 140
WebGL
about 11, 42
Facebook, bridging to 131-140
Facebook friends, visiting in 140-145
fundamentals, URL 42
key components, for drawing 2D triangle 43-47
shader languages 43, 44
used, for teaching math 253-260
versus X3D 14, 15

WebGL applications
building, with Facebook 131
webGLStart() function 146
World Wide Web Consortium. *See* **W3C**

X

X3D
versus WebGL 14, 15
X3D objects
building 13
building, objectives 13
positioning, transformation used 17, 18
X3DOM
about 14
URL 14, 206
X3D scenes
interactivity, adding to 18, 19
lights, adding to 18, 19
X3D with the Document Object Model. *See*
X3DOM
XHTML file 206
XML 152
XMLHTTPRequest() function 142

Thank you for buying
WebGL HOTSH©T

About Packt Publishing

Packt, pronounced 'packed', published its first book "*Mastering phpMyAdmin for Effective MySQL Management*" in April 2004 and subsequently continued to specialize in publishing highly focused books on specific technologies and solutions.

Our books and publications share the experiences of your fellow IT professionals in adapting and customizing today's systems, applications, and frameworks. Our solution based books give you the knowledge and power to customize the software and technologies you're using to get the job done. Packt books are more specific and less general than the IT books you have seen in the past. Our unique business model allows us to bring you more focused information, giving you more of what you need to know, and less of what you don't.

Packt is a modern, yet unique publishing company, which focuses on producing quality, cutting-edge books for communities of developers, administrators, and newbies alike. For more information, please visit our website: www.packtpub.com.

About Packt Open Source

In 2010, Packt launched two new brands, Packt Open Source and Packt Enterprise, in order to continue its focus on specialization. This book is part of the Packt Open Source brand, home to books published on software built around Open Source licences, and offering information to anybody from advanced developers to budding web designers. The Open Source brand also runs Packt's Open Source Royalty Scheme, by which Packt gives a royalty to each Open Source project about whose software a book is sold.

Writing for Packt

We welcome all inquiries from people who are interested in authoring. Book proposals should be sent to author@packtpub.com. If your book idea is still at an early stage and you would like to discuss it first before writing a formal book proposal, contact us; one of our commissioning editors will get in touch with you.

We're not just looking for published authors; if you have strong technical skills but no writing experience, our experienced editors can help you develop a writing career, or simply get some additional reward for your expertise.

Learning Three.js: The JavaScript 3D Library for WebGL

ISBN: 978-1-78216-628-3   Paperback: 402 pages

Create and animate stunning 3D graphics using the open source Three.js JavaScript library

1. Create and animate beautiful 3D graphics directly in the browser using JavaScript without the need to learn WebGL.

2. Learn how to enhance your 3D graphics with light sources, shadows, and advanced materials and textures.

3. Each subject is explained using extensive examples that you can directly use and adapt for your own purposes.

Game Development with Three.js

ISBN: 978-1-78216-853-9   Paperback: 118 pages

Embrace the next generation of game development and reach millions of gamers online with the Three.js 3D graphics library

1. Develop immersive 3D games that anyone can play on the Internet.

2. Learn Three.js from a gaming perspective, including everything you need to build beautiful and high-performance worlds.

3. A step-by-step guide filled with game-focused examples and tips.

Please check **www.PacktPub.com** for information on our titles

Leap Motion Development Essentials

ISBN: 978-1-84969-772-9   Paperback: 106 pages

Leverage the power of Leap Motion to develop and deploy a fully interactive application

1. Comprehensive and thorough coverage of many SDK features.

2. Intelligent usage of gesture interfaces.

3. In-depth, functional examples of API usage explained in detail.

Torque 3D Game Development Cookbook

ISBN: 978-1-84969-354-7   Paperback: 380 pages

Over 80 practical recipes and hidden gems for getting the most out of the Torque 3D game engine

1. Clear step-by-step instructions and practical examples to advance your understanding of Torque 3D and all of its subsystems.

2. Explore essential topics such as graphics, sound, networking, and user input.

3. Helpful tips and techniques to increase the potential of your Torque 3D games.

Please check **www.PacktPub.com** for information on our titles